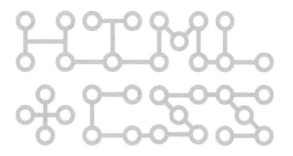

FOUNDATIONS OF WEB DESIGN:
INTRODUCTION TO HTML AND CSS

Thomas Michaud

FOUNDATIONS OF WEB DESIGN: INTRODUCTION TO HTML AND CSS

Thomas Michaud

New Riders

www.newriders.com

To report errors, please send a note to errata@peachpit.com

New Riders is an imprint of Peachpit, a division of Pearson Education.

Copyright © 2014 by Thomas Michaud

Project Editor: Michael J. Nolan

Production Editor: Katerina Malone

Development Editor: Margaret Anderson/Stellarvisions

Technical Editor: Chris Mills

Copyeditor: Jennifer Needham

Proofreader: Patricia Pane

Indexer: Rebecca Plunkett

Cover & Interior Designer: Jonathon Wolfer

ISBN 13: 978-0-321-91893-2

ISBN 10:   0-321-91893-2

9 8 7 6 5 4 3 2 1

Printed and bound in the United States of America

To my grandmother, Nonnie; you pushed me to never stop learning.

And to my wife, Erica; you always sustain me.

I hear and I forget. I see and I remember. I do and I understand.

~ Confucius

ACKNOWLEDGMENTS

I don't know if I can thank enough people (or thank them enough) for all the support they've provided during the writing of this book. If I leave someone out, just let me know on Twitter @coldcoffee!

First off, I give thanks to my Creator, who has sustained me throughout the writing of this book—all things are truly possible.

Thank you to my amazing, beautiful, and patient wife, Erica, and wonderful kids, Dylan and Natalie, who have been a tremendous support and were extremely accommodating while I worked long hours writing this book. I'm going to be ever so grateful to be a part of the family again. I also give thanks to my mother-in-law, Mary, who helped watch the kids when my wife needed a break—you are truly a gift!

I'd like to thank my team at Peachpit Press: Michael Nolan, who took a chance on an unknown teacher; and Margaret Anderson, an amazing developmental editor, who helped to make my words clearer than I could have done on my own, kept me on task, and rapped my knuckles when necessary. I owe a great debt to Chris Mills, my tech editor, who has always been one of my web heroes, for all his suggestions and corrections. Thank you to Katerina Malone, Jennifer Needham, and Patricia J. Pane, who caught all big, small, and in-between mistakes, and Rebecca Plunkett for indexing the book.

Thanks also to my friends—Marc & Sharon, Kai & Kristi, Rob & Sara, Rudy & Stefanie, Tracy & Lori, Brad & Lori, and many others—who constantly gave me support and encouragement.

Thank you to my students—all of you whom I've taught over the past six years—who were the inspiration behind this book. Special thanks go to Jonathon Wolfer, my longtime student, who designed my book.

To iconmonstr (http://iconmonstr.com/) for many of the icons at the start of each chapter and within Chapter 13.

To the brilliant and funny Dr. Leslie Jensen-Inman, who saw something in me I didn't and recommended me to Michael Nolan: I'm so thankful for our email conversation, which began two years ago, about elevating web design in higher education—and for (most of all) your friendship.

Heartfelt thanks to my mom and dad for all those years of support and love … I sure wish dad could have lived to see his youngest getting a book published.

CONTENTS

I am always doing that which I can not do, in order that I may learn how to do it.
~ Pablo Picasso

WELCOME TO FOUNDATIONS OF WEB DESIGN: HTML & CSS

Since Sir Tim Berners-Lee, a research scientist, proposed and developed an internet-based hypertext system back in 1989, and then, in the early 1990s, developed the first HTML documents, HTML has been the backbone for creating websites. While style sheets have been a part of markup languages since the 1980s, CSS (Cascading Style Sheets), which was created to separate presentation (design) from content (markup documents), was first adopted in the mid-1990s; since then, CSS has become the standard styling language for the Web. Today, HTML and CSS need to be a part of every hobby and professional web designer's toolkit.

WHO THIS BOOK IS FOR

This book is written primarily for two types of readers:

- Absolute beginners at hand-coding HTML and CSS

- Those who have used a drag-and-drop website-builder application, but may have little to no idea what all those letters (`p`, `q`, `b`, etc.), numbers (`h1`, `h2`, etc.), and words (`strong`, `span`, `div`, etc.) inside the angled brackets (`< >`) really are

You may wish to learn HTML and CSS to help build a personal website (professional or for family) or to look to take a step toward working in the field of web design. Either way, I believe you'll find this book, and the accompanying resources, to be helpful in your journey.

OBJECTIVES

The objective of *Foundations of Web Design: HTML & CSS* is to provide a fundamental knowledge of HTML (**H**yper**t**ext **M**arkup **L**anguage) and CSS (**C**ascading **S**tyle **S**heets). Learning is accomplished through hands-on coding demonstrations—in the book and in online video tutorials—and challenges. Additionally, you can download assignments in which you'll be asked to develop a basic website based upon chapter material, a one-page promotional site for a midterm project, and a personal website—professional, family, or client—for your final project.

ONLINE ASSIGNMENT REVIEWS

If you are a self-learner—and not in a classroom directed by an instructor—you will be able to submit your work online for questions and reviews.

DESCRIPTION

The different parts of this book work to build your knowledge and skill in a slightly different manner than other books of this type.

PART 1: BASICS

In Chapters 1-5, you'll learn the basics of creating and coding HTML and CSS documents. While it may seem very elementary, it lays an important foundation for the subsequent chapters.

PART 2: WORKING TOGETHER

In Chapters 6-8, you will start to see how HTML and CSS work together in developing more complex web pages through the use of attributes, selectors, typography, and the all-important box model. This is either where it "clicks" for many students or where they become "lost." Make sure you take your time and work through each demonstration (multiple times, if necessary).

PART 3: LAYOUT AND INTERACTIVITY

Chapters 9-12 will teach you how to create layouts that are responsive for different devices, how to develop navigation elements that help users find information on your website, and how to design and use forms.

PART 4: NEXT STEP

Chapters 13 and 14 talk about the tasks that are involved in developing a website from beginning to end, and about additional skills a web designer needs—giving you a foretaste of what you can do next and pointing toward where you can learn those skills.

CONVENTIONS USED

Code examples, notes, and asides will have different typographical styles from the normal body text.

CODE EXAMPLES

HTML code that is being used as a current example is a bright blue color:

```
<h1>This is a header</h1>
```

HTML code that has been previously shown but is part of a new example is shown in a muted blue color:

```
<h1>This is a header</h1>
<p>This is a paragraph</p>
```

FILES

When downloading files, you'll find they are all compressed in the .zip format and will need to be uncompressed (or extracted) prior to use.

>>> *NEED HELP EXTRACTING? VIDEO TUTORIALS ARE AVAILABLE ON THE WEBSITE IF YOU DO NOT KNOW HOW TO UNCOMPRESS A ZIP FILE.*

When referencing folder and document names for demonstration, the names will be in bold lettering:

foldername

document.html

document.css

If you see a forward slash (**/**) between two names

fowd_ch02_folder/01-book.html

it's telling you that the document (**01-book.html**) is located in a specific folder (**fowd_ch02_folder**).

CSS code that is being used as a current example is a bright magenta color:

```
h1 {color: orange;}
```

CSS code that has been previously shown but is part of a new example is shown in a muted magenta color:

```
h1 {
color: orange;
font-size: 2em;
}
```

Sometimes lines of code are intended to be written on a single line, but the book requires a line wrap. An arrow shows where a line break occurs for print formatting purposes only and should be ignored.

```
<blockquote cite="http://alistapart.
com/article/uncle-sam-wants-you-to-
optimize-your-content-for-mobile">
```

TIPS & NOTES

>>> *TIP: TIPS & NOTES PROVIDE REMINDERS ABOUT THE CURRENT TOPIC OR STEP.*

 SIDEBARS

Sidebars help you learn more about a topic through related information.

REQUIREMENTS

In order to work through the assignments and projects in this book, you do not need expensive software or hardware.

TEXT EDITOR

You will need a code text editor—not a text editor that came with your computer— to write HTML and CSS. An excellent, and free, editor I would recommend is Komodo Edit (http://activestate.com/komodo-edit) for Windows, Mac, and Linux. Other free alternatives include Notepad++ for Windows, TextWrangler for Mac, and Bluefish for Linux.

>>> *NOTE: THE WEBSITE HAS LINKS AND TUTORIALS TO HELP YOU INSTALL AND SET UP KOMODO EDIT.*

IMAGE EDITOR

If you have Photoshop or Photoshop Elements, those are fine but a bit much for what you need at this point. Pixlr (http://pixlr.com/editor/) is a great free application that works directly in your browser. Additional image editors are included on the website.

BROWSER

It would be best to download one or two modern—standards-compliant— browsers such as Chrome, Firefox, or Opera (**Figure 1**). All of these can be installed on Linux, Mac, and Windows systems. The screenshots you'll see in this book were primarily taken while using Opera on Mac, unless otherwise noted.

FIGURE 1
Chrome, Firefox, and Opera are open-source browsers that keep current with many web standards and are available on multiple operating systems.

>>> *NOTE: IT'S BEYOND THE SCOPE OF THIS BOOK TO HAVE MAC USERS SET UP A WINDOWS OPERATING SYSTEM TO RUN INTERNET EXPLORER. WINDOWS USERS ALSO CANNOT INSTALL THE LATEST VERSION OF SAFARI. THERE'S MORE ON MULTI-BROWSER TESTING IN CHAPTER 13 ON THE WEBSITE.*

 INTERNET EXPLORER

If you're a Windows user, you might be accustomed to using Internet Explorer (referred to throughout this book as IE). It's fine to continue using it, but the examples in this book will primarily work for version 8 (IE8) and above. Microsoft has stopped supporting IE6, and IE7 lags behind web standards common in most browsers. Check your version of IE by selecting About Internet Explorer under the Help tab (**Figure 2**).

> SAFARI

If you're a Mac user, Safari is pre-installed on your computer and has kept up good support of web standards. However, make sure your version of Safari is as up to date as possible. At minimum, you should have Safari 5, but it would be best to have Safari 6. To check your version of Safari, simply select About Safari under the Safari menu (**Figure 3**).

WEB HOSTING & DOMAIN REGISTRATION

In the final set of assignments and projects, you will need to host your website online. Instructions on how to register a domain name, set up a free hosting account, and uploading files are supplied on the corresponding website.

FIGURE 2
How to check your version of IE.

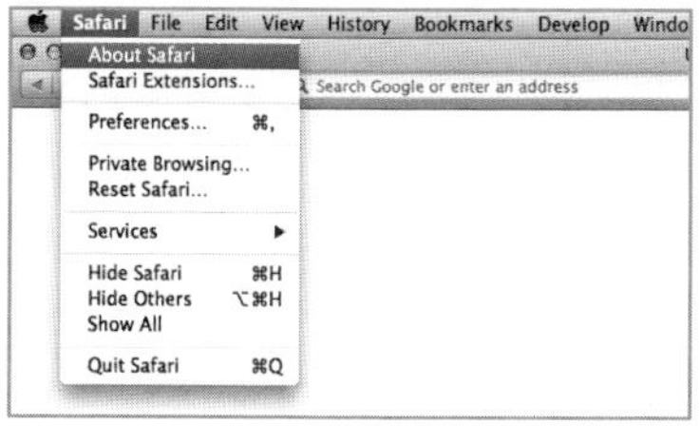

FIGURE 3
How to check your version of Safari.

BOOK + WEBSITE = ENHANCED LEARNING

What's different about this book?

While the book does contain a substantial amount of information and examples by itself, it's not intended to be a bulky, comprehensive resource on its own.

The corresponding website, found at **http://foundationsofwebdesign.com**, provides a great deal of additional material:

CHAPTER DOWNLOADS

At the beginning of a chapter that has files and documents to download, you'll see the following message:

CHAPTER CODE

>>> *THE CODE EXAMPLES FOR THIS CHAPTER CAN BE DOWNLOADED FROM THE WEBSITE (HTTP://FOUNDATIONSOFWEBDESIGN.COM).*

FORUMS AND RESOURCES

Additionally, the website has a forum where you can answer questions, submit website assignments for review, download assignments, and find additional resources related to each chapter topic.

VIDEO DEMONSTRATIONS

Video tutorials are provided for each chapter to enhance and reinforce what is taught in the book. Why the combination of print and video? We learn best when we can combine the use of as many senses as possible, and, between the book and videos, I'm hoping (for most of you) to hit at least three (sight, hearing, and touch) of the five senses. The videos also supply a few advantages:

- You see me walk through each step of a demonstration.

- You work right along with the video.

- You can pause and replay if anything doesn't make sense.

STRUCTURE

How should you approach the material?

1. Read through the chapter and work through the demonstrations.

2. Watch the videos and work through the demonstrations.

3. Work on the assignment/projects (PDFs available on the site).

TEACHERS

If you're a teacher and wish to adopt this textbook for your class, I've provided the following materials to download from the website:

• Course syllabus

• Assignments

• Two projects

• Rubrics for grading

These documents can be modified to fit your class needs.

 FLIPPED CLASSROOM

My classes use the "flipped classroom" model, which means students read and watch video demonstrations outside of class and work on assignments and projects during the class time. This allows the teacher to work as a guide and revisit concepts students don't understand. There is more information online, and I am happy to talk to you about this model if you're interested in finding out more.

LET'S GET STARTED

With the introduction behind you, it's time to jump in and get going on your first HTML document.

If you hold a cat by the tail

you learn things you cannot

learn any other way.

~ Mark Twain

PART

—

01

THE BASICS

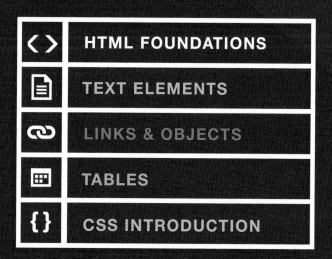

‹ ›	**HTML FOUNDATIONS**
📄	**TEXT ELEMENTS**
🔗	**LINKS & OBJECTS**
▦	**TABLES**
{ }	**CSS INTRODUCTION**

HTML FOUNDATIONS

—

01

>>> CHAPTER CODE

THE CODE EXAMPLES FOR THIS CHAPTER CAN BE DOWNLOADED FROM THE WEBSITE (HTTP://FOUNDATIONSOFWEBDESIGN.COM).

Every year, I look into the eyes of my HTML and CSS introductory class students and know most are there because they have to be—and they are terrified at the idea they have to learn to hand-code a website. Some are nontraditional, older students who always wanted to learn how but are overwhelmed by the technology and terminology. However, by the end of the course, many are surprised to find they can "get it"; some even decide to continue on and eventually find work in the field of web design and development.

One thing everyone can agree upon is that it has become more essential for individuals and businesses to have a web presence. Whether you plan on creating websites as a hobby or getting into the field as a web designer or developer, it's important to learn the foundational framework of modern websites. In this chapter, you'll begin your journey by learning how to create an HTML document and the skeletal elements that make up its framework.

GETTING STARTED

So, at this point, you should be ready to get your feet wet learning HTML. You should have a code editor installed (see the introduction) and open, and have the folder for this chapter (**fowd_ch01_folder**) downloaded and on your desktop (or another location you can easily find).

>>> *NEED HELP? IF YOU GET LOST OR HAVE PROBLEMS, THE FOLDER CONTAINS SOLUTIONS TO THE EXERCISES IN THIS CHAPTER. FOR FURTHER ASSISTANCE, USE THE FORUM ON THE WEBSITE.*

CREATING AN HTML DOCUMENT

Your first step is to create a new HTML document—much like creating a new word-processing document.

STEP 1.1.1

Create a new document in your text editor:

File > New > New File

KEYBOARD SHORTCUT: CTRL+N ON WINDOWS AND LINUX; COMMAND+N ON MAC.

STEP 1.1.2

Save the document into your **fowd_ch01_folder**:

File > Save As

KEYBOARD SHORTCUT: SHIFT+CTRL+S ON WINDOWS AND LINUX; SHIFT+COMMAND+S ON MAC.

STEP 1.1.3

You'll see a dialogue window open that asks you what you want to name the document and where you want to save it (**Figure 1.1**).

01

For the name of the
document, enter
index.html.

02

The location of the
document should
be set as the
fowd_ch01_folder.

03

Click Save.

The HTML document
is now ready to accept
HTML elements!

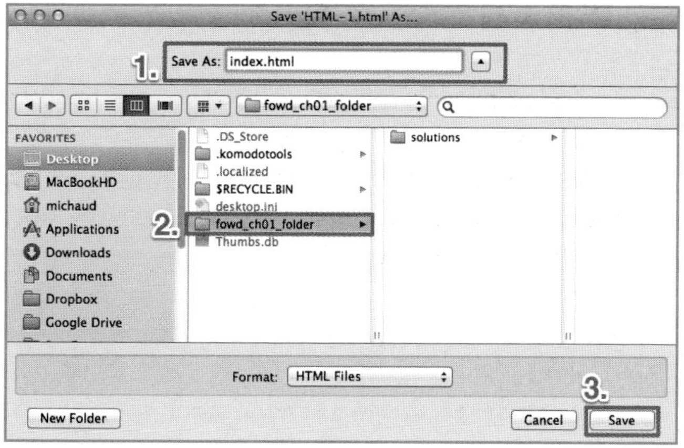

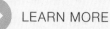

FIGURE 1.1
The dialogue window for saving your document.

NAMING FILES & FOLDERS

When naming documents and folders, remember these
basic rules:

- Write all document and folder names in lowercase:
  portfolio.html.

- Use dashes or underscores between names:
  about_us.html, about-us.html, or aboutus.html,
  not about us.html.

>>> *LEARN MORE ABOUT DOCUMENT AND FOLDER NAMING
ON THE WEBSITE.*

LEARN MORE

Check out the website to learn more
about HTML, browsers, and the
history of the Internet.

WHY "INDEX"?

Every website is contained within a
directory on a web server (a directory
like those on your computer), and
each HTML page is a separate
document within that directory.
When you go to a website (for
example, www.smashingmagazine.
com), the web server—which hosts
the website—is set up to deliver
a default document. The default
document typically starts with
the name "index" and can have a
number of different format names,
e.g., .html, .php, .htm, .aspx. Visit
the website for additional resources
about default file names.

HTML VERSIONS

While there are different HTML versions you could choose from, for the purposes of this book HTML5 will be used. Check out the website if you need to know about other versions.

WORLD WIDE WEB CONSORTIUM

Led by Web inventor Tim Berners-Lee and CEO Jeffrey Jaffe, the World Wide Web Consortium (W3C) is an international community working together to develop web standards.

HTML STRUCTURE

An HTML document is about presenting content. In order for browsers to recognize the document as HTML, you need to write specific elements defining your HTML document and indicating what version of HTML you're using.

DOCTYPE

The `<!doctype html>` declaration tells the browser what type of HTML document you're creating and what rules should apply to it, as defined by the World Wide Web Consortium (W3C).

>>> *USE LOWERCASE: SOMETIMES YOU'LL SEE THE WORD DOCTYPE ALL LOWERCASE OR ALL UPPERCASE—EITHER WAY IS FINE. ALL EXAMPLES IN THIS BOOK WILL USE LOWERCASE TAGS.*

STEP 1.2.1

Add the HTML5 doctype to the first line of your **index.html** document.

```
<!doctype html>
```

HTML ELEMENT

The `html` element is the root HTML object in your document, and it surrounds all the other objects (HTML tags) in the document.

>>> *REMEMBER: THE ONLY TWO DIRECT DESCENDANTS OF THE `html` ELEMENT ARE THE head AND body ELEMENTS. ONLY THE doctype GOES BEFORE THE OPENING `<html>` TAG, AND NOTHING COMES AFTER THE CLOSING `</html>` TAG.*

STEP 1.2.2

In the **index.html** document, add the html element after the doctype.

```
<!doctype html>
<html>
</html>
```

HEAD ELEMENT

After the opening `<html>` tag comes the `head` element. Consider this the "brains" of the outfit—it does some critical thinking and communicating to the browser. It holds the elements that

- Provide a website title for display on browser title bars, bookmarks, and search engine results— `<title></title>`

- Help define metadata— `<meta>`

- Link to style sheets— `<link></link>` (see Chapter 5)—and scripts— `<script></script>` (see Chapter 14)

STEP 1.2.3

Add the `head` element after the opening `<html>` tag.

```
<!doctype html>
<html>
    <head>

    </head>
</html>
```

BODY ELEMENT

The `body` element contains the information (such as headings, paragraphs, tables, and forms) that users actually see and interact with when using a website. When we look at people, we see their bodies (but not necessarily the bones that give their bodies structure). So, if you want to relate this to some basic anatomy, the `body` is the skin (content) and bones (HTML tags) of your document. The opening `<body>` tag is placed immediately after the closing `</head>` element, and the closing `</body>` tag is placed immediately before the closing `</html>` tag.

STEP 1.2.4

In your **index.html** document, place the `<body></body>` tags after the closing `</head>` tag.

```
<!doctype html>
<html>
    <head>

    </head>
    <body>

    </body>
</html>
```

>>> REMEMBER: *SAVE AFTER EACH ADDITION YOU MAKE TO THE DOCUMENT.*

You now have the basic skeletal framework for the HTML document. If you save the document and view it in a browser, you'll only see a blank page (**Figure 1.2**).

In the next two sections, we'll cover the next level of detail—the elements that fit within the `head` and `body` elements.

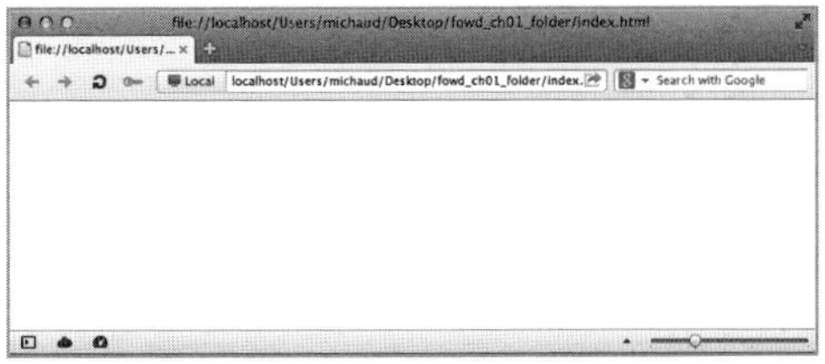

FIGURE 1.2
The skeletal framework for HTML only gives you a blank canvas.

HEAD ELEMENTS

While there are other (optional) elements—discussed later in the book—placed between the opening and closing `html` tags, the one required element is the `title` element.

TITLE ELEMENT

The `title` element is contained within the `head` element, and its content (words between the opening and closing tags) is displayed in the title bar of the browser. For example, www.cnn.com has

```
<title>CNN.com International -
Breaking, World, Business, Sports,
Entertainment and Video News</title>
```

I've highlighted where that shows up in the browser's title bar and tab in Opera (**Figure 1.3**).

STEP 1.2.5

In your document, place the `<title>` `</title>` tags after the opening `<head>` tag.

```
<head>

    <title>My Website</title>

</head>
```

After you save your document—Ctrl+S (Windows/Linux) or Command+S (Mac)—view the **index.html** document in the browser (**Figure 1.4**).

META ELEMENT

The `meta` element holds metadata to give the browser more information about the website.

⟫⟫ *NOTE: THERE IS ONE STRIKING DIFFERENCE YOU'LL FIND BETWEEN THE* `<meta>` *TAG AND OTHER TAGS SUCH AS* `html, head, body, AND p:` *IT'S A SELF CLOSING TAG—THERE IS NO CLOSING* `</meta>` *TAG.*

The information contained in the `meta` element may tell the browser how to render the document or index the document content with keywords; or you can define your own metadata. While there is not a set of standard metadata properties, one of the most useful is the `charset` attribute.

FIGURE 1.3
The title bar and tab display the content of the title element.

HTML ATTRIBUTES

HTML attributes provide additional information about HTML elements. They are discussed in more detail in Chapter 6.

STEP 1.2.6

In your HTML document, place the `meta` element above the title element, and give it a `charset` attribute with the value of `utf-8`.

```
<head>
    <meta charset="utf-8">
    <title>My Website</title>
</head>
```

>>> *NOTE: WEB CODERS ARE ENCOURAGED TO USE THE VALUE OF "UTF-8". WHY? LET'S JUST SAY IT ALLOWS YOU TO ENCODE A LOT OF CHARACTERS FOR YOUR DOCUMENT AND WILL ALLOW THE BROWSER TO HANDLE PRETTY MUCH ANY LANGUAGE YOU MIGHT WANT TO INCLUDE.*

 CHARACTER ENCODING

The character encoding defines what character set the web page is written in. If you need to use special characters in your website:

copyright ©
ampersand &
greater-than >
less-than <

the character set will help the browser to display these using character entities.

© = ©
& = &
> = >
< = <

If you don't use character entities for these (and other) special characters, the browser can display unexpected results—as some are specifically reserved HTML characters.

The website has more information on the use of special characters.

FIGURE 1.4
The title appears in the browser title bar and tab.

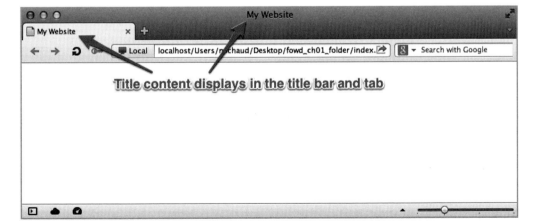

LANGUAGE ATTRIBUTE

While we're on the topic of attributes, you can identify what the language for the website content is by using the `lang` attribute in the `html` element.

STEP 1.2.7

Add the `lang` attribute, with the value of `en-us`, to the `html` element.

```
<!doctype html>
<html lang="en-us">
<head>
```

BODY ELEMENTS

To conclude this chapter, you'll get your first (very basic) introduction to adding and structuring the content that will be displayed in the browser.

STRUCTURING CONTENT

The content you place between the `body` tags is what is displayed in the window of the browser.

STEP 1.3.1

If you simply add a few lines of text:

```
<body>
    My Website: HTML &amp; CSS
➥ This website will be about my
➥ adventures in learning HTML
➥ &amp; CSS
</body>
```

the browser will display it as a single line of text (**Figure 1.5**).

<image type="segment"></image>

> OTHER LANGUAGES

You can place the `lang` attribute in other HTML elements to identify other languages within the content of your website.

```
<p>In a speech by John F.
Kennedy, he said,
➥<q lang="de">Ich bin ein
➥ Berliner</q>.</p>.
```

Screen readers would then use a German pronunciation for "Ich bin ein Berliner," rather than English.

FIGURE 1.5
Content to be displayed in the browser is added within the `body` element.

CHARACTER ENTITY IN USE

Did you see a special character entity used? The & gives you the & symbol. Since it's often reserved as a character in programming, you should use the character entity & when you need the & symbol.

To add structure to the content, you'll need elements that work within the body element. While the text elements will be covered more in-depth in Chapter 2, it's good to see how they help to structure the content.

BLOCK-LEVEL ELEMENTS

Block-level elements are those elements that usually force a new line after the element is closed: </div>, </p>, </li>, </dd>. Block-level elements can only appear within the <body> element and can contain other block-level and inline-level elements (which we'll cover later). One exception to this rule: The paragraph element (<p>...</p>) cannot contain other block-level elements.

STEP 1.3.2

Between the body's opening and closing tags, wrap the first line of text with the <h1></h1> tags and the second line of text with the <p></p> tags.

```
<body>
    <h1>Foundations of Web Design</h1>
    <p>This website will be about my
➡ adventures in learning HTML &amp;
➡ CSS</p>
</body>
```

Viewing the website in the browser, you see the content now has some structure (**Figure 1.6**).

What did those <h1></h1> and <p></p> tags just do? Besides displaying each line of text in different sizes and weights (more on that in Chapter 2), they allow you to give meaningful structure (also referred to as semantic markup) to your content.

The h1 (top-level header) block-level element is like the title element for the body—it tells the visitor the name of the website (like Google, Facebook, Twitter, CNN, etc.).

The p (paragraph) block-level element defines blocks of single-line sentences or paragraphs.

DIV ELEMENT

The block-level div element is a very generic element—it gives no meaning to the content—but it's very commonly used for grouping content (by subject or functionality) into arbitrary structural sections (or divisions) within a document.

FIGURE 1.6
Content with semantic structure.

STEP 1.3.3

Add the opening `<div>` tag above the `h1` element and the closing `</div>` tag after the `p` element.

```
<body>
<div>
  <h1>My Website: HTML &amp; CSS</h1>
  <p>This website will be about my
  adventures in learning HTML &amp;
  CSS</p>
</div>
</body>
```

Save the document and then preview the document in the browser (**Figure 1.7**).

While the `div` element does not cause the text to display any differently, you'll find it can be used quite effectively with CSS to change the way your content is displayed (Chapters 8 and 9). Although this example is pretty limited, you'll come to find, as you progress, the `div` element is used (and often misused) quite extensively to structure websites (**Figure 1.8**).

FIGURE 1.7
The content within the `div` element does not display differently.

HTML5 ALTERNATIVE

The `section` element was introduced in HTML5 to provide a more meaningful element than the `div` for defining sections of content within a website. The W3C Specification says:

>>> *THE `<section>` ELEMENT IS AN ELEMENT DESIGNED TO PROGRAMMATICALLY DESIGNATE SECTIONS OF DOCUMENT CONTENT. IT REPRESENTS THE SECTION OF A DOCUMENT THAT IS GROUPED AROUND A GENERAL THEME AND OFTEN COMES WITH A SPECIFIC HEADING.*

While the `section` element doesn't do away with the `div` element, it does have a more specific purpose in breaking the content of a page into different functions or subject areas, or breaking an article or story up into different sections (**Figure 1.9**).

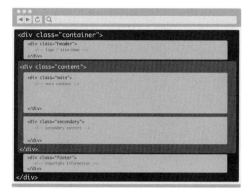

FIGURE 1.8
An illustration of a common `div` structure.

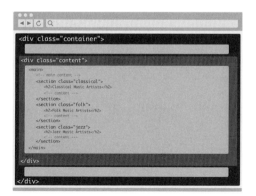

FIGURE 1.9
A basic illustration of using
the `section` element.

*▶▶▶ IF YOU WISH TO SEE AN EXAMPLE (FROM WWW.MOZILLA.ORG) OF THE SECTION ELEMENT, OPEN **HTML5-SECTION-EXAMPLE.HTML** IN YOUR TEXT EDITOR.*

Beyond the book ... While the use of HTML5 elements is something you will need to know, it's beyond the scope of this book to go into any great detail for the new elements: `section`, `article`, `aside`, `header`, `footer`, `nav`. In Chapter 6, the `aside`, `header`, `footer`, and `nav` will be discussed briefly.

WRAPPING THINGS UP

In this chapter, you were introduced to using your code editor to create an HTML document and add in the foundational `doctype`, `html`, `head`, and `body` elements. These, along with the `title` and `div` elements and the `lang` and `charset` attributes, are pieces you'll use in every HTML document you create.

In the next chapter, you'll get further into the HTML structural text elements that are used to mark up the meaning of your text content.

▶▶▶ WEBSITE REMINDER: THERE IS ADDITIONAL CONTENT TO DOWNLOAD AND VIDEOS TO VIEW FOR THE FOUNDATIONAL HTML ELEMENTS, AS WELL AS AN ASSIGNMENT TO TEST YOUR SKILLS!

TEXT ELEMENTS

—

02

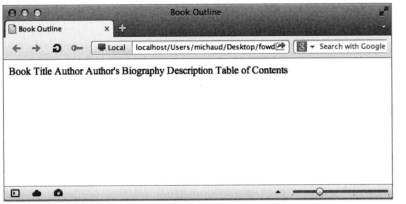

FIGURE 2.1
Text with no
HTML structure.

›››› CHAPTER CODE

*THE CODE EXAMPLES FOR THIS CHAPTER
CAN BE DOWNLOADED FROM THE WEBSITE
(HTTP://FOUNDATIONSOFWEBDESIGN.COM).*

In the first chapter, we looked at the basic containing elements for a web document: the head and body elements. In this chapter, we'll focus specifically on text elements that are contained within the body element.

HANDS ON

The HTML document **fowd_ch02_folder /01-book.html** contains:

```
<!DOCTYPE html>
<html lang="en-us">
<head>
    <meta charset="utf-8">
    <title>Book Outline</title>
</head>
<body>
    <!-- Book Website -->
    Book Title
    Author
    Author's Biography
    Description
    Table of Contents
</body>
</html>
```

While you'll see that each line of text between the `<body>...</body>` tags is on a separate line in the text editor, it will look quite different in your browser. Open the **01-book.html** document in your web browser (**Figure 2.1**).

Notice that all the text (while it has spaces between each word) runs together. To correct this, you need to add some additional structure to the content, using HTML text elements.

OUTLINE

When thinking about using the text elements in an HTML document, it's helpful if you think about basic writing skills. Let's say you are creating a (simple) website about the book *The Grapes of Wrath* by John Steinbeck. The

first thing you might do is create an outline of the topic headings (**Figure 2.2**).

The book's title is the most important piece of information; after that, each topic is a sub-topic within the main topic—the book. For example, because the description is about the book, not the author, it is at the same level as the Author topic, and not a sub-topic of it. The only exception is "Author's Biography," a sub-sub-topic (under "Author," which is a sub-topic of "Book Title").

TEXT HEADERS

You will use the outline topics above to set up a parallel structure of text heading elements for your page about *The Grapes of Wrath*.

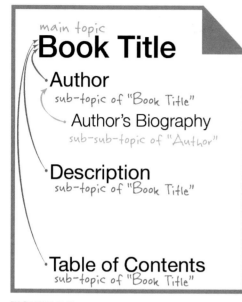

FIGURE 2.2
Possible outline.

MAIN TOPIC

`<h1>...</h1>`

The `h1` element denotes the most important topic heading—in this case "Book Title" (it's what your website is about).

STEP 2.1.1

Replace `Book Title` with `The Grapes of Wrath`, and add the opening `<h1>` tag before and the closing `</h1>` tag after the title:

`<h1>The Grapes of Wrath</h1>`

SUB-TOPICS

`<h2>...</h2>  thru  <h6>...</h6>`

STEP 2.1.2

Let's move on to the next example in the outline. If the book title *The Grapes of Wrath* is the main topic, you can determine from the outline what sub-topic heading elements are needed. "Author" is a sub-topic and should be wrapped within the `h2` element. Replace `Author` with `John Steinbeck` and wrap it with an `h2` element.

`<h2>John Steinbeck</h2>`

STEP 2.1.3

Next we have the "Author's Biography." The biography is a sub-sub-topic of the book's title, subsidiary to the author. So, what level heading would it receive? If you said `h3`, you'd be correct! This time no text needs to change; simply wrap Author's Biography with the opening `<h3>` and closing `</h3>` tags:

`<h3>Author's Biography</h3>`

STEP 2.1.4

Following the biography, the next topic is the "Description." Is the description of the author (John Steinbeck) or the book (*The Grapes of Wrath*)? The book, correct? So, instead of continuing down the hierarchy to `h4`, you go back up to the `h2` element (since *The Grapes of Wrath* is an `h1` element). Wrap the word Description with the `h2` element tags.

`<h2>Description</h2>`

STEP 2.1.5

Finally, the list of topics concludes with "Table of Contents." Again, this topic is a sub-topic of the book and not of the author, so we'll stick with the h2 element to surround Table of Contents.

```
<h2>Table of Contents</h2>
```

This is now what you should have in your text editor:

```
<!DOCTYPE html>
<html lang="en">
<head>
    <meta charset="utf-8">
    <title>Book Outline</title>
</head>
<body>
    <!-- Book Website -->
    <h1>The Grapes of Wrath</h1>
    <h2>John Steinbeck</h2>
    <h3>Author's Biography</h3>
    <h2>Description</h2>
    <h2>Table of Contents</h2>
</body>
</html>
```

Save your document and open it in a browser (**Figure 2.3**).

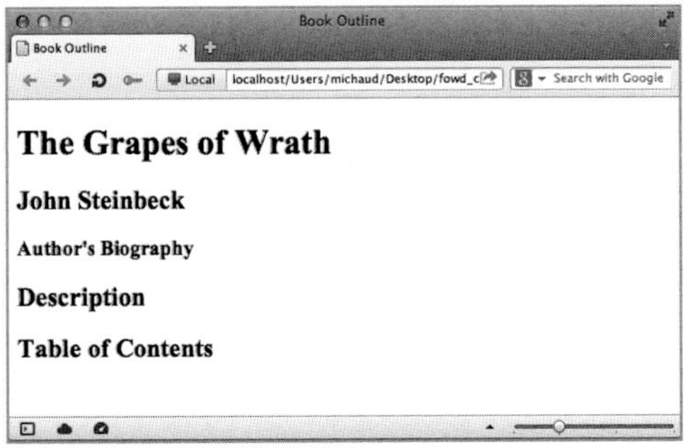

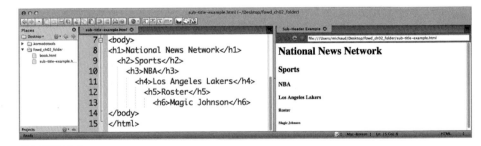

FIGURE 2.3
The book website's structure is starting to take shape!

KEEP THE ORDER

There are actually six levels of text heading elements: h1, h2, h3, h4, h5, h6. When using them, you should never skip levels in the sequence—so, you shouldn't go from h1 to h3 or h4 to h6. Of course, you do not need to use all six levels; you will rarely need more than three or four.

How does the browser render each heading? Open **02-sub-title-example.html** and view the default display of the document in the browser (**Figure 2.4**).

FIGURE 2.4
Notice the decreasing font sizes for each sub-level heading.

`<p>...</p>`

The `p` (paragraph) element is the most basic of all block-level elements. The `p` element cannot contain *any* other block-level element but can surround inline-level elements (see sidebar on block- and inline-level elements).

```
<p>This is some text</p>
```

BLOCK-LEVEL ELEMENTS

Block-level elements have a line break before and after each element (thereby creating a stand-alone block of content). Block-level elements, other than the `<p></p>` element, can contain other block-level elements, but all can contain inline-level elements.

INLINE-LEVEL ELEMENTS

Inline-level elements do not form new blocks of content; the content is distributed inline and contained within block-level elements or other inline-level elements. Some inline elements help to define text or data in a document: `<strong>` helps to strongly emphasize text and `<q>` denotes a quotation. Others, like the `<span>` element offer no semantic information.

STEP 2.1.6

Go ahead and add some text after

```
<h3>Author's Biography</h3>
```

⟫⟫ REMINDER

THE TEXT FOR THE BOOK EXAMPLE IS IN THE **FOWD_CH02_FOLDER/ BOOK TEXT COPY.TXT** DOCUMENT.

Add the following text:

John Ernst Steinbeck, Jr. (February 27, 1902 – December 20, 1968) was an American writer. He is widely known for the Pulitzer Prize-winning novel The Grapes of Wrath (1939) and East of Eden (1952) and the novella Of Mice and Men (1937). As the author of twenty-seven books, including sixteen novels, six non-fiction books, and five collections of short stories, Steinbeck received the Nobel Prize for Literature in 1962.

STEP 2.1.7

Add an opening `<p>` tag before the word "John" and a closing `</p>` tag after "1962."

You should now have:

```
<h3>Author's Biography</h3>
<p>John Ernst Steinbeck, Jr. (February 27, 1902 – December 20, 1968) was an American writer. ... Steinbeck received the Nobel Prize for Literature in 1962.</p>
```

STEP 2.1.8

Now, do the same for the book's description. Place the following text (also found in the **book text copy.txt** document) after `<h2>Description</h2>`:

```
Set during the Great Depression, the
novel focuses on the Joads, a poor fam-
ily of tenant farmers driven from their
Oklahoma home by drought, economic hard-
ship, and changes in financial and agri-
cultural industries. Due to their nearly
hopeless situation, and in part because
they were trapped in the Dust Bowl, the
Joads set out for California. Along with
of other "Okies", they sought jobs, land,
dignity, and a future.
```

STEP 2.1.9

Finally, wrap the paragraph with a `p` element:

```
<p>Set during the Great Depression, the
novel … they sought jobs, land, dignity,
and a future.</p>
```

Save your document and open it in a browser (**Figure 2.5**).

`<blockquote>…</blockquote>`

The book's description was taken from another source, so let's look at how you can credit the original author. Since this is a rather lengthy quote, you should use the `blockquote` element (rather than the inline `q` element). The `blockquote` element handles large blocks of text and can contain other elements, in this case the `p` element.

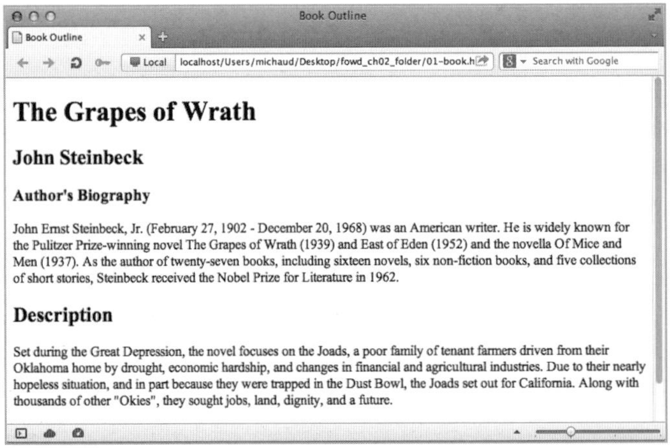

STEP 2.1.10

Add the opening `<blockquote>` tag before the opening `<p>` tag and the closing `</blockquote>` tag after the closing `</p>` tag:

```
<blockquote>
    <p>Set during the Great Depression,
    the novel … they sought jobs, land,
    dignity, and a future.</p>
</blockquote>
```

FIGURE 2.5
The result of adding the paragraph elements.

Save your document and open it in a browser. You'll notice the browser (by default) indents any text within the `blockquote` element (**Figure 2.6**).

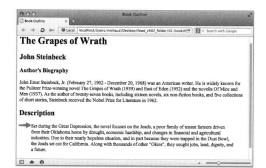

FIGURE 2.6
The result of adding the `blockquote` element.

Because a blockquote, by definition, comes from a source, adding citations within the `blockquote` element will make it more useful to your website's visitors

CITE ATTRIBUTE

The opening `<blockquote>` tag can contain the `cite` attribute, in which you can insert the absolute URL online reference of the quote or a relative URL (pointing to a page within your site). In this case, the quote was taken from Wikipedia, and the absolute URL is http://en.wikipedia.org/wiki/The_Grapes_of_Wrath.

STEP 2.1.11

Add the `cite` attribute to the opening `<blockquote>` tag with the URL value in quotation marks.

```
<blockquote cite="http://en.wikipedia.
org/wiki/The_Grapes_of_Wrath">
    <p>Set during the Great Depression,
    the novel … they sought jobs, land,
    dignity, and a future.</p>
</blockquote>
```

If you refreshed the preview of your website in the browser after doing this step, you'll notice this does nothing to change the website from the user's point of view. However, the data is stored and tagged (and it may be displayed in the future), so it's a great attribute to get into the habit of using.

`<cite>…</cite>`

Another way to record a citation in conjunction with the `blockquote` element is the inline `cite` element. The `cite` element identifies a source of reference for your visitors (book, play, website, etc.): in this case, Wikipedia.

STEP 2.1.12

Just *before* the closing `</blockquote>` tag, create a new line and add Wikipedia.

Wrap Wikipedia within a `<cite>…</cite>` element.

```
<blockquote cite="…">
    <p>…</p>
    <p><cite>Wikipedia</cite></p>
</blockquote>
```

>>> *HOLD ON: DON'T DELETE THE CONTENT! SORRY. JUST WANTED YOU TO KNOW THE CONTENT WAS LEFT OUT OF THE CODE EXAMPLE SO YOU CAN SEE ONLY WHAT YOU NEED TO ADD.*

CREATING LISTS

`<li>…</li>`

Save your document and open it in a browser. Notice that "Wikipedia" is visible, as well as indented (because it resides within the `blockquote`) and italicized (the result of how the browser styles the `cite` element by default) (**Figure 2.7**).

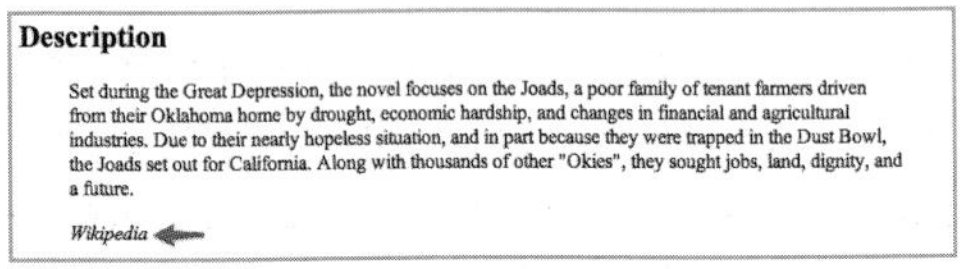

Description

Set during the Great Depression, the novel focuses on the Joads, a poor family of tenant farmers driven from their Oklahoma home by drought, economic hardship, and changes in financial and agricultural industries. Due to their nearly hopeless situation, and in part because they were trapped in the Dust Bowl, the Joads set out for California. Along with thousands of other "Okies", they sought jobs, land, dignity, and a future.

Wikipedia ◀━

FIGURE 2.7
The browser italicizes text within the `cite` element by default.

The `li` element enables you to make lists. Lists cannot stand alone, but must be used within either the unordered `ul` element (such as a bulleted list) or the ordered `ol` element (such as a numbered list). Lists play roles in a large portion of our lives—step-by-step instructions, grocery shopping lists, recipe instructions, etc.—and lists are an important part of websites too.

EXTRA CREDIT: CLICKABLE CITATIONS

While we have not covered anchor tags yet, here's a foretaste of what you'll soon learn. You can add a link to the website for your Wikipedia citation:

```
<cite>
<a href="http://en.wikipedia.org/wiki/The_Grapes_of_Wrath">Wikipe-
dia</a>
</cite>
```

The anchor tag transforms plain text into a clickable link that will take visitors to the Wikipedia page.

Place an opening `<li>` and closing `</li>` around each of the first four chapters of the book.

```
<h2>Table of Contents</h2>
<li>Chapter 1</li>
<li>Chapter 2</li>
<li>Chapter 3</li>
<li>Chapter 4</li>
```

The `li` element doesn't mean much without defining what *type* of list you have (ordered or unordered). Sometimes lists don't need to be in a particular order, such as when you have a book about home repair and you need only the chapter specifically on how to replace floor tiles. Or, maybe you're making a list to purchase items at a grocery store.

`<ol>…</ol>`

Chapters in a book, where the order is important, should be defined as an *ordered* list with the `<ol>…</ol>` tags.

STEP 2.1.14

Wrap the `<ol>…</ol>` tags around the list items:

```
<ol>
  <li>Chapter 1</li>
  <li>Chapter 2</li>
  <li>Chapter 3</li>
  <li>Chapter 4</li>
</ol>
```

You'll notice the browser (by default) places numbers sequentially before each list item (**Figure 2.8**).

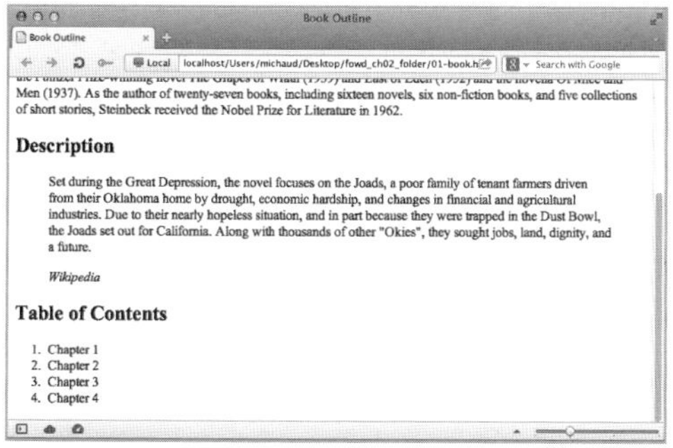

FIGURE 2.8
The list shows sequential numbering.

Since the chapters are already named "Chapter 1," "Chapter 2," and so forth, it might seem redundant to have the same numbers before and after "Chapter." Later on, we'll look at how you can use CSS to change the style of your list (change bullets to blocks, change numbers to letters, or even add custom images). But, for this example, we'll just keep the numbers.

`<ul>…</ul>`

Where order is not important in a list, the unordered list element can be used. Say you wanted to list out some other books written by John Steinbeck and place those in a list. For this demonstration, the list can be added after the chapters.

STEP 2.1.15

Since the "Other Works" are by the author (not about the book), it will be at the same sub-level as the "Author's Biography"— the `h3` header level.

```
<h3>Other Works</h3>
```

Then, within the `<ul></ul>` tag, type out a couple of his works: *Of Mice and Men* and *East of Eden*. Wrap the book titles in `<li></li>` tags and you're done:

```
<ul>
  <li>Of Mice and Men</li>
  <li>East of Eden</li>
</ul>
```

Now, save and preview the document again to see the result. You'll notice the browser (by default) placed bullets • before each book title (**Figure 2.9**).

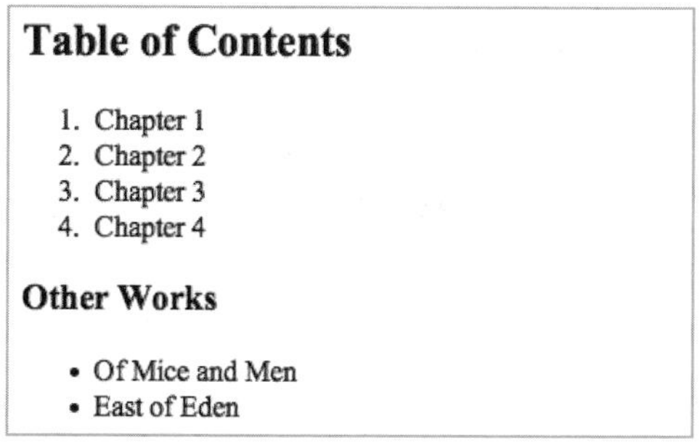

FIGURE 2.9
The list shows as a bulleted list.

DESCRIPTION LISTS

I want to briefly talk about another type of list called the "description list."

>>> *DESCRIPTION LISTS WERE FORMERLY CALLED DEFINITION LISTS IN HTML4, BUT THEY ARE THE SAME ELEMENT.*

I love these lists because they are so flexible in their usage. An article posted back in 2004, by Russ Weakley at Max Design, beautifully demonstrates how you can use description lists (http://maxdesign. com.au/articles/definition/). Basically, the description list comprises three elements: `dl`, `dt`, and `dd`.

You can build your description list in the **03-description-list.html** document.

`<dl>…</dl>`

The `dl` element simply identifies the description list and is the container for the term (`dt`) and description (`dd`) elements.

`<dt>…</dt>`

The `dt` element is the term or name that will be defined in the list. A term might be "Football," which will be followed with a `dd` element containing a description of football.

```
<dl>
    <dt>Football</dt>
    …
</dl>
```

>>> **MULTIPLE TERMS**

THE GREAT THING ABOUT DESCRIPTION LISTS IS THAT YOU'RE NOT LIMITED TO A SINGLE DT ELEMENT, NOR SHOULD YOU LIMIT YOURSELF TO A SINGLE TERM IN A DESCRIPTION LIST. FOR EXAMPLE, YOU COULD LIST OTHER SPORTS IN THIS SAME LIST (FOOTBALL, BASEBALL, BASKETBALL, ETC.)!

`<dd>…</dd>`

The `dd` element is the description list's description or value of the term. You can actually have multiple descriptions per term. The term "Football" has different meanings depending upon where you grew up. For most of the world, "Football" means the game where you kick a ball into a goal, but for many in America, "Football" is the game with a quarterback and a wide receiver, and the ball is kicked through a goalpost. In a description list, you can add both descriptions.

STEP 2.2.2

```
<dl>

    <dt>Football</dt>

    <dd>Football refers to a number of
    sports that involve, to varying de-
    grees, kicking a ball with the foot
    to score a goal.
    </dd>

    <dd>American football, known as
    football in the United States, is a
    team sport played between two teams
    of 11 players with an oval ball on a
    rectangular field 120 yards long and
    53.3 yards wide with goalposts at
    either end.</dd>

</dl>
```

Let's see how a description list is rendered by default in the browser (**Figure 2.10**).

ADDITIONAL TEXT ELEMENTS

There are a few text elements that you'll come across that are not block-level but inline and can help to give additional meaning to your content. However, remember that you should really use these tags to provide meaning (often referred to as "semantic HTML") and not "style" (that's what CSS is for).

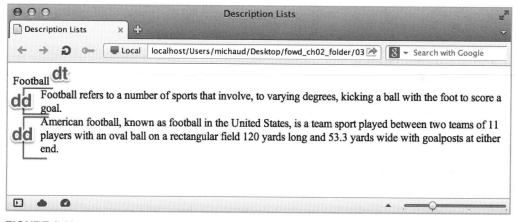

FIGURE 2.10
Notice the descriptions are indented
(like the blockquote).

SEMANTIC HTML = MEANINGFUL HTML

Semantic HTML is a fancy term for HTML where the element names have meaning— they tell you something about the element. The code `<h1>Major heading</h1>` is semantic: screen readers or bots looking at your site will identify this element as a major heading. However, this example `<p><b>Major heading</b></p>` could look exactly like a heading, but the HTML tells you nothing about the role of the element.

`<b>...</b>`

The b inline element is short for "bold"—I'm sure you've seen the "B" icon quite often in word processing documents. While it is not semantic, you can use it to highlight text within a paragraph.

```
<p><b>Reminder</b>: Do not touch the wet
paint.</p>
```

The browser renders "Reminder" in bold type (**Figure 2.11**).

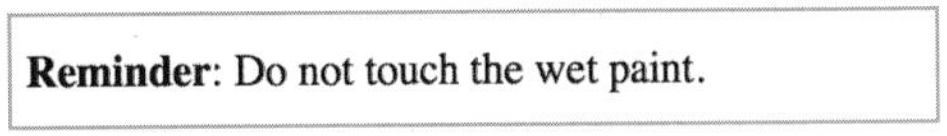

`<strong>...</strong>`

The strong inline element helps give "strong" importance to text and (like the b element) is displayed in bold type.

```
<p>It's <strong>essential</strong>
you remember to turn your paper in on
time.</p>
```

As you can see, there's no difference in how the browser renders the strong and the b elements by default (**Figure 2.12**).

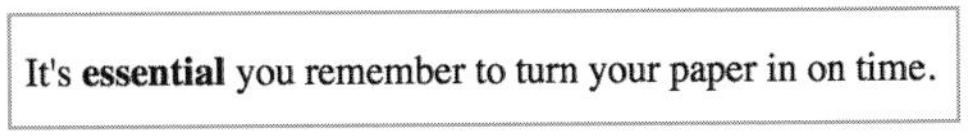

Reminder: Do not touch the wet paint.

FIGURE 2.11
Bold text has a heavier weight than normal text.

It's **essential** you remember to turn your paper in on time.

FIGURE 2.12
Text with the strong element is also rendered with bold type.

B VS STRONG

So, you might ask, what's the difference between the b and strong elements? Excellent question! The developers over at Mozilla (the people who develop Firefox) give us this answer (https://developer.mozilla.org/en-US/docs/HTML/Element/strong):

> It is often confusing to new developers why there are so many ways to express the same thing on a rendered website. Bold and Strong are perhaps one of the most common…
>
> Perhaps not, strong is a logical state, and bold (b) is a physical state.
>
> Logical states separate the appearance from the meaning. The strong element's physical appearance could be something other than "bold." You could express "strongly emphasized" text as a different color, underlined, or a different size, without changing the "meaning."
>
> A "physical" state can't be separated from its appearance. There is no getting around something that uses the b element looking anything other than "bold." If we changed its appearance, it would be confusing.

In short, <b></b> gives no extra meaning or importance, but is a pure highlight.

`<i>...</i>`

The `i` inline element helps to offset some text from other text, without conveying any extra emphasis or importance. Again, like a word processing program with the big "I" button, the browser italicizes the text (**Figure 2.13**).

```
<dl>
    <dt>Meeting Time</dt>
    <dd><i>Time:</i> 10:45am</dd>
    <dd><i>Location:</i> My Office</dd>
</dl>
```

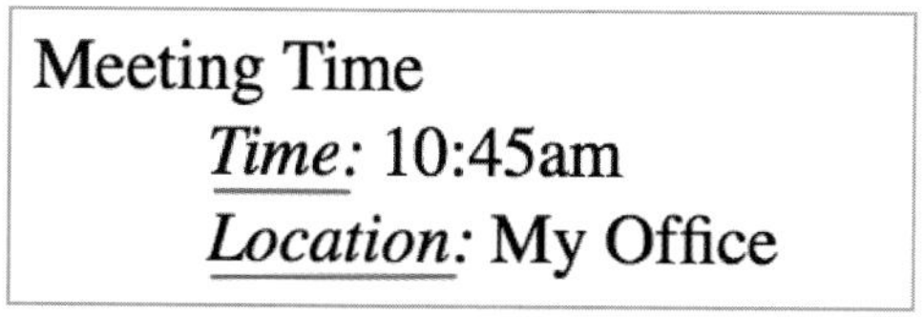

FIGURE 2.13
The first words in each description are italicized with the `i` element.

>>> *NOTE: SOMETIMES THE BROWSER HAS TO ARTIFICIALLY SLANT THE TYPE IF THERE IS NO ITALIC FORMAT FOR A FONT, AND IT LOOKS A LITTLE ODD.*

> **ADDITIONAL USAGES FOR I**

From the w3.org: the `i` element could be a taxonomic designation, a technical term, an idiomatic phrase from another language, a thought, or a ship name.

```
<p>It was<i>raining cats and
dogs</i> outside</p>
```

`<em>...</em>`

If it's important to you for tags to have more meaning—and you are emphasizing some word—then you would use the `em` element. Again, the browser renders the text with italic type, but the `em` element means you're emphasizing (stressing) an idea (**Figure 2.14**).

```
<p>I have a <em>great</em> fear of
heights</p>
```

I have a *great* fear of heights

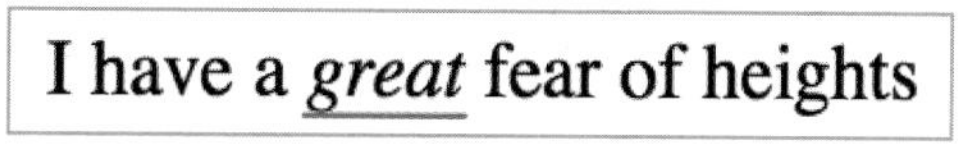

FIGURE 2.14
Can I *emphasize enough* how much I fear heights?

STEP 2.3.1

With the `b`, `strong`, `i`, and `em` elements under your belt, return to the **01-book.html** document. According to literary rules, you need to add one of these elements to some text in the author's biography: When you type out the name of a written work (a book, full-length play, film, longer musical composition, or periodical), you should italicize the title.

So, let's surround each book title with the `<i>...</i>` tags.

```
<h3>Author's Biography</h3>
<p>John Ernst Steinbeck, Jr. (February
27, 1902 - December 20, 1968) was an
American writer. He is widely known for
the Pulitzer Prize-winning novel <i>The
Grapes of Wrath</i> (1939) and <i>East
of Eden</i> (1952) and the novella <i>Of
Mice and Men</i> (1937). As the author
of twenty-seven books, including sixteen
novels, six non-fiction books, and five
collections of short stories, Steinbeck
received the Nobel Prize for Literature
in 1962.</p>
```

The titles are now properly formatted
(Figure 2.15).

Author's Biography

John Ernst Steinbeck, Jr. (February 27, 1902 - December 20, 1968) was an American writer. He is widely known for the Pulitzer Prize-winning novel *The Grapes of Wrath* (1939) and *East of Eden* (1952) and the novella *Of Mice and Men* (1937). As the author of twenty-seven books, including sixteen novels, six non-fiction books, and five collections of short stories, Steinbeck received the Nobel Prize for Literature in 1962.

FIGURE 2.15 Titles of books are italicized.

ADDING COMMENTS

```
<!-- comments -->
```

While not a "structural element," a great feature of HTML is that it enables you to add comments to the code without those comments showing up when your website is viewed. However, you or others working in the markup can see the comments.

You should have noticed a number of comments in each HTML document used in this chapter:

```
<!-- Book Website -->
```
in **01-book.html**

```
<!-- em means we're emphasizing a word -->
```
in **04-bold-italic.html**

When you viewed these documents in the browser, these comments did not show up! Any text you place between the opening `<!--` tag and the closing `-->` tag is rendered as a comment.

WHY USE COMMENTS?

To help you remember what you were doing

To help others working on your code know what you're doing

To note where additions or changes have been or need to be made

HELPFUL HOOK ELEMENT

```
<span>...</span>
```

If the `div` element is the most general of block-level elements, the `span` element **(05-span.html)** is the most general of all inline elements: it provides no semantic value; it does not change visual styling. It's one of the most useful elements, as it provides a *hook* for styling—it identifies content that you might want styled in a specific manner. This is accomplished by attaching a `class` attribute to each `span` with a repeating value.

```
<p>Which American University:</p>
<ul>
    <li>has a mascot that is a <span
class="mascot">Buckeye</span>?</li>
    <li>has a mascot that is a <span
class="mascot">Jayhawk</span>?</li>
    <li>has a mascot that is a <span
class="mascot">Tar Heel</span>?</li>
</ul>
```

The `class` attribute will be covered in Chapter 6, "HTML Attributes." But you can see that the value of `mascot` has now been applied to every `span` element you're using around the name of each mascot.

FIGURE 2.16
The list with the span inline element.

As you can see from the screenshot, there's no visible change to reveal use of the span element—yet. (**Figure 2.16**).

FIGURE 2.17
The applied CSS changes the look of the span element.

When we get into CSS, you will learn how you can style the value of the class selector like so:

```
.mascot {font-weight: bold; color: red;}
```

Then your list will appear as shown in **Figure 2.17**.

FURTHER EXPLORATION

In addition to the span element, there are many other elements that can act as hooks to change the display of type or help define text. Some of the most common are listed below, and I will provide links and examples on the website for further study and exploration.

<abbr>...</abbr>	<dfn>...</dfn>	<kbd>...</ kbd>	_{...}
<code>...</code>	<hr>	<pre>...</pre>	^{...}
<del>...</del>	<ins>...</ins>	<small>...</small>	<var>...</var>

 The <br> element is unique, it does not provide a hook. It simply provides a line break—which can be very useful.

WRAPPING THINGS UP

With text elements, there are a lot of things to consider when considering what is "semantic" (meaningful) when marking up your text. While there are some areas that are pretty consistent (headings, paragraphs, lists), there will be gray areas when you wonder which element is best.

Now that you have the foundations of the "ML" (markup language) in HTML structure, it's time to start learning about the "HT" (hypertext) portion with links. Additionally, in the next chapter, you'll learn how to add objects (images and movies) into a page and how to prepare images to be "web-ready."

DOWNLOAD REMINDER: THERE IS BONUS CONTENT TO DOWNLOAD FOR ADDITIONAL WORK ON TEXT ELEMENTS AND AN ASSIGNMENT TO TEST YOUR SKILLS!

LINKS & OBJECTS

—

03

>>> CHAPTER CODE

THE CODE EXAMPLES FOR THIS CHAPTER CAN BE DOWNLOADED FROM THE WEBSITE (HTTP://FOUNDATIONSOFWEBDESIGN.COM).

As web designers, we want users to interact with and be informed by our websites. This chapter looks at how you can make your pages more interactive with hypertext links, which allow you to link multiple HTML documents to each other and to link your website with other websites. We'll also look at how you can embed objects—images and videos—into your HTML document.

LINKS

The <a>...</a> (anchor) element brings the "Hypertext" to HTML (Hypertext Markup Language) and helps you to link to a destination by using the href (hypertext reference) attribute. Your destination could be a place within your document, another page on your website, a link to a file or document to download, or a website other than your own. So, it's an *extremely* important element.

I've developed a homepage (**index.html**) for your demonstration website on which you need to link the chapters listed to their specific HTML pages. When you open up the **index.html** document, you'll find the following list:

```
<ol>
    <li>Global Structures</li>
    <li>Text Elements</li><
    li>Links and Objects</li>
</ol>
```

STEP 3.1.1

To make "Global Structures" link to the **global-structures.html** document, you need to wrap the text with an anchor tag.

```
<ol>
    <li><a>Global Structures</a></li>
    <li>Text Elements</li>
    <li>Links and Objects</li>
</ol>
```

INDEX.HTML = HOMEPAGE

While a book may have the "index" at the back, the first page a web server looks to open is a document named "index." While you might see other suffixes (.php or .cfm), the name "index" is commonly used to denote the "homepage" of a website.

HREF ATTRIBUTE

In order to make the anchor tag useful, you need the href attribute. href stands for "hypertext reference," and it allows you to reference where your link is going.

Keep this attribute in your memory, as you'll use it again for another HTML element!

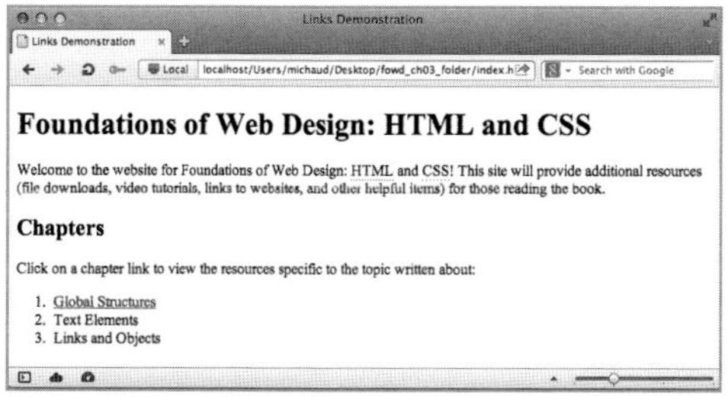

STEP 3.1.2

Reference the **global-structures.html** document using the href attribute; the value of the attribute will be the document **global-structures.html**.

```
<ol>
  <li><a href="global-structures.html">
  Global Structures</a></li>
  <li>Text Elements</li>
  <li>Links and Objects</li>
</ol>
```

>>> REMEMBER

*YOU MUST SELECT **FILE** > **SAVE** FROM THE MENU—OR CTRL+S (PC/LINUX) OR COMMAND+S (MAC)—BEFORE PREVIEWING THE CHANGES TO YOUR HTML DOCUMENT.*

Preview the document in your browser. "Global Structures" should appear blue and underlined (**Figure 3.1A**).

Moving your cursor over the link will cause the cursor to change from an arrow to a hand icon—indicating that you can click on the link (**Figure 3.1B**).

When you click on the link, the browser loads the new document you referenced **(global-structures.html)** (**Figure 3.2**).

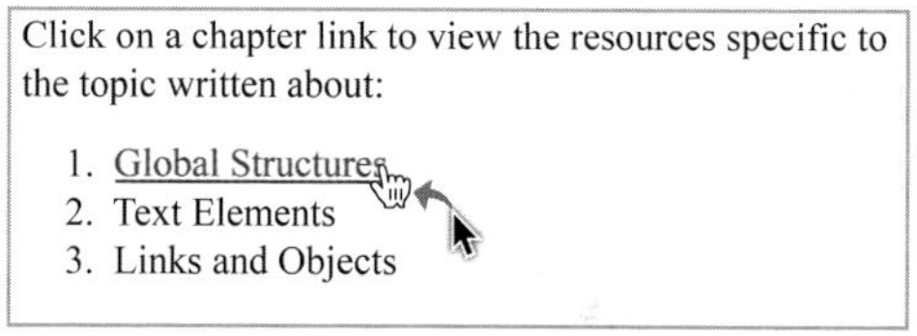

FIGURE 3.1B
Hovering over a hyperlink will change the cursor from an arrow to a hand.

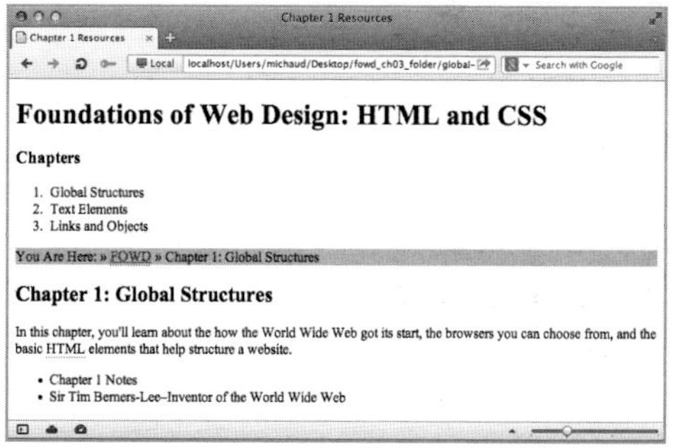

FIGURE 3.1A
How a hypertext link looks.

FIGURE 3.2
The linked document opens in the browser.

I've already applied a link to the abbreviation "FOWD" in the **global-structures. html** document in a **breadcrumb trail**. Click the "FOWD" link and you'll return to the **index.html** (home) page.

After you return to the **index.html** page, notice "Global Structures" is now purple and not blue (**Figure 3.3**). By default, browsers color unexplored links blue and visited links purple—you'll learn how to change these colors with CSS.

STEP 3.1.3

Open **global-structures.html** in a code editor. Down toward the end of the document, you'll see the following code:

```
<ul>
    <li>Chapter 1 Notes</li>
    <!-- http://en.wikipedia.org/wiki/
    Tim_Berners-Lee -->
    <li>Sir Tim Berners-Lee
➡ &ndash;Inventor of the World Wide
    Web</li>
</ul>
```

Sometimes we want users to download a PDF (or other document) or a file, and all we need to do is create a link referencing the document or file.

Add a link for "Chapter 1 Notes" and have the `href` attribute reference a PDF document (**chapter01-notes.pdf**) included in the example folder. It's also good to inform your visitors what type of document they'll view and its size, so add (PDF / 84kb) after the closing anchor tag.

```
<ul>
    <li><a href="chapter01-notes.
➡ pdf">Chapter 1 Notes</a> (PDF /
➡ 84kb)</li>
    <!-- http://en.wikipedia.org/wiki/
    Tim_Berners-Lee -->
    <li>Sir Tim Berners-Lee
    &ndash;Inventor of the World Wide
    Web</li>
</ul>
```

You now have a link to the PDF document (**Figure 3.4**).

STEP 3.1.4

Creating a link to go from your website to someone else's requires that the `href` attribute value contain an **absolute URL path**.

 BREADCRUMBS

A **breadcrumb** is a navigation trail that helps users keep track of where they are within a website (or an application)—like dropping breadcrumbs behind you on a path. You can provide links back to pages they have navigated through to get to the current page or (in hierarchical site structures) the parent pages of the current page.

LEARN FROM EXTRA CODE

Sometimes in a document you'll see code I haven't covered, but which helps "style" or "structure" the document. Study the extra code and use it as a reference in this—and future—examples.

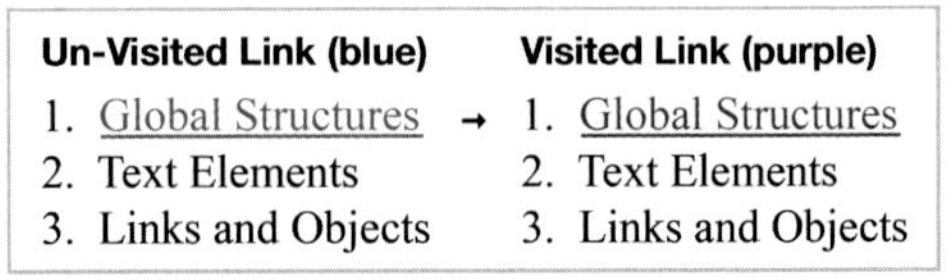

Un-Visited Link (blue)		Visited Link (purple)	
1. Global Structures	→	1. Global Structures	
2. Text Elements		2. Text Elements	
3. Links and Objects		3. Links and Objects	

FIGURE 3.3
Links that have been clicked (or visited) turn from blue to purple.

FILE SIZE INDICATION

Whenever you provide a link where the user will download (or view in a browser) an item (document, image, video, file), you should indicate the file size. It's not nice to interrupt someone's reading by surprising them with an unexpectedly huge download!

FIGURE 3.4
Links to documents look no different than links to pages.

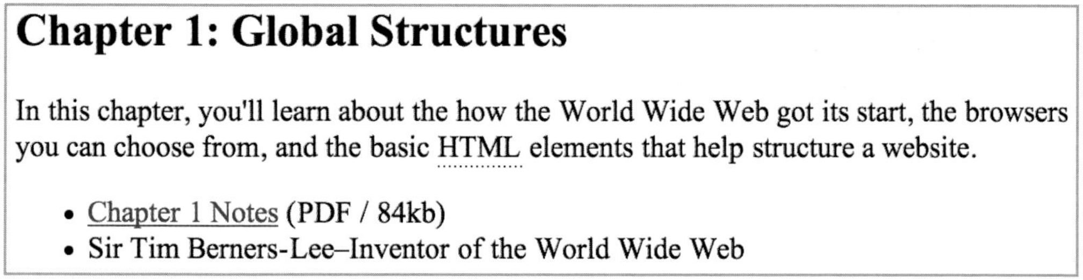

Chapter 1: Global Structures

In this chapter, you'll learn about the how the World Wide Web got its start, the browsers you can choose from, and the basic HTML elements that help structure a website.

- Chapter 1 Notes (PDF / 84kb)
- Sir Tim Berners-Lee–Inventor of the World Wide Web

RELATIVE VS. ABSOLUTE PATHS

Remember, a URL is the website address (http://google.com).

A **relative path** is used when your links reference the same website, but different documents.

```
<a href="index.html">Home</a>
```

http://mysite.com/**index.html** (goes to the homepage)

```
<a href="contact.html">About
➥ Me</a>
```

http://mysite.com/**contact.html** (goes to the "Contact" page)

You could also use a **"root relative" path**. This tells the link to start at the root folder (the folder that holds the all files and folders of the website) and then go from there. Simply add a slash (/) sign before the document or folder name.

```
<a href="/about/thomas-michaud.
➥ html">Contact Me</a>
```

http://mysite.com/**about/thomas-michaud.html** (goes to the root folder for mysite.com, then searches for the "about" folder and then the HTML document).

An **absolute path** includes the document plus the domain name.

```
<a href="http://anothersite.
➥ com/product.html">Their
➥ Products</a>
```

You need an absolute path (also known as a URL) when you leave your site and go to someone else's website.

The second list item is the text: Sir Tim Berners-Lee—Inventor of the World Wide Web. Using the absolute URL `http://en.wikipedia.org/wiki/Tim_Berners-Lee` for your `href` attribute value, create a link using the anchor tag just around the text `Sir Tim Berners-Lee`.

```
<ul>
    <li><a href="chapter01-notes.
➥ pdf">Chapter 1 Notes</a> (PDF /
➥ 84kb)</li>
    <!-- http://en.wikipedia.org/wiki/
    Tim_Berners-Lee -->
    <li><a href="http://en.wikipedia.
➥ org/wiki/Tim_Berners-Lee">Sir Tim
    Berners-Lee</a>&ndash;Inventor of
    the World Wide Web</li>
</ul>
```

If you view your website, you'll notice that "Sir Tim Berners-Lee" is now a hyperlink (**Figure 3.5**).

When you click on the link, the browser navigates away from the demonstration page to the Wikipedia page about Sir Tim Berners-Lee (**Figure 3.6**).

FIGURE 3.6
The link to Wikipedia's article about Sir Tim Berners-Lee.

FIGURE 3.5
Your link to the Wikipedia article about Sir Tim Berners-Lee.

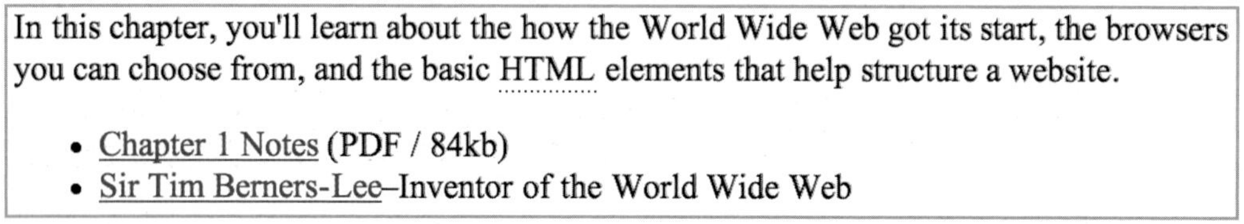

In this chapter, you'll learn about the how the World Wide Web got its start, the browsers you can choose from, and the basic HTML elements that help structure a website.

- Chapter 1 Notes (PDF / 84kb)
- Sir Tim Berners-Lee–Inventor of the World Wide Web

FRAGMENT IDENTIFIER

While you can link to files, other documents, and other websites, you can also link to elements within a page using fragment identifiers. A fragment identifier points to a subordinate resource within the parent document. At the top of a document, you could have the href attribute's value reference an ID (represented by the # sign) attribute:

```
<a href="#topicName">Go to Topic Name</a>
```

Further down, in the same document, you would have an id attribute with the value of topicName, and the previous link would link to the point in the document where this ID appears:

```
<h2 id="topicName">Topic Name</h2>
```

The URL address would then say http://mysite/id-link.html**#topicName.**

View this example in **id-link.html**, in the Chapter 03 folder.

OBJECTS: IMAGES

The <img> element, like the meta element, has no closing tag and is thus referred to as an empty element. As with the a (anchor) element, you must use attributes to make this element work. As a matter of fact, the img element requires two attributes to be technically correct (or valid):

The src attribute tells the img element where the image you wish to embed on your page is located.

The alt attribute helps screen readers (software that works with browsers for visually impaired visitors) to describe the image. Some browsers use this attribute to show text if the image fails to load.

FIGURE 3.7
The Back button is one of the most (if not the most) commonly used buttons in the browser.

THE BACK BUTTON

In order to return to your original site from a new site, you must use the browser's Back button (**Figure 3.7**).

SCREEN-READING SOFTWARE

Screen-reader software, working closely with the computer's Operating System (OS), interprets the content displayed on the screen and then presents it to the user using text-to-speech, sound icons, or a Braille output device. Web pages built using well-structured code provide the best interaction with screen readers and the best result for the visitor with special accessibility needs.

For more information, visit www.nomensa.com/blog/2005/what-is-a-screen-reader/.

LIMITED DEMONSTRATION

FOR THE PURPOSE OF THIS DEMONSTRATION, I WILL ONLY SHOW HOW TO ADD AN IMAGE THAT HAS ALREADY BEEN PREPARED FOR DISPLAY ON A WEBSITE. AS READERS WILL HAVE ACCESS TO DIFFERENT IMAGE EDITORS TO PREPARE IMAGES FOR THE WEB, THE WEBSITE HAS VIDEO TUTORIALS ON HOW TO PREPARE IMAGES IN VARIOUS FORMATS (JPG, PNG, AND SVG) FOR THE WEB USING VARIOUS IMAGE EDITORS.

STEP 3.2.1

Open the **objects.html** document and on line 16, you'll see the following code:

```
<h3>JPG:</h3>
<p>Good for photographs and artwork that
has gradients</p>
<!-- place JPG sample here -->
```

STEP 3.2.2

After the comment, add the

`<img>` element:

```
<img>
```

STEP 3.2.3

To find the image in our project folder, use the `src` attribute and the value will look for the `flower.jpg` in the `images` folder.

```
<img src="images/flower.jpg">
```

After you make changes, save the document (use Control + S [PC/Linux], Command + S [Mac]) and view objects. html in the browser (**Figure 3.8**).

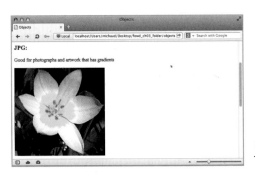

FIGURE 3.8
The image displays in the browser.

STEP 3.2.4

For screen-reading software, add the `alt` attribute with a detailed description:

```
<img src="images/flower.jpg" alt="A
picture of a beautiful, white, flower
with yellow in the center">
```

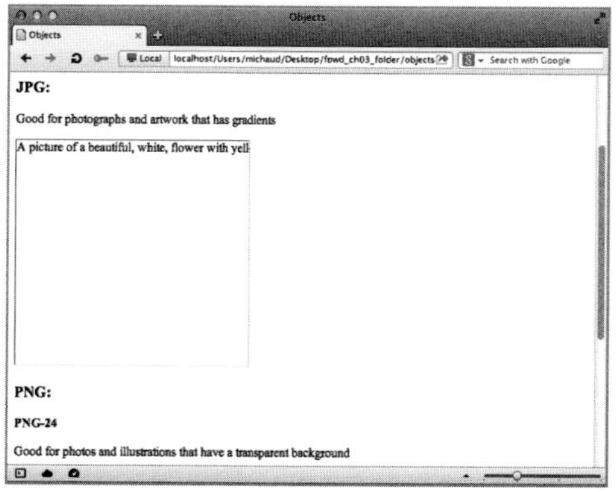

FIGURE 3.9
Adding the `width` and `height` of the image provides a placeholder for images to appear in once they've loaded.

STEP 3.2.5

Finally, add the `width` and `height` attributes (the dimensions of the image) to the `img` element:

```
<img src="images/flower.jpg" alt="A
picture of a beautiful, white, flower
with yellow in the center" width="300"
heigth="282">
```

>>> **DIMENSIONS IN PIXELS:** *ADDING IN THE DIMENSIONS OF THE IMAGE DOES NOT REQUIRE YOU TO ADD IN THE PX, AS THE VALUE IS PIXEL BY DEFAULT.*

Adding the width and height values stops the unsightly user experience you get when your browser keeps rearranging the layout as new images pop into view (**Figure 3.9**).

>>> **RESIZING:** *IT'S BEST TO RESIZE IMAGES BEFORE YOU USE THEM ON THE WEB. DO NOT USE THE width AND height ATTRIBUTE VALUES TO RESIZE LARGE IMAGES DOWN OR UP IN SIZE!*

TITLE ATTRIBUTE

The `title` attribute can also be applied but is optional. While the attribute is not well supported for touch- or screen-reader devices, users on desktop browsers can hover their mouse over an object containing the `title` attribute and see a displayed message.

```
<img src="" alt="" width=""
height="" title="message
displayed on mouse hover">
```

For more on the accessibility of the `title` attribute, view: http://blog.paciellogroup.com/2010/11/using-the-html-title-attribute/.

OBJECTS: VIDEO

There are several ways to create a video, upload it to your server, and add it to your website, but you have to consider browser support for the HTML5 video formats (MP4, OGG, WEBM) vs. Flash video, and which video formats play (or don't play) on which browser. A simple solution is to use hosted services (like YouTube and Vimeo) that do all the hard work for you and then give you links to share your video. Sweet!

STEP 3.3.1

Head over to YouTube and do a search for a very popular video: "MOVE - STA Travel Australia" (**Figure 3.10**).

Below the video, you'll see a set of options. Select Share and then Embed (**Figure 3.11**). If you wish, de-select "Show suggested videos when the video finishes."

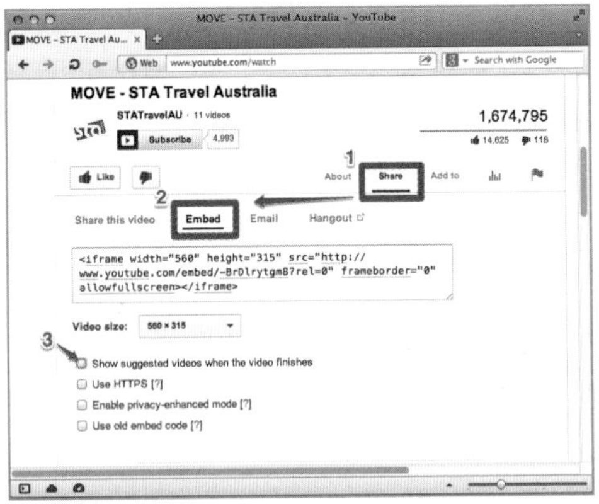

STEP 3.3.2

`<iframe>…</iframe>`

The first option that YouTube provides is the `iframe` element to embed the video.

FIGURE 3.10
"MOVE – STA Travel Australia" by STA Travel Australia.

FIGURE 3.11
Options for embedding a video.

```
<iframe width="560" height="315"
src="http://www.youtube.com/embed/-
BrDlrytgm8?rel=0" frameborder="0"
allowfullscreen></iframe>
```

The `iframe` element (iframe is short for "inline frame") allows you to embed another website's content into your own. The three following attributes are pretty important when using the `iframe` element: `src`, `width`, and `height`.

You've already worked with the `src` attribute while using the `img` element. It looks for the "source" of your content: `src="http://www.youtube.com/embed/-BrDlrytgm8?rel=0"`.

WIDTH AND HEIGHT ATTRIBUTES

Next we'll look at the `width` and `height` attributes, since they really work in conjunction with each other. The values for these attributes are set in pixels but don't require you to add the `px` after the number. YouTube provides some pre-sized and custom options (**Figure 3.12**).

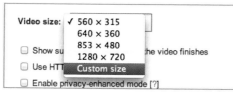

FIGURE 3.12
Options for video height and width.

FIGURE 3.13
The Custom size option automatically calculates the correct width and height ratio for the video.

```
<iframe width="600" height="338" src="http://
www.youtube.com/embed/-BrDlrytgm8?rel=0" frameborder="0"
allowfullscreen></iframe>
```

FIGURE 3.14
The width and height values are automatically updated.

STEP 3.3.3

Select Custom size. Enter the value "600" into the first box and you'll see that the box next to it automatically generates a number—in this case, it's "338" (**Figure 3.13**).

Why does it do this? YouTube automatically calculates the correct aspect ratio so the video doesn't look "squished" or "pulled." So, while you could hand-code this into the code that is supplied, YouTube quickly calculates the correct size and (magically) places it in your code (**Figure 3.14**)!

ADDITIONAL ATTRIBUTES

Finally, when embedding video, services will insert a couple of other attributes: `frameborder` and `allowfullscreen`.

The `frameborder` attribute simply tells the browser either to draw a border (`frameborder="1"`) or not to draw a border (`frameborder="0"`) by attributing the value of 1 or 0.

`allowfullscreen` tells the browser to allow the video to be played full screen, if the option (usually on the video player) is clicked.

STEP 3.3.3

Add the `<iframe>` code into the **objects. html** document under the "Objects: Videos" topic.

```
<h2>Objects: Videos</h2>
<p>Adding videos to your site can
be easy or complex. For our example,
we're going to stick with the basics
and bring in a video hosted on
YouTube. You can sign up for your
own free account, upload videos,
and embed those videos on your own
website.</p>
<!-- place YouTube sample here -->
<!-- iframe option -->
<iframe width="600" height="338"
src="http://www.youtube.com/embed/-
BrDlrytgm8?rel=0" frameborder="0"
allowfullscreen></iframe>
<!-- object option -->
```

Refreshing the browser shows the embedded video on your page (**Figure 3.15**).

FIGURE 3.15
The video from YouTube on your web page.

FIGURE 3.16
The object element for older browsers.

Another option for embedding video is to use the `object` element. This option helps when you need to embed Flash video to support older versions of Internet Explorer. If you select "Use old embed code," you'll see the `iframe` element change to the `object` element (**Figure 3.16**).

`<object>...</object>`

You'll notice the `object` element still contains your `width` and `height` attributes, and that's about it. Pretty simple.

```
<object width="560" height="315">
  <param name="movie" value="//www.
  youtube.com/v/-BrDlrytgm8?hl=en_
  US&amp;version=3&amp;rel=0"></
  param><param name="allowFullScreen"
  value="true"></param>
  <param name="allowscriptaccess"
  value="always"></param>
  <embed src="//www.youtube.
  com/v/-BrDlrytgm8?hl=en_
  US&amp;version=3&amp;rel=0"
  type="application/x-shockwave-
  flash" width="560" height="315"
  allowscriptaccess="always"
  allowfullscreen="true"></embed>
</object>
```

`<param>...</param>`

The `param` (parameters) element sets the parameters on the object element and, in this case, is helping to give support for older versions of Internet Explorer to set values when playing the video.

```
<object width="560" height="315">
❶ <param name="movie" value="//www.
  youtube.com/v/-BrDlrytgm8?hl=en_
  US&amp;version=3&amp;rel=0"></param>
❷ <param name="allowFullScreen"
  value="true"></param>
❸ <param name="allowscriptaccess"
  value="always"></param>
  <embed src="//www.youtube.
  com/v/-BrDlrytgm8?hl=en_
  US&amp;version=3&amp;rel=0"
  type="application/x-shockwave-
  flash" width="560" height="315"
  allowscriptaccess="always"
  allowfullscreen="true"></embed>
</object>
```

1 The first `param` element embeds the video from YouTube with the URL from the value attribue.

2 The second `param` element sets the permission for the user to play the video full screen (if set to false, the video will not be allowed to viewed full screen).

3 The third `param` element sets the permission for the browser to access the Flash video on YouTube so it can play in the HTML document where it's embeded.

The `embed` tag has nothing to do with the `object` and `param` tags, but it brings in support to allow the video to display for browsers (other than the older versions of IE) to play the video.

So, to play video for older versions of IE, you need the `object` and `param` tags, and the `embed` tag for all other browsers.

OUT WITH THE OLD ... BUT NOT YET

You only need to use the "old embed code" when dealing with older document types and browsers that only support Flash video and reject the newer HTML5 video encodings. However, if you want the video to display on mobile devices, make sure you use the new `<iframe>` embed code.

WRAPPING THINGS UP

Now you know how to harness the power of hypertext by using the `<a>…</a>` element with the `href=""` attribute to link documents. Don't forget, while you can link to files, other documents, and other websites, you can also link to elements within a page using fragment identifiers (`href="#topicName"`).

Additionally, you can now add images and hosted video to your pages. Don't forget to check out the video demonstrations on the website for more detailed instructions on how to prepare images for the web. While using hosted video is a great beginning method to adding video and audio to your website, in the future, you'll come to use such elements as:

`<audio>…</audio>` for sound content
`<canvas>…</canvas>` for drawing graphics
`<svg>…</svg>` to draw scalable vector graphic images
`<video>…</video>` to embed video content.

⟫ *CHECK OUT THE WEBSITE'S VIDEO TUTORIALS ON HOW TO WORK WITH THESE ELEMENTS AND AN ASSIGNMENT TO TEST YOUR SKILLS!*

In the next chapter, you'll look at how you can add data (like a spreadsheet) by using the `table` elements.

TABLES

—

04

>>> CHAPTER CODE

THE CODE EXAMPLES FOR THIS CHAPTER CAN BE DOWNLOADED FROM THE WEBSITE (HTTP://FOUNDATIONSOFWEBDESIGN.COM).

What are HTML tables used for? Think of spreadsheets or data you want to organize and present. Maybe you have statistics, a schedule, or a project you need to organize. Let's see how each element is used.

TABLE ELEMENT

The `table` element allows you to arrange and present data in rows and columns of cells. However, it can't do much without its supporting cast: the `tr` (table row), `td` (table data cell), and `th` (table header) elements. So, let's start out by using these basic elements with some common attributes.

STEP 4.1.1

Open the table.html document in the **fowd_ch04_folder** and enter a table element inside the `div` element.

```
<div class="container">
    <table>
    </table>
</div> <!-- end .container -->
```

TABLE HEADINGS

The `th` element holds the heading of each column. Let's say you're developing a reading list of your favorite books and you want columns for the authors, for the book titles, and for indicating if you've read each book.

STEP 4.1.2

Add the three `th` elements with the column topics within the `<table>` tags.

```
<table>
    <th>Author(s)</th>
    <th>Book Title</th>
    <th>Read?</th>
</table>
```

Save your document and view the result in the browser (**Figure 4.1**).

YEARS PAST

Did you know that web designers used to design layouts using table elements! Well, it's not so crazy considering that tables were one way—before there was adequate CSS support—to make sure your layout looked the same from browser to browser. However, in modern web design, page layout is not the purpose of tables.

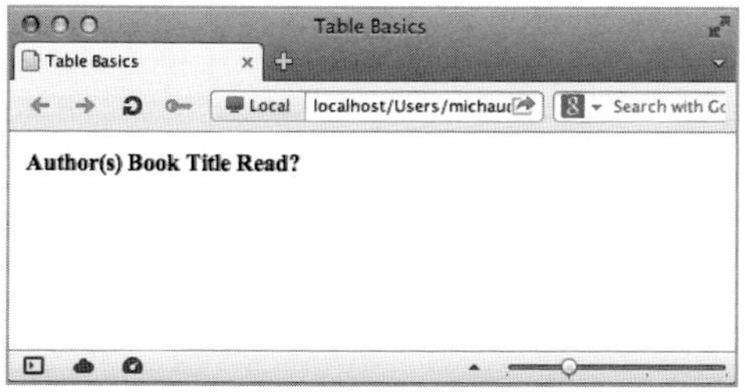

TABLE ROWS

The `tr` element defines the rows of your table. While the three `th` elements already display as a "row," the `tr` element gives structure and meaning to a row—and a table can have lots of rows.

```
<table>
<tr>
    <th>Author(s)</th>
    <th>Book Title</th>
    <th>Read?</th>
</tr>
</table>
```

The next row will add data about one of your favorite books. The data for each book will be contained in a row, between a set of `<tr>` `</tr>` tags. The first book is John Steinbeck's *The Grapes of Wrath*, which you will affirm you've read.

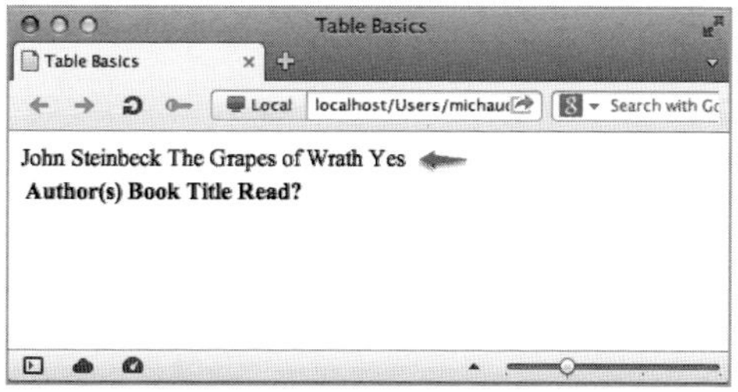

```
<table>
<tr>
    <th>Author(s)</th>
    <th>Book Title</th>
    <th>Read?</th>
</tr>
<tr>
    John Steinbeck
    The Grapes of Wrath
    Yes
</tr>
</table>
```

When you view this site, notice that the data is above (not below) each heading and not within the borders of your table (**Figure 4.2**).

In order to get the data in the correct spot, you need to add another set of tags around each piece of data using the `td` element.

FIGURE 4.1
Table headers are bold by default.

FIGURE 4.2
Unstructured table row.

TABLE DATA CELL

The td element defines the cells of your table and contains your data.

STEP 4.1.3

In the example, the book's name, the author's name, and your "yes" or "no" (whether or not you've read the book) are your data. Each item of data needs to be within a td element.

```
<table>
<tr>
    <th>Author(s)</th>
    <th>Book Title</th>
    <th>Read?</th>
</tr>
<tr>
    <td>John Steinbeck</td>
    <td>The Grapes of Wrath</td>
    <td>Yes</td>
</tr>
</table>
```

Now each cell of data is below the header it matches (**Figure 4.3**).

TABLE BORDER

In order to see your table a little more easily, you're going to add a border around it. Although we've not discussed CSS (Cascading Style Sheets), this method is best for displaying borders.

STEP 4.1.4

Add styles, within the <style></style> tags located in the head element, to show the border for the table, th, and td elements within your HTML document (**Figure 4.4**).

```
<head>
  <meta charset="utf-8">
  <title>Table Demo</title>
  <style>
    table, th, td{
      border: 1px solid #333;
    }
  </style>
</head>
```

FIGURE 4.3
Structured table data.

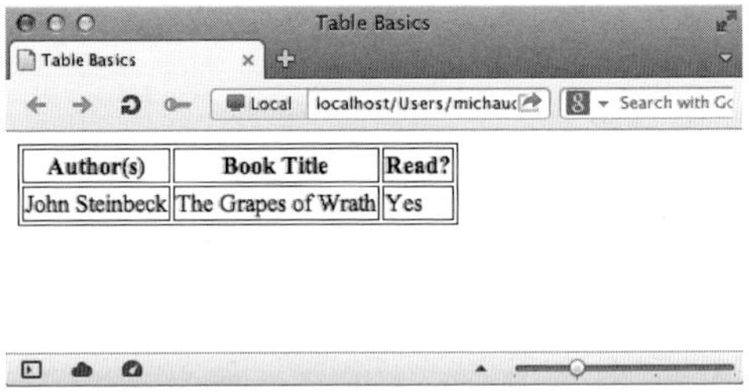

FIGURE 4.4
Your CSS styles create a border around your table and data cells.

ADDING STYLES

While it's good practice to keep your content (HTML) separate from your design (CSS), the style element allows you to add CSS to your HTML document. It must be contained within the *head* element.

We'll get more in-depth into CSS in Chapter 5.

BAD HTML

In the past, the border for a table and its data was displayed using the (now) deprecated border attribute.

```
<table border="1">
```

Deprecated HTML tags and attributes are those that have been (or will soon be) removed from the HTML specification. It is recommended that you not use these HTML tags because they may become obsolete.

For a list of deprecated HTML elements and attributes, view http://webdesign.about.com/od/htmltags/a/bltags_deprctag.htm.

ORDER HEADERS AND DATA

Each td has to be ordered according to the th. So your first td element should relate to the first th element, the second td element relates to the second th element, and so on (**Figure 4.5**).

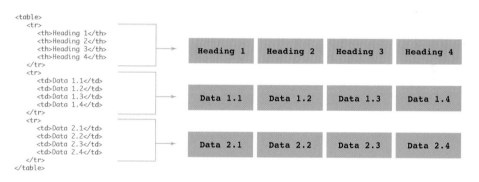

FIGURE 4.5 Illustration of an ordered layout for table headers and table data.

TABLE CAPTION

The `caption` element gives an overall title to the table. In this case, maybe you'd call it "My Reading List"—it's actually a list of books that I have either read or want to read.

STEP 4.1.5

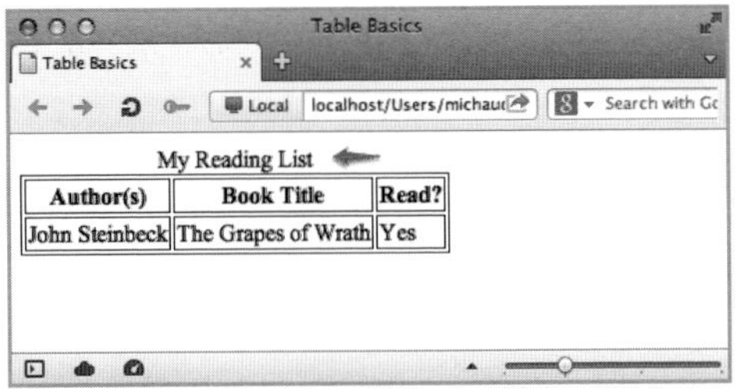

The `caption` element for the table comes right after the opening `<table>` tag. Go ahead and add it to your code.

```
<table>
<caption>My Reading List</caption>
<tr>
    <th>Author(s)</th>
    <th>Book Title</th>
    <th>Read?</th>
</tr>
<tr>
    <td>John Steinbeck</td>
    <td>The Grapes of Wrath</td>
    <td>Yes</td>
</tr>
</table>
```

Notice the text for the caption is placed above the table headers, but outside of the border (**Figure 4.6**).

FIGURE 4.6
The caption is added to the top of the table, but not within the border.

TABLE HEADER

The `thead` element helps to group your table header (`th`) cells.

STEP 4.1.6

In this table, the header row is where the `th` elements are: "Book Title," "Author(s)," and "Read?" Simply add the opening `<thead>` tag before the opening `<tr>` tag and add the closing `</thead>` tag immediately after the closing `</tr>` tag for that row.

```
<table>
<caption>My Reading List</caption>
<thead>
<tr>
    <th>Author(s)</th>
    <th>Book Title</th>
    <th>Read?</th>
</tr>
</thead>
    ...
</table>
```

TABLE BODY

The `tbody` element groups the body—the set of rows where the content resides—of the table.

STEP 4.1.7

Place the `tbody` tags around the book list.

```
<table>
<caption>My Reading List</caption>
<thead>
<tr>
    <th>Author(s)</th>
    <th>Book Title</th>
    <th>Read?</th>
</tr>
</thead>
<tbody>
<tr>
    <td>John Steinbeck</td>
    <td>The Grapes of Wrath</td>
    <td>Yes</td>
</tr>
<!-- additional table rows and data
are stored in the tbody element -->
</tbody>
</table>
```

TABLE FOOTER

The `tfoot` element groups the summary (footer) area of the table. The summary of a table could show the copyright information for the data, give credit to who has created (or edited) the list, provide totals of column values, or indicate when the table was last updated.

STEP 4.1.8

After the closing of the `</tbody>` tag, add the `<tfoot></tfoot>` tags. Within the `tfoot` element, add a `tr` element and `td` element with the data Updated March 5, 2013.

MULTIPLE BODIES

It is possible to have more than one `tbody` inside a `table`. This is covered with the `rowspan` attribute in the bonus material for this chapter you can download on the website.

>>> NOTE: THE FOLLOWING EXAMPLE FOR PLACING tfoot APPLY ONLY TO THE MODERN HTML5 DOCUMENT. HOWEVER, THERE ARE STILL MANY HTML4 AND XHTML DOCUMENTS IN USE, SO IF THAT'S YOUR SITUATION, SEE THE ASIDE ON PAGE 52.

```
<table>
<caption>My Reading List</caption>
<thead>
    <tr>
    ...
    </tr>
</thead>
<tbody>
    <tr>
    ...
    </tr>
<!-- additional table rows and data are
stored in the tbody element -->
</tbody>
<tfoot>
    <tr>
    <td>Updated March 5, 2013</td>
    </tr>
</tfoot>
</table>
```

Now you'll view your document with the addition of your new elements (**Figure 4.7**).

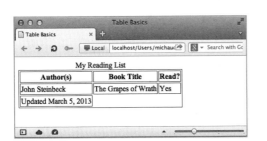

FIGURE 4.7
The data in the `tfoot` now displays at the bottom of the table layout.

FOOTER PLACEMENT FOR HTML4 AND XHTML

If you're going to be developing (or updating) a website that has a DOCTYPE for HTML4 or XHTML Strict (plenty of websites still use them), you'll need to place the `tfoot` after the `thead` and before the `tbody` element.

```
<table>
    <caption></caption>
    <thead></thead>
    <tfoot></tfoot>
    <tbody></tbody>
</table>
```

MEANINGFUL MARKUP BUT NO STYLE

While the `thead`, `tbody`, and `tfoot` elements will not change the look of your table, they will add some meaning (semantics) and provide hooks to style your table. Although these elements are not required, I'd recommend their use, as there are additional benefits that go beyond the scope of this book.

SPANNING COLUMNS

The `colspan` attribute allows you to expand a data cell to span multiple columns in the table. So, in the example, you have the `thead` that consists of one row with three columns of data (**Figure 4.8**).

And, in the `tbody`, you currently have one row with three `td` elements (**Figure 4.9**).

However, the `tfoot` element has one row (`tr` element) and only one `td` element (**Figure 4.10**).

STEP 4.1.9

You can tell that `td` element to span multiple columns by adding the attribute `colspan` (short for "column span") and assigning a value (in this case, you want it to expand to three columns wide).

```
<tfoot>
<tr>
  <td colspan="3">Updated March 5, 2013</td>
</tr>
</tfoot>
```

The result gives you a `tfoot` element that spans all three columns (**Figure 4.11**).

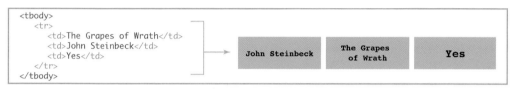

FIGURE 4.8
Your table heading has three columns.

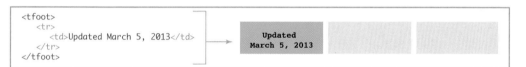

FIGURE 4.9
Your table body has three columns of data.

```
<tfoot>
    <tr>
        <td>Updated March 5, 2013</td>
    </tr>
</tfoot>
```

FIGURE 4.10
Your table footer has only one column of data.

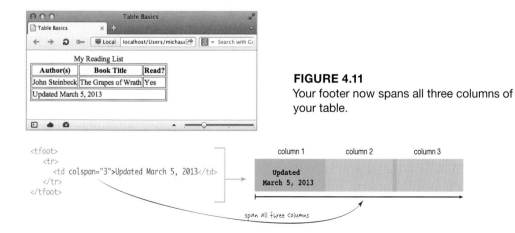

FIGURE 4.11
Your footer now spans all three columns of your table.

```
<tfoot>
    <tr>
        <td colspan="3">Updated March 5, 2013</td>
    </tr>
</tfoot>
```

span all three columns

WRAPPING THINGS UP

You now have the basic foundation of how to structure your data with the table element and the basic supporting cast. While they're not the easiest elements to mark up, tables can be extremely useful for box scores, budgets, etc. In the next chapter, we'll take a break from HTML markup and I'll introduce you to the design side of the Web with CSS—allowing your right brain to play a little.

DOWNLOAD REMINDER

>>> *THERE IS BONUS CONTENT TO DOWNLOAD FOR ADDITIONAL MARKUP FOR THE TABLE ELEMENT AND AN ASSIGNMENT TO TEST YOUR SKILLS!*

{}

CSS: INTRODUCTION

—

05

>>> CHAPTER CODE

*THE CODE EXAMPLES FOR THIS CHAPTER
CAN BE DOWNLOADED FROM THE WEBSITE
(HTTP://FOUNDATIONSOFWEBDESIGN.COM).*

After four chapters, I'm sure you're sick of just looking at HTML and black-and-white text in the browser. I don't blame you! After all, the book does have the words "Web Design" in the title! Well, in this chapter, you'll learn some of the basics of how to style a website with CSS (Cascading Style Sheets).

THE POWER OF CSS

If you wish to see the power of CSS in action, visit CSS Zen Garden (http://csszengarden.com/). Here you can see how different designers responded when asked to use the same HTML document but develop their own CSS document. When the last submission was accepted in 2007, there were 213 official designs—that's 213 different designs for one HTML document (**Figure 5.1**)!

I was fortunate enough to have my submission accepted and added to the official list (**Figure 5.2**).

FIGURE 5.1
A sample of the 213 official CSS designs.

NEW SUBMISSIONS BEING ACCEPTED

As of this writing, Dave Shea, the creator of CSS Zen Garden, has reopened submissions for the site's tenth anniversary (http://mezzoblue. com/archives/2013/05/07/10_years/)!

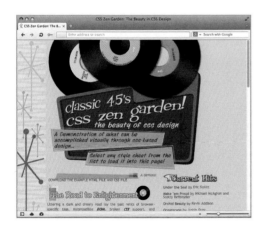

FIGURE 5.2
My CSS Zen Garden Design #183.

SELECTORS

In Cascading Style Sheets (CSS), you can select HTML elements and style them with a number of properties. CSS is written rather differently than HTML, but you'll pick it up quickly.

The **selector** is how you specify the HTML element (h1, p, span, etc.). The **property** identifies the aspect of the element you wish to style (color, border, font-family, etc.). Finally, the **value** is where you indicate exactly how you want the property to display for that selector (red, 20px, left, right, etc.). The property and value together (such as the color property and red value) are called a **declaration**.

The entire group—a selector, like the h1 HTML element, plus a declaration—makes up a CSS **rule**:

selector {declaration;}

```
h1 { color: red; }
```

The selector, the opening curly bracket ({), the declaration (property and value), and the closing curly bracket (}) compose the whole **CSS rule** (**Figure 5.3**).

FIGURE 5.3
An example of how to select an HTML element in CSS.

STEP 5.1.1

Let's look at a basic example (**fowd_ch05_ examples/01-selector.html**). It contains HTML that has an h1 element with the text "My Website."

```
<body>
    <h1>My Website</h1>
</body>
```

The CSS, which is located (for now) in the head element, is within another HTML element called the style element (one of four ways you can apply CSS style to HTML). We'll talk more about the different ways to apply CSS to markup in just a moment.

```
<head>
    <meta charset="utf-8">
        <title>CSS Selector</title>
        <style>
        h1 {
            color: red;
        }
        </style>
</head>
```

The CSS rule above selects the h1 element and modifies its color property from the default black you've been seeing to the value of red. The browser shows the result (**Figure 5.4**).

MULTIPLE DECLARATIONS

CSS rule sets can also contain multiple declarations (properties and values) (**Figure 5.5**).

You'll notice we separate each declaration with a semicolon (;). This tells CSS that you're done with the property–value combination.

SEMICOLON REQUIREMENTS

The last declaration doesn't require a semicolon, but it's a good habit to use one.

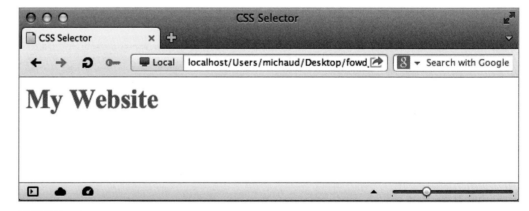

FIGURE 5.4
CSS transformed the h1 element's default black text to red.

STEP 5.1.2

There is a lot more to this … a lot more, but even now your head might be spinning—mine certainly was when I was first learning this stuff back in 2002. For some of you, it all may make perfect sense. In order to familiarize you with these concepts, let's add to your CSS!

Returning to the example you were just looking at, **01-selector.html**, the CSS I gave you is modifying the `color` property of the selected `h1` element. By default, the browser makes all text black, but this CSS changes its value to `red`. What else could be modified? You can use the `font-size` property to increase the size of your font.

```
h1 {
    color: red;
    font-size: 6em;
}
```

So, you've added a new property (`font-size`) and value (`6em`) and ended with a semicolon, creating a new declaration. The browser shows the results (**Figure 5.6**).

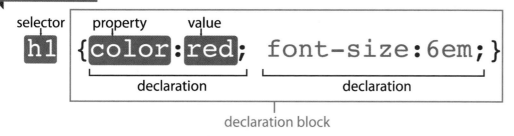

CSS Rule Set

declaration block

FIGURE 5.5
A CSS rule set comprises a selector and a declaration block.

FIGURE 5.6
The `h1` element's font size is now much larger.

EXPANDED DECLARATIONS

While you can write your CSS rule set in a "compact" style where one declaration appears right after the other, it can get a little tough to distinguish each declaration when there are quite a few in the same selector. To begin with, write CSS rule sets in expanded format, where each declaration is on a separate line, making it easier to read (**Figure 5.7**).

I've gone through the structure of CSS in painstaking detail because it's extremely important that you understand how CSS is written. Cascading Style Sheets is

a set of rules containing selectors and declarations that allow you to control how your site looks—so you're not stuck with the default settings that browsers employ.

ADDING CSS TO HTML

Now, remember that I said there were multiple ways to apply CSS style to a document? There are four methods:

- Embedded CSS in the `head` of an HTML document

- Inline CSS, inserted directly into the opening tag of the HTML element

- A separate CSS document linked to an HTML document

- A separate CSS document imported into an HTML document

EMBEDDING CSS

I've already shown you one method: embedding CSS into your HTML document inside the `style` element,

which must be contained within the `head` element.

```
<head>
    <style>
        h1 { color: red; }
    </style>
</head>
```

Benefit of embedded CSS: This can be useful for quick testing of rules or changes to a single page.

Downside of embedded CSS: It has to be loaded every time the HTML document is loaded and could slow down the page. Also, embedded rules cannot be applied to multiple HTML documents, limiting their reusability and efficiency. Additionally, it's desirable to separate content (HTML) from design (CSS) to keep documents lightweight and easy to manage.

INLINE CSS

Inline styles are applied directly to the opening HTML element tag via a `style` attribute.

```
<h1 style="color:red;">My Website</h1>
```

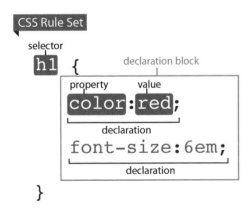

FIGURE 5.7
Expanded CSS rule set.

Benefits of inline CSS: Inline CSS is useful for testing a single, simple style and for rigid content management systems that don't allow you to add your own style sheet (but that's for a different book).

Downside of inline CSS: Inline CSS is difficult to change if you have to hunt through lots of HTML to find all of the inline CSS styles in your HTML documents. It adds to the HTML document size and combines content with design (which are best separated). Seriously, try to avoid this method.

LINK TO AN EXTERNAL CSS DOCUMENT

It's a good idea to put CSS rules into their own document (separating presentation styles from content) and insert a link to that document in each HTML document. Use the link element (within the head element) in order to accomplish this task.

```
<head>
<meta charset="utf-8">
<title>...</title>
<link rel="stylesheet" href="css/styles.css">
</head>
```

REL ATTRIBUTE

The rel attribute specifies the relationship between the HTML document and the linked style sheet.

Benefits of linked CSS: This separates design from content. You can link to a single CSS document from each of your HTML documents and get a consistent look throughout your website. If you make a change in a single CSS document, the change is instantly applied to all HTML documents that link to that style sheet! Also, these CSS documents are "stored" in browser memory (cache) when a user visits a site, and thus the site will load faster the next time the user visits (since it doesn't have to load the documents again).

Downside of linked CSS: When you are first learning and have only one HTML document, it might seem like extra work to have two files to manage. But as soon as you have multiple HTML files, you'll see that it's a much simpler approach. In fact, there aren't any downsides, if you link your CSS documents correctly. Remember, this is the goal you're trying to achieve—separating content (HTML) from design (CSS).

WHEN WOULD
YOU NOT LINK?

If your website is a simple one-page website, you could stick with the embedded CSS method, as it will load more efficiently.

CHALLENGE: MOVE CSS OUT OF HTML

Your challenge is to move all the CSS rule sets in the document **02-externalcss.html** to their own CSS document (**styles.css**)—and to move that document into its own folder (**css**). Finally, use the `link` element so the **styles.css** document can apply your CSS rules to the **02-externalcss.html** document (**Figure 5.8**).

To help you along, here are the steps to take to make the move:

CREATE A CSS DOCUMENT

STEP 5.2.1

Creating a document to contain the CSS rules is really simple—even simpler than creating an HTML document! A CSS document ends with the suffix ".css" and contains no HTML. You can give whatever name you want to your document, but a common name is "styles.css."

STEP 5.2.2

CREATE A FOLDER FOR CSS

To help file your CSS documents separately from your HTML documents, it's a good idea to keep them in their own folder called "css" (remember to keep it all lowercase).

WHY DOES CSS GET ITS OWN FOLDER?

It's best to keep CSS documents in their own folder, as websites end up having multiple CSS documents. As you progress further along, you'll also find that other code languages (like JavaScript) often reside in their own folders. It's just an easy way to keep the languages you use organized.

MOVE YOUR CSS

STEP 5.2.3

Move your CSS rules from the `head` of the HTML document to the new **styles.css** style sheet document. Don't move any HTML with it, and don't leave any CSS behind (**Figure 5.9**).

 WHY "STYLES.CSS"?

You can actually name CSS documents most anything you want, but try to keep the names meaningful (to you and anyone else working on the project). A document name like "styles" could signify that the CSS document will contain the styles for any and all pages in your website. However, you could use a name like "site" or "common" if it's more appropriate.

Remember Case Sensitivity: Just like HTML documents and attribute values, CSS document names are case sensitive. A CSS document named styles.css is not the same as Styles.Css. Also, all suffixes (.html and .css) and folder names (css) should be lowercase!

THE HREF ATTRIBUTE IS USED IN THE LINK ELEMENT TOO

The `href` attribute allows you to add a hypertext reference link to an internal document (relative URL) or external document (absolute URL).

REMOVE ONLY THE CSS

02-externalcss.html

`<html>`

`<style>`

`</style>`

```
body{
    background-color:#235f93;
    font-size: 100%;
}
.container {
    width:90%;
    max-width:960px;
    min-width:340px;
    margin: 0 auto;
    font-family: sans-serif;
    padding: 2.0833333%;
    background-color:#2d7abc;
    border-radius:6px;
}
h1{
    color:#9bc4e7;
}
p{
    font-family: Georgia, serif;
    color: #efefef;
    font-size:1em;
    line-height:1.25em;
}
```

styles.css

`{css}`

FIGURE 5.9
Move (cut and paste) only your CSS rule sets to the **styles.css** document.

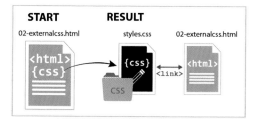

FIGURE 5.8
Move the CSS rules from the HTML document into their own CSS document.

LINK TO YOUR CSS

STEP 5.2.4

In the final step, use the `link` element with the `href` attribute to attach the `styles.css` document in the `css` folder to the **02-externals.html** document.

```
<link rel="stylesheet" href="css/styles.css">
```

SOLUTION

Now, test out your result and see if the **02-externalcss.html** document uses the rules from the **styles.css** document (**Figure 5.10**).

If you have any problems or want to check your answer, I've provided a final result in the **solutions** folder and a video tutorial walk-through on the website.

IMPORT A CSS DOCUMENT

Using the `@import` rule is similar to using the link option: this rule can be used within a CSS document to chain other CSS documents together.

You could create one CSS document called **layout.css** for layout properties (covered in Chapters 8, 9, and 10) and then another CSS document called **type.css** for typography rules (covered in Chapter 7). If you `link` to **layout. css** using the link element in the HTML documents, you could add the `@import "type.css";` rule in **layout.css** to import **type.css** into it, thereby saving you the trouble of adding an additional link element to every document in the site to apply **type.css** to your pages.

```
@import "type.css";
```

Benefits of imported CSS: Rather than adding lots of link elements to the HTML document, rules load through the CSS document.

Downside of imported CSS: While this is supported by all browsers, older versions of Internet Explorer can be a bit buggy.

Now that you have a basic understanding of how you can use CSS rules to design your page, let's focus on some of the most common (and basic) selectors you'll need to know.

VIDEO TUTORIALS:

If you wish to see examples of how each method of hooking CSS to HTML documents works, check out the Chapter 5 videos on the website.

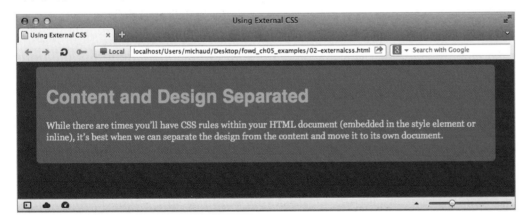

FIGURE 5.10
The external CSS document now styles the HTML document.

SELECTOR TYPES

So far in this chapter we've only looked at element selectors, which select what to style based on an element name. In this section we'll revisit them, as well as look at some of the other common selector types that you'll use in your web design work. These include the following:

- Universal selector

- Element selector

- Selector groupings

- Combinators (such as child selectors)

- Class selectors

UNIVERSAL SELECTOR

You can select all elements in your website by using the universal selector, which takes the form of an asterisk (*).

STEP 5.3.1

In the **03-selector_universal.html** document, in-between the `style` tags, change all of the text `color` (property) from the default black to `green` (value).

```
* { color: green; }
```

Open the document in a browser and you'll see that all the text in the document has been changed from the default black to green (**Figure 5.11**).

 UNIVERSALLY SLOOOOOW

Be careful when using the universal selector (*), as it's the least efficient of all selectors—causing your page load to slow down more than the other selectors we'll be talking about.

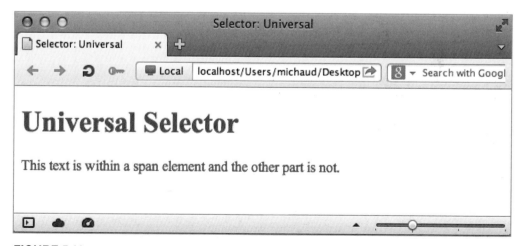

FIGURE 5.11
The color of the text is now green for all elements.

ELEMENT SELECTOR

One of the most common selectors is the element selector, which selects all instances of an HTML element on the page (or site). You want to change that h1? You can do that. Need to style your paragraphs (the p elements)? You can do that too. All you need to do is simply type the element name (e.g., h1, p, span, blockquote, ul, li, etc.) without the less-than (<) and greater-than (>) symbols.

STEP 5.4.1

Open **04-selector_element.html** and add the following CSS rule within the style tags in the head element:

```
p { color: blue; }
```

Open the document in a browser to see the results (**Figure 5.12**).

SELECTOR GROUPING

For an example of the next type of selector, open the file **05-selector_grouping.html**.

STEP 5.5.1

Let's say you want the h1 and h2 elements to have a line under the text. You could select each HTML element separately and write the following properties and values:

```
h1 { text-decoration: underline; }
h2 { text-decoration: underline; }
```

STEP 5.5.2

However, if you had to do this for each of the text heading elements (h1 thru h6), your CSS document could get pretty lengthy. You'll come to find, as you progress in your CSS skills, that there are a lot of HTML elements that have similar (repeating) declaration blocks. Wouldn't it be better if you could group these similar rules? You can! CSS allows you to group selectors by using commas. So, the h1 and h2 rules above can be rewritten into a single rule set:

```
h1,h2 { text-decoration: underline; }
```

The browser shows that both h1 and h2 are now underlined (**Figure 5.13**).

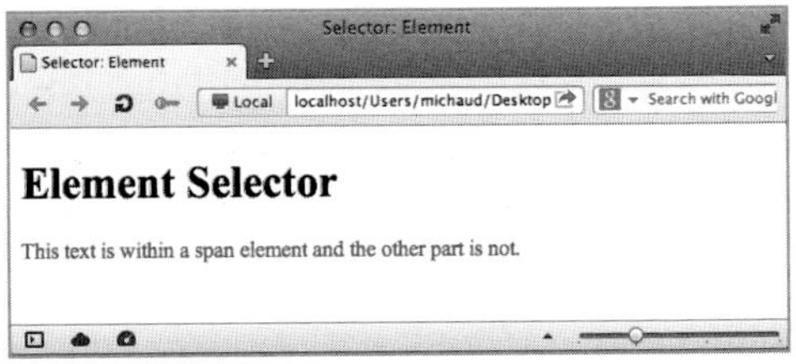

FIGURE 5.12
The color of the paragraph is blue.

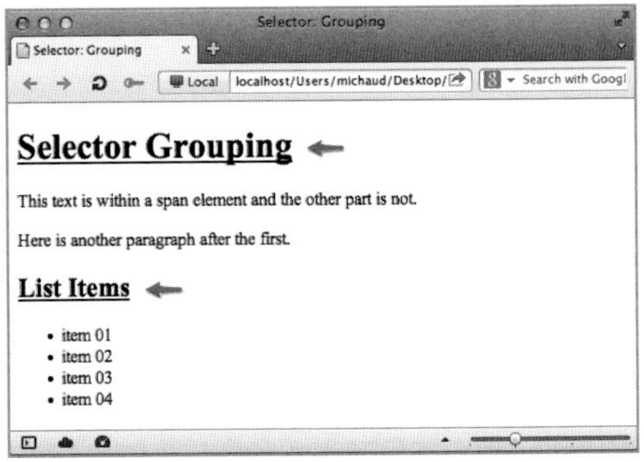

FIGURE 5.13
You now have a line under your text.

COMBINATORS

What if you want to select elements by their location (or relationship to other elements)? You can use certain symbols to help combine selectors and specify their relationships. We'll delve into each of these combinators in more detail:

- Descendant selector

- Child selector

- Adjacent sibling selector

- General sibling selector

Open the example document **06-selectors_ combinators.html**, and all this family tree terminology will make more sense as you work through some examples.

FAMILY RELATIONSHIPS

Think of elements as relating to each other in terms of parents and children. You are a descendant of your parents (and grandparents) and have probably inherited some of their characteristics, such as eye color or hair color. In a similar manner, related elements can share and inherit styles.

In HTML code, when one element follows after another, they are called siblings. Specifically, the opening tag of the second element comes after the closing tag of the first:

```
<h1>…</h1>
<h2>…</h2><!--sibling of the h1 element-->
<p>…</p><!--sibling of the h2 element-->
```

Elements can also be inside of other elements. The elements contained within a parent element's tags are called children.

```
<p><span>This text is within a span
element</span> and the other part is
not.</p> <!-- the span is a child of
the p element -->

<ul>
    <li>…</li>
    <li>…</li>
    <!-- li are children of the ul -->
</ul>
```

You should never have tags that overlap, where one element opens within—but closes outside of—the other. Elements should either be siblings or child/parent, otherwise your HTML is faulty!

DESCENDANT SELECTORS

Descendant selectors will apply a style rule to all elements that are descendants of a specified element.

STEP 5.6.1

In **06-selectors_combinators**, notice that you have two lists: unordered (ul) and ordered (ol). What if you want to select only the list items (li) from the unordered list and change their color to blue? Select the li element in your CSS rule, like so:

```
h1,h2 {
    text-decoration: underline;
}
/*Descendant ( ) Selector */
li { color: blue; }
```

This rule changes all the li text to blue (**Figure 5.14**).

STEP 5.6.2

But you want to select only the list items in the unordered list, so add the `ul` element before the `li`, separated by a space.

```
ul li { color: blue; }
```

Now the rule focuses specifically on the `li` elements within the parent `ul` element (**Figure 5.15**).

CHILD SELECTOR

Child selectors are even more specific than descendant selectors, performing a similar function but selecting only the *immediate* children of a specified element. The child combinator uses the greater-than sign (>) between the two elements.

STEP 5.6.3

In **06-selectors_combinators**, change the paragraphs' (p) `color` property to `green`, but limit it to only those paragraphs contained within a `div` element. To do this, simply add a greater-than sign (>) between the `div` element and the `p` element.

```
/*Child (>) Selector */
div>p { color: green; }
```

Refresh your browser and see that the first two paragraphs (not contained within the `div` element) are still black, but the paragraphs within the `div` element are green (**Figure 5.16**).

>>> NOTE: *THE ORDER OF THE ELEMENTS IS KEY. THE ELEMENT YOU ARE STYLING IS THE CHILD (OR DESCENDANT OR SIBLING) AND ALWAYS COMES AFTER THE CONTAINING ELEMENT (OR SIBLING).*

ADJACENT SIBLING SELECTOR

Adjacent sibling selectors select the sibling element that immediately follows the element listed first. The adjacent sibling combinator uses the plus character (+).

STEP 5.6.4

Sticking with the example code in **06-selectors_combinators**, create a new rule that selects only the paragraph (p) immediately *following* the h1 element.

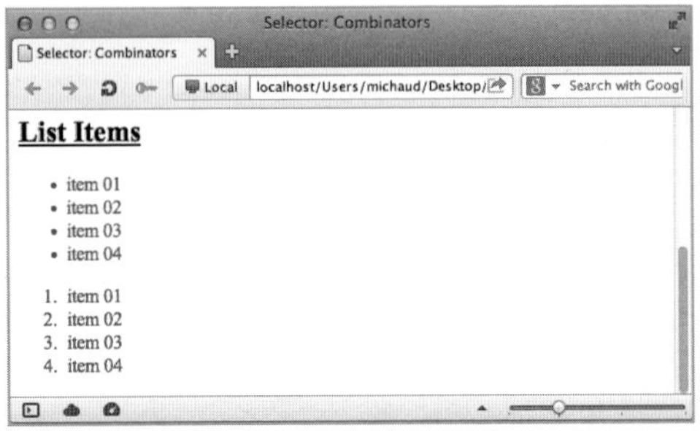

FIGURE 5.14
All list items are blue.

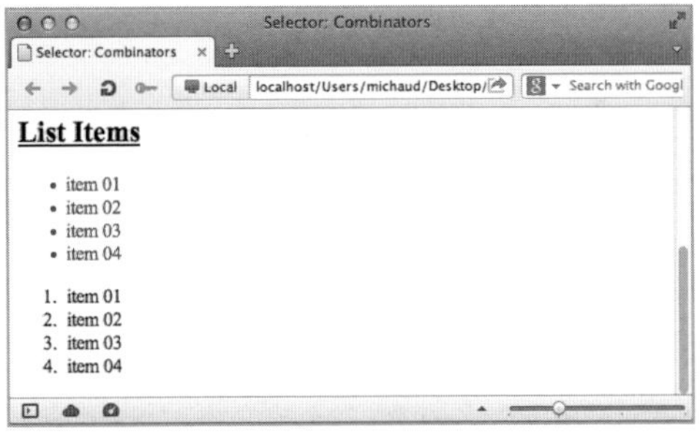

FIGURE 5.15
Only the unordered list items are blue as a result of using the descendant selector.

DESCENDANT VS. CHILD SELECTORS

While descendant selectors will select elements inside other elements at any level of hierarchy, child selectors only select immediate children.

```
/*Adjacent (+) Sibling Selector */
h1+p { font-size: 24px; }
```

Now the paragraph (p) that comes immediately *after* the h1 element has a larger font size than the other paragraphs (**Figure 5.17**).

GENERAL SIBLING SELECTOR

The general sibling selector is a CSS3 rule (we've been dealing with CSS2.1 thus far) that matches elements that are siblings of a stated element. It uses the tilde character (~). Unlike the adjacent sibling selector, it will select **all** siblings of the element. The elements don't have to be adjacent siblings, but they need to have the same parent.

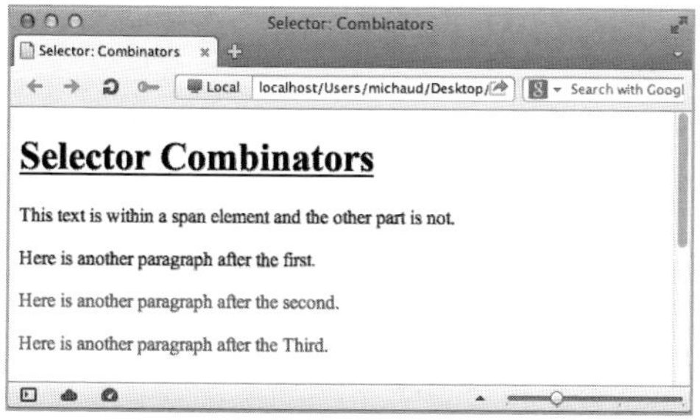

CSS1 was the first CSS specification, published by the W3C (World Wide Web Consortium) in 1996.

CSS2 was a superset to CSS1, published by the W3C in 1998.

CSS2.1 corrected errors in CSS2. While the final publication was in 2011, its origins go back to 2004.

CSS3 (also know as CSS Level 3) is different from earlier versions of CSS: it's divided into several separate documents (modules). Some CSS3 modules have better support than others across modern browsers, and some are still very experimental. As of June 2012, there were over 50 modules published from the CSS working group, and only four had been published as formal recommendations.

(For more on the history of CSS, visit http://en.wikipedia.org/wiki/Cascading_Style_Sheets.)

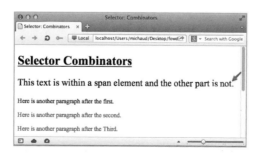

FIGURE 5.16
Only the last two paragraphs, the children of the div element, should be green.

FIGURE 5.17
Only the paragraph immediately following the main header should have larger text size.

HTML

```
<h1>Selector Combinators</h1>
```

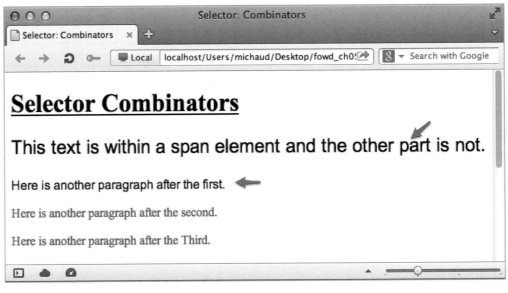

FIGURE 5.18
Diagram showing how the sibling selector works.

FIGURE 5.19
The paragraphs that are siblings of the `div` do not use the Arial font.

STEP 5.6.5

In **06-selectors_combinators**, create a new rule that selects all paragraph (p) elements that are siblings of the h1 element and sets the `font-family` property to the value `Arial`.

```
/*General (~) Sibling Selector */
h1~p { font-family: Arial; }
```

This rule styles all paragraphs (p) that are siblings to the h1 to use the font Arial, but not the paragraphs that are siblings to the `div` element (**Figure 5.18**).

Here is the result showing our first two paragraphs in the Arial font and the last two in the default Times font (**Figure 5.19**).

CLASS SELECTORS

A class selector begins with a period/full stop (.) symbol. The CSS rule will then apply wherever that class is designated in your HTML.

STEP 5.7.1

In the **07-selectors_class_id.html** document, you'll see two description lists. You want to italicize the elements where the `class` attribute has the value of `book` (**Figure 5.20**).

```
<dl id="steinbeck">
    <dt class="author">John Steinbeck</dt>
    <dd class="book">Of Mice and Men</dd>
    <dd class="book">The Grapes of Wrath</dd>
</dl>
<dl id="wells">
    <dt class="author">H.G. Wells</dt>
    <dd class="book">The Time Machine</dd>
    <dd class="book">War of the Worlds</dd>
</dl>
```

So, the CSS should have the following rule, with a period preceding the selected class attribute.

```
/*class (.) Selector */
.book {
    font-style: italic;
}
```

ID SELECTORS

By contrast, an ID selector begins with the pound/hash (#) symbol. Since `id` attributes must have a unique value, the ID selector cannot match more than one element per HTML document.

STEP 5.7.2

Using the ID selector, you can target each author with an individual style. From your HTML elements, select the `id` attribute with the unique value of steinbeck and turn the font color `red` (**Figure 5.21**).

```
/*ID (#) Selector */
#steinbeck {
    color: red;
}
```

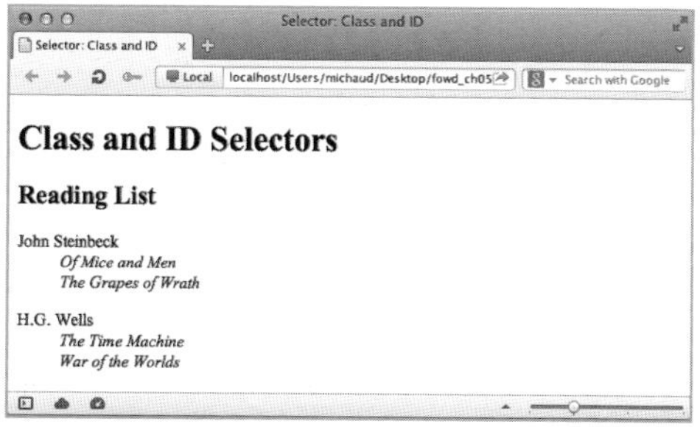

FIGURE 5.20
All of the book titles are now italicized.

FIGURE 5.21
Only the list with the unique `id` attribute value of steinbeck is red.

GENERAL SIBLING SUPPORT

As of this writing, the general sibling selector has pretty good support in all major browsers other than Internet Explorer 7 and below.

MORE ON THE CLASS AND ID SELECTORS

In Chapter 6, we'll go further in-depth on the use of the class and ID selectors.

PSEUDO-CLASSES

With pseudo-classes, you can modify element properties based on user interaction. For example, have you ever seen a link on a website change color when you hover your cursor over the link (**Figure 5.22**)?

Pseudo-classes are similar to classes, but they are not explicitly present in the HTML; they don't need to be added to your code. Basically, they are keywords in CSS that can be added to a selector to specify a special state of the element.

In just a moment, we'll look at how you can achieve the **hover** effect using the pseudo-class `:hover` selector with the anchor element selector (`a`). We're going to discuss the pseudo-classes that style links in their various states:

- Unvisited (not yet clicked)

- Visited

- Hover (cursor is over the link)

- Active (link is being clicked)

- Focus (the focus of the keyboard is on this link)

All pseudo-class selections begin with a colon (`:`) and appear immediately after the HTML element selection (no whitespace).

:LINK PSEUDO-CLASS

In the example document **08-selectors_pclasses.html**, there are a number of links that point to some popular search engine websites (**Figure 5.23**).

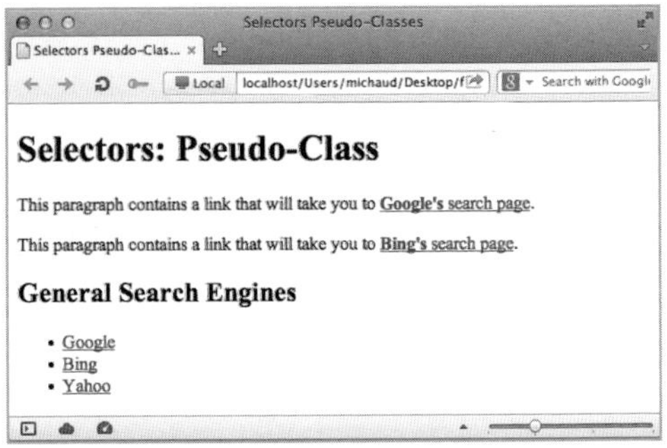

FIGURE 5.23
The hyperlink default style is blue and underlined.

STEP 5.8.1

Before moving on, click the link in the paragraph that will take you to "Google's search page" (**Figure 5.24**).

FIGURE 5.22
Sometimes the underline disappears from a link when you hover your cursor over it.

STEP 5.8.2

After you visit Google's search page, click the **Back** button to return to your document. You should see that the first link in the paragraph and list below is now purple and underlined (**Figure 5.25**).

In the HTML, links use the anchor element.

```
<a href="http://google.com">
<strong>Google's</strong> search page
</a>
```

To change the `color` property of the hypertext links from the default value `blue` to `orange`, select the anchor (*a*) element and the *a* element with the `:link` pseudo-class to change the color:

```
/* simple selector */
a, a:link { color: orange; }
```

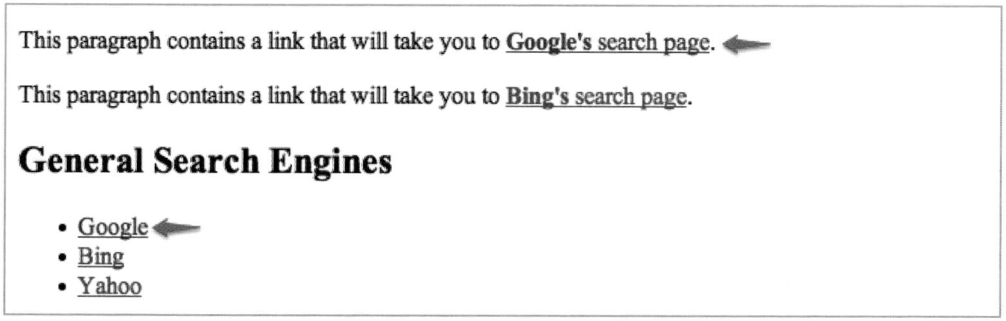

Selectors: Pseudo-Class

This paragraph contains a link that will take you to <u>Google's search page</u>.

FIGURE 5.24
The blue underlined text indicates a link you can click.

This paragraph contains a link that will take you to **<u>Google's search page</u>**. ←

This paragraph contains a link that will take you to **<u>Bing's search page</u>**.

General Search Engines

- <u>Google</u> ←
- <u>Bing</u>
- <u>Yahoo</u>

FIGURE 5.25
Default styles for visited links are purple and underlined.

THE BROWSER REMEMBERS WHERE YOU GO

When you visit a website, your browser caches (stores) the pages you visit in a "history" log and subsequently changes the color properties of any anchor tags that point to that page.

A AND A:LINK SELECTORS

The *a* selector covers all the link states without the need for a pseudo-class. Use `a:link` to style links that are un-visited, un-hovered, and not active.

So, use *a* for things like font-family (if you want links to appear in a different font), then use `:link` for the standard formatting—and `:visited`, `:hover`, and `:active` for special styles that you only want apply to those situations.

When you view the page again, you'll find all the links have changed from the default blue to orange (**Figure 5.26**)!

:VISITED PSEUDO-CLASS

Since the link to "Google's search page" has been clicked, perhaps it should change appearance to provide feedback telling the visitor that they've clicked a link. This type of feedback can be helpful when there's a list of links and a visitor wants to visually "check off" where they've been.

STEP 5.8.3

Adding the `:visited` pseudo-class to the `a` element will allow you to style the hypertext link when the link has already been clicked:

```
/* :visited pseudo-class selector */
a:visited { color: red; }
```

The visited link should now be red (**Figure 5.27**).

Selectors: Pseudo-Class

This paragraph contains a link that will take you to Google's search page.

This paragraph contains a link that will take you to Bing's search page.

General Search Engines

- Google
- Bing
- Yahoo

FIGURE 5.26
The orange links.

Selectors: Pseudo-Class

This paragraph contains a link that will take you to Google's search page.

This paragraph contains a link that will take you to Bing's search page.

General Search Engines

- Google
- Bing
- Yahoo

FIGURE 5.27
The visited link is now styled as red.

>>> *NOTE: IF THE LINK COLOR DIDN'T CHANGE TO RED, CLICK ON THE LINK AND THEN RETURN TO THE PAGE (CLICKING THE BACK BUTTON) TO SEE THE CHANGE OCCUR.*

>>> *DID YOU SEE: THE CHANGE IN COLOR TO THE VISITED LINK ALSO OCCURS FOR THE IDENTICAL LINK YOU DID NOT CLICK ("GOOGLE" IN THE LIST UNDER "GENERAL SEARCH ENGINES"). THE BROWSER SEES THE SAME LINK LOCATION IN THE ANCHOR TAG (`href="http://google.com"`) AND APPLIES THE CSS RULE TO ALL ANCHOR TAGS THAT POINT TO THE SAME PLACE. PRETTY SWEET!*

:HOVER PSEUDO-CLASS

By adding the `:hover` pseudo-class to the anchor element (`a`), you give users immediate feedback when their cursor passes over the link (even briefly).

Let's say you want to remove the underline from the text of the link when the user's cursor is over it.

STEP 5.8.4

The CSS property to call on is `text-decoration`, and the value of `none` will remove the underline.

```
/* :hover pseudo-class selector */
a:hover { text-decoration: none; }
```

Return to your browser and move your cursor over a link (any link), and you should notice the underline disappear (**Figure 5.28**).

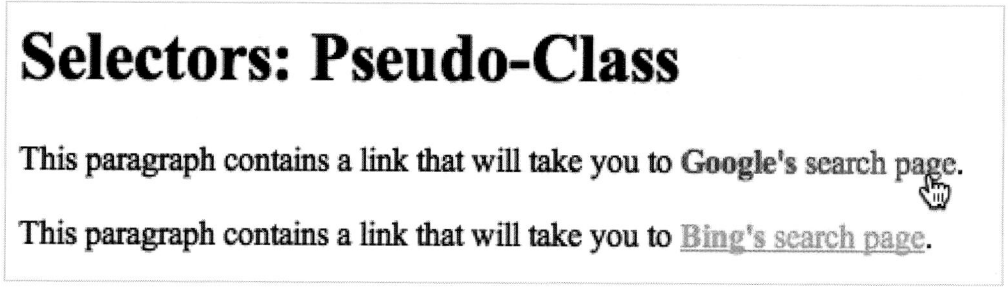

Selectors: Pseudo-Class

This paragraph contains a link that will take you to **Google's** search page.

This paragraph contains a link that will take you to Bing's search page.

FIGURE 5.28
The text underline vanishes when you hover over the link.

CHALLENGE

With the information you've just learned,

- Style the links, in any state, to appear without the underline.

- Style the links, upon hover, to show the underline.

Take a look at how my links work (**Figure 5.29**).

If you have problems, I've provided the solution for you in the **08-selector_challenge.html** document.

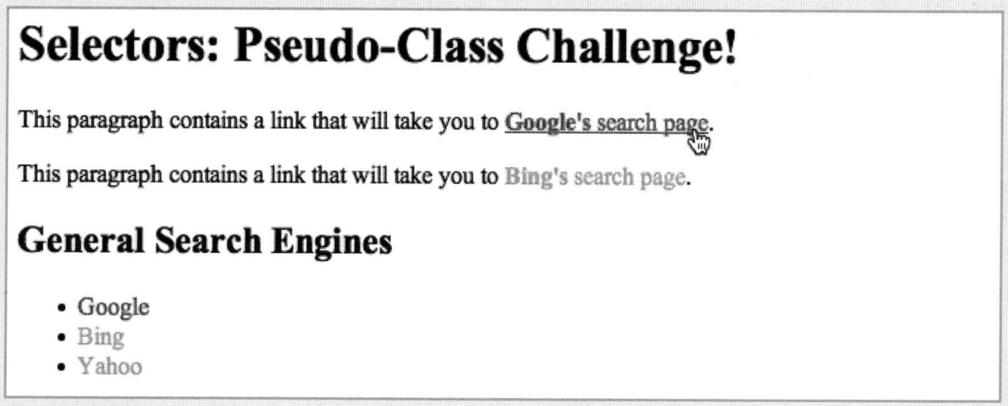

Selectors: Pseudo-Class Challenge!

This paragraph contains a link that will take you to Google's search page.

This paragraph contains a link that will take you to Bing's search page.

General Search Engines

- Google
- Bing
- Yahoo

FIGURE 5.29
The underline should show up when the cursor hovers over the link.

> THE ORDER OF THINGS

To avoid any problems of inherited styles (see the appendix on Inheritance and Specificity), it's best to use the following order for the pseudo-classes:

```
:link
:visited
:hover
:active
```

To remember the order of these pseudo-classes, people often use the words **LoVe HAte** (with L, V, H, and A being the first letters of the pseudo-classes).

:ACTIVE PSEUDO-CLASS

The `:active` pseudo-class allows you to give feedback to the user when the element is *activated*—an example would be when you press a button on a mouse to click a link.

STEP 5.8.5

To add a rule when the user clicks the link, simply add the `:active` pseudo-class to the anchor (`a`) selector. Let's modify the `color` property to be `green`.

```
/* :active pseudo-class selector */
a:active { color: green; }
```

When you hover over the link and press the mouse button (make sure you keep it held down), you'll notice the link loses its underline (from the `a:hover` rule) and the color becomes green (**Figure 5.30**).

While providing feedback for clicking something may seem like a small detail, it can help users clearly see where they clicked.

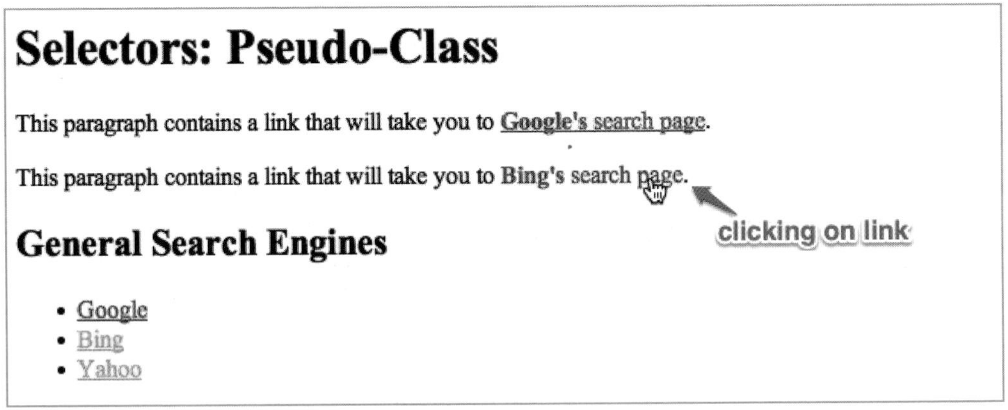

FIGURE 5.30
Feedback when the user "activates" an element.

FOCUS ON ORDER

Where does :focus fit in the order of **LoVe HAte**? Some say the :hover and :focus rules should be combined so those using the keyboard get the same visual cues as those not using the keyboard.

```
a:hover, a:focus {
  text-decoration: none;
}
```

MORE PSEUDOS

Now, I've covered the most common pseudo-class selectors, but there are more, including pseudo-element selectors! Head over to the website and find out about :first-child, :last-child, :nth-child, :before, :after, and many other pseudo selectors.

:FOCUS PSEUDO-CLASS

While the pseudo-classes we've used thus far are good, they leave out those visitors using a keyboard for navigation. The :focus pseudo-class selects links that are the current focus of the keyboard.

STEP 5.8.6

Add :focus to your anchor (*a*) selector and give the background-color property a value of yellow.

```
/* :focus pseudo-class selector*/
a:focus { background-color: yellow; }
```

>>> *THE RESULT IS BEST SEEN IN CHROME.*

Using your keyboard to navigate through the site, click the **Tab** key until it cycles to the link. When the link becomes the focus of the keyboard, the browser will apply a yellow background to the link— and in Chrome you might see a bluish border (**Figure 5.31**).

FIGURE 5.31
Navigation with the keyboard brings focus on your link.

WRAPPING THINGS UP

In this chapter, you've started to harness the power of CSS using an assortment of selectors, pseudo-classes, and pseudo-elements. You also know how CSS can be added to your document and that it's best to keep content (HTML) and presentation (CSS) separate. In the upcoming chapters, most of the CSS will be located in an external CSS document.

In the next chapter, the journey continues with CSS selectors and their relationships with some commonly used HTML attributes that help provide additional information for HTML elements.

>>> *DOWNLOAD REMINDER: THERE IS BONUS CONTENT TO DOWNLOAD FOR ADDITIONAL INFORMATION ON CSS SELECTORS AND AN ASSIGNMENT TO TEST YOUR SKILLS!*

PART

—

02

WORKING TOGETHER

⟨/⟩	**HTML ATTRIBUTES**
{/}	**CSS: STYLING TEXT**
⬡	**BOX MODEL**

HTML ATTRIBUTES

—

06

THE CODE EXAMPLES FOR THIS CHAPTER CAN BE DOWNLOADED FROM THE WEBSITE (HTTP://FOUNDATIONSOFWEBDESIGN.COM).

Attributes permit you to assign additional information to HTML elements. You've already seen some in action—like the `href` attribute used with the `<a>`...`</a>` element. I'm covering only a few of the most essential attributes you need for a good foundation. However, there are many, many (many) more at your disposal.

>>> **BAD ATTRIBUTES**

THERE ARE MANY ATTRIBUTES BEYOND THE BASICS, BUT THERE ARE SOME YOU SHOULD NOT USE. SOME ARE OBSOLETE AND SOME LOOK TO STYLE CONTENT (A TASK WHICH SHOULD BE RESERVED FOR CSS). THE COMPANION WEBSITE POINTS OUT SEVERAL OF THE MOST NOTORIOUS BAD-GUY ATTRIBUTES.

Of all the attributes, there are two that you'll see often that are extremely important for connecting CSS to elements: `id` and `class`. One more attribute that merits exploration is the `role` attribute.

HTML: CLASS ATTRIBUTE

HTML tags allow you to specify the type of element, such as `<p>`...`</p>` = paragraph, `<h1>`...`</h1>` = top-level heading, `<div>`...`</div>` = generic division or section. You can add a `class` attribute—with one or more values—to assign one or more subtypes to the element. The best way to learn is to get your hands dirty using the `class` attribute and assigning it values.

Upon opening **01-class-attribute.html**, in the Chapter 6 sample folder, you will see description lists of car manufacturers and their nationalities (**Figure 6.1**).

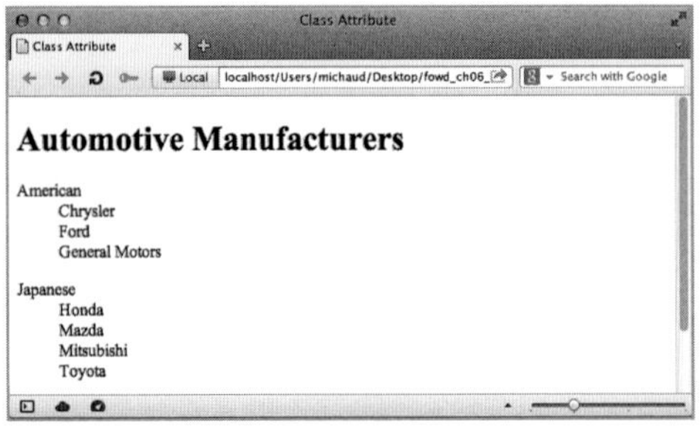

```
<!--list of American Manufacturers-->
<dl>
    <dt>American</dt>
    <dd>Chrysler</dd>
    <dd>Ford</dd>
    <dd>General Motors</dd>
</dl>

<!--list of Japanese Manufacturers-->
<dl>
    <dt>Japanese</dt>
    <dd>Honda</dd>
    <dd>Mazda</dd>
    <dd>Mitsubishi</dd>
    <dd>Toyota</dd>
</dl>
```

FIGURE 6.1
A list of automotive manufacturers.

While there are two separate `dl` lists, they're not differentiated from any other description lists (which may not contain information about automotive manufacturers). If you want to identify all lists that contain manufacturers (because you could add France, Germany, or Russia), you could consider assigning a value of `mfg` (short for "manufacturer") to each opening `<dl>` element. Now the question arises: Which attribute should be used, `class` or `id`?

⟫⟫ HERE'S A SET OF RULES YOU NEED TO MEMORIZE

`class` ATTRIBUTE VALUES CAN BE USED UN-LIMITED TIMES IN THE SAME DOCUMENT ON DIFFERENT ELEMENTS—AND ACROSS MULTIPLE DOCUMENTS.

`id` ATTRIBUTE VALUES CAN **ONLY** BE USED **ONCE** IN THE **SAME** DOCUMENT—BUT CAN BE USED AGAIN IN **DIFFERENT** DOCUMENTS. (FIGURE 6.2)

class **attributes**

class="dog" →
class="dog" →
class="dog" →
class="dog" →

GO

You can use that same class+value combination as much as you want in a single document.

`<html>`

id **attributes**

id="dalmatian" →

STOP

You can't use that same id+value combination again in this document.

You can use it again in another document

`<html>`

FIGURE 6.2
An illustration to help determine which attribute to use.

The answer to the question is: Use the `class` attribute.

STEP 6.1.1

So, add the `class` attribute with the value `mfg` to the opening `dl` elements.

```
<!--list of American Manufacturers-->
<dl class="mfg">
    <dt>American</dt>
    ...
</dl>


<!--list of Japanese Manufacturers-->
<dl class="mfg">
    <dt>Japanese</dt>
    ...
</dl>
```

If this affects nothing visually, what is the class attribute (and its value) doing? It allows you to assign a subtype specific to what the dl elements contain—and gives you a design "hook" for your CSS. In this case, you will assign a subtype of manufacturers for a given country. The "manufacturer" is a general topic for the specific topic of "American" or "Japanese" manufacturers (Ford, Honda, General Motors, Toyota, etc.).

MULTIPLE VALUES

The class attribute can also accept multiple values! All you need to do is separate the values with a space. If you look further down in your **01-class-attribute.html** document, you'll see paragraphs with class attributes.

```
<h2>FAQ</h2>
<p class="faq">What cars have the best
fuel economy?</p>
<p class="faq important">Are flying
vehicles in our future?</p>
```

Both paragraphs have one value (faq) in common, but the second paragraph also contains a second value (important).

Additionally, if there were other elements that merited the important value, we could add that value to an existing class attribute or add a class attribute as needed.

So, now that you've seen some basic uses of the class attribute in HTML, let's see how you can use it to style your document with CSS.

CSS: CLASS SELECTOR

Open the **01class.css** document.

In order to select the class attribute, simply type a period (.) … Yeah, a period. Weird. So, make sure you get this straight (**Figure 6.3**):

- HTML attribute: class

- CSS class selector: . (period)

```
HTML
  <ul class="dogs">
      ...
  </ul>

CSS
  .dogs{background:lightblue;}
```

> **DON'T CROSS-ATTRIBUTE**
>
> It's extremely important that you **never** use the same value for both the class and id attributes. Why? While there are a few reasons I could list, it simply becomes very confusing to keep the values organized between the two attributes.

> **REMEMBER: CSS HAS ITS PLACE**
>
> Your CSS rules will now be written within their own **.css** documents, found in the **css** folder. The HTML documents already have the link element set up.

FIGURE 6.3
In CSS, the period (.) can be used to represent the class attribute.

STEP 6.2.1

Immediately after the class selector (.), write the `class` attribute name. So, the HTML `class="mfg"` attribute and value combination would be selected by the following CSS rule:

```
.mfg { }
```

>>> REMEMBER: ATTRIBUTE VALUE NAMES ARE SENSITIVE

*ATTRIBUTE VALUES ARE CASE SENSITIVE. WHEN WRITING THE ATTRIBUTE VALUE IN CSS, IT MUST BE WRITTEN **EXACTLY** THE SAME WAY IT WAS IN HTML. THE HTML VALUE myName IS NOT THE SAME AS THE CSS VALUE myname (IT MUST BE WRITTEN myName).*

STEP 6.2.2

Now, add the following CSS declarations to the rule:

```
.mfg {
    padding: 10px;
    border: 1px solid black;
    width:  260px;
}
```

When you view your HTML document in the browser, you see the intended result (**Figure 6.4**).

STEP 6.2.3

Let's also style the paragraphs below the lists. Remember, both have the value of `faq` for the `class` attribute. Your CSS rule set would use the (.) period to select the `class` attribute and add the value `faq` immediately after.

```
.faq {
    margin-left: 20px;
    padding-left: 5px;
    border-left: 2px solid red;
}
```

After writing out the CSS declarations (and saving your document), refresh the browser to see how both paragraphs are now indented, with a red line to their left and a little space between the line and the first letter (**Figure 6.5**).

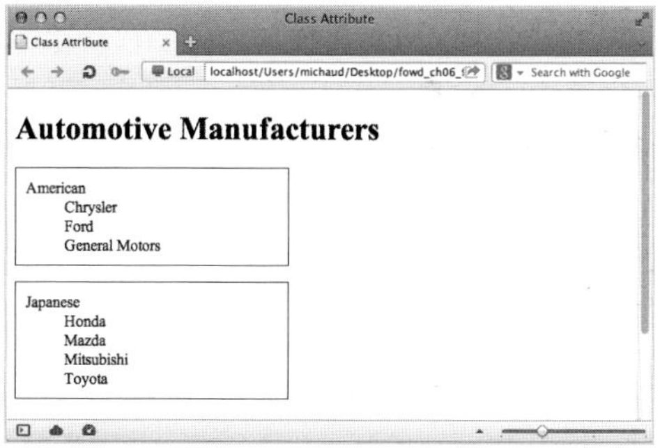

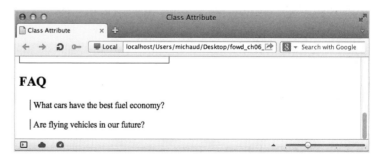

FIGURE 6.4
With one CSS rule, there are borders around both lists!

FIGURE 6.5
Both paragraphs have been styled by selecting the same `class` value.

STEP 6.2.4

Let's also add another rule below your `.faq` rule that selects the `class` attribute (.) with the value of `important`.

```
.important {
    font-weight: bold;
    color: red;
}
```

Viewing the results, you see that the new rule styled the last paragraph's text to become bold and red. However, the paragraph still has all the characteristics from the previous rule, since there were two values applied to the `class` attribute (**Figure 6.6**).

HTML: ID ATTRIBUTE

The `id` attribute is similar to the `class` attribute in that it doesn't style the document directly, but allows you to apply a unique identifier to an HTML element.

⟫ REMEMBER:
ONCE IS ENOUGH

*WHATEVER VALUE YOU GIVE TO THE `id` ATTRIBUTE CAN ONLY BE USED **ONCE** PER DOCUMENT.*

In the **02-id-attribute.html document**, you will return to your car manufacturer lists. Although you subtyped each `dl` element with the `class` attribute and `mfg`, it might be valuable to identify each list uniquely!

 CAUTION: OVERRIDING RULES

Be careful using multiple class values, because you could have conflicting declarations between two or more rules that style the same properties with different values.

HTML

```
<div class="faq important">...</div>
```

CSS

```
.faq {
    margin-left: 20px;
    padding-left: 5px;
    border-left: 2px solid red;
}
.important {
    font-weight: bold;
    color:  red;
    margin-left: 10px;
}
```

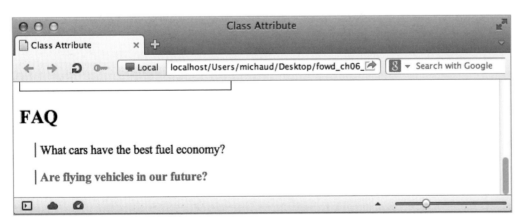

FIGURE 6.6
An element with two class values retains styles of a previous CSS rule while adding on new styles.

STEP 6.3.1

The first `dl` element will receive the `id` attribute with the value of `american`.

```
<!--definition list for American
Manufacturers-->
<dl id="american" class="mfg">
    <dt>American</dt>
    ...
</dl>
```

STEP 6.3.2

Next, add an `id` attribute with the value of `japanese` to the second definition list.

```
<!--definition list for Japanese
Manufacturers-->
<dl id="japanese" class="mfg">
    <dt>Japanese</dt>
    ...
</dl>
```

>>> REMEMBER THE ID RULES

ONCE YOU'VE USED A VALUE FOR THE `id` ATTRIBUTE, YOU CANNOT USE IT AGAIN IN THE SAME DOCUMENT. HOWEVER, YOU CAN USE THE SAME ID+VALUE COMBINATION IN ANOTHER HTML DOCUMENT.

`id` ATTRIBUTES ALLOW ONLY ONE VALUE: `id="content"`.

`id` ATTRIBUTE VALUES CANNOT HAVE SPACES: `id="main content"` *(THIS WOULD BE TWO VALUES).*

`id` ATTRIBUTE VALUES ARE CASE SENSITIVE: `id="mainContent"` *IS DIFFERENT FROM* `id="maincontent"`.

Now that you know the basics of using the `id` attribute, let's use it in CSS.

> USING ID VS. CLASS ATTRIBUTES

While the purpose of this demonstration is to help you understand how the HTML `id` attribute works, it should be used with great caution. In CSS, ID selectors are very powerful—in terms of specificity—and can create unnecessary headaches. I believe you'll find the `class` attribute to be a better solution than the `id` attribute, as it's more flexible and easier to use in CSS. To read more on this topic, I suggest checking out Harry Roberts's website CSS Wizardry (http://csswizardry.com/).

So, a production site might use the `class` attributes for all values:

```
<dl class="american mfg">
    <dt>American</dt>
    ...
</dl>
<dl class="japanese mfg">
    <dt>Japanese</dt>
    ...
</dl>
```

CSS: ID SELECTOR

As you saw in Chapter 5, CSS uses the # sign (commonly called a hash or pound) to select the HTML `id` attribute (**Figure 6.7**). This makes as much sense as using the period (.) for the `class` attribute. Anyway, so you have this clear:

- HTML attribute: `id`

- CSS ID selector: #
  (pound, number, or hash)

Like the CSS class (.) selector, the value comes immediately after the # sign (with no spaces).

FIGURE 6.7
The ID selector in CSS selects the `id` attribute and value from HTML.

STEP 6.4.1

Open the CSS document **02id.css**. You'll write a rule that selects the `american` value of the `id` (#) attribute and apply a `lightblue` value to the `background-color` property.

```
#american {
    background-color: lightblue;
}
```

In the browser, the style is applied to the description list that has the `id` attribute with the value of `american` (**Figure 6.8**).

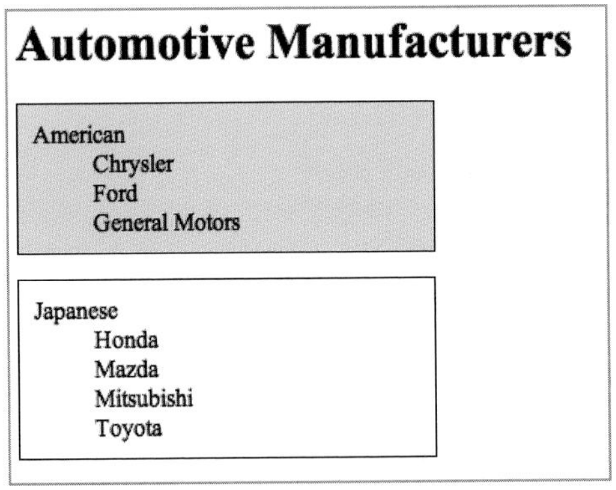

FIGURE 6.8
Your first list has been uniquely styled.

STEP 6.4.2

Next, add another CSS rule using the ID (#) selector with the value of `japanese` and apply a `lightsalmon` value to the `background-color` property.

```
#japanese {
    background-color: lightsalmon;
}
```

Both `dl` elements still have some similar styles because of the rule sets that style the `class` attributes, but you now have used the `id` attributes to uniquely identify and style each list (**Figure 6.9**).

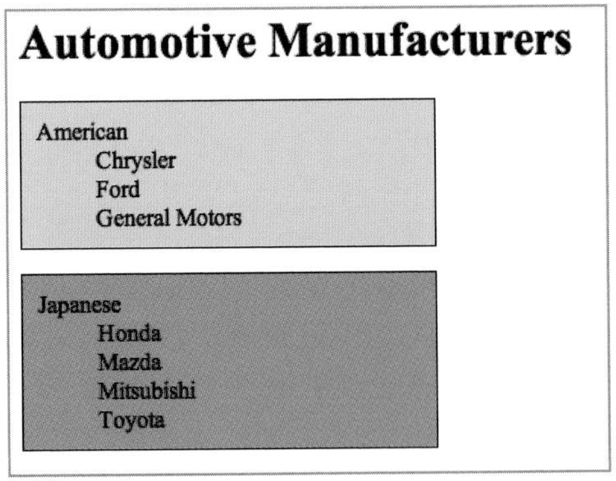

FIGURE 6.9
The second list has been uniquely styled too!

SPECIFICITY POWER OF ID SELECTORS

STEP 6.4.3

With the ID (#) selector you can be much more specific with your CSS selectors. Just to show you how much more powerful the ID (#) selectors are than class (.) selectors, add a new rule using the class (.) selector with the `mfg` value and apply a `green` value to the `background-color` property.

```
#american { background-color: lightblue; }
#japanese{ background-color: lightsalmon; }
.mfg { background-color: green; }
```

You might think that your two lists (that both have the `class` attribute with the value of `mfg`) would now have a green background color. However, when you refresh your page, you'll notice there is no green background for either list (**Figure 6.10**).

REMEMBER: IDS WEIGH MORE THAN CLASS SELECTORS

*AS MENTIONED PREVIOUSLY, THERE IS SPECIFIC CSS MATH WITH REGARD TO SELECTORS: THE ID (#) SELECTOR **TRUMPS** THE CLASS (.) SELECTOR. SO, IF YOU'RE NOT GETTING THE RESULTS YOU EXPECT, YOU MIGHT HAVE A 100-POUND ID SELECTOR SQUASHING YOUR 10-POUND CLASS SELECTOR.*

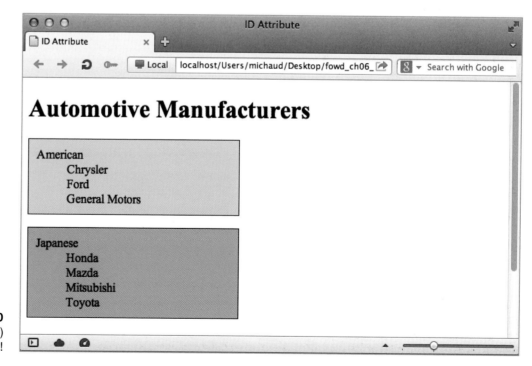

FIGURE 6.10
The CSS specificity power of the `id` (#) attribute trumps the `class` (.) attribute!

ROLE ATTRIBUTES OR
HTML5 TAGS?

Even if you're using HTML5
elements, you should still use the
ARIA landmark role attribute to
help structure your document—
until there is more widespread
support for the new HTML5 tags.

HTML: ROLE ATTRIBUTE

Another attribute worth noting is the
WAI-ARIA (Web Accessibility Initiative—
Accessible Rich Internet Applications)
landmark `role` attribute. This attribute
has some great benefits. First, it's really
geared to help websites become more
accessible to users with disabilities—
screen-reading browsers utilize the `role`
attribute in ways other browsers don't
(see the website for more information).
Second, it helps to describe your
document's structure for assistive
devices (and bots from search engines).

> *Adding ARIA landmarks to your existing
> site, or to a site you are developing,
> provides useful global navigation features
> and aids understanding of content
> structure for users. Over time the necessity
> of explicitly assigning landmarks will lessen
> as browsers build in ARIA landmark roles
> to newer HTML element semantics. There
> is widespread support for ARIA landmarks
> in browsers and screen readers.*

Steve Faulkner

The Paciello Group Blog

http://blog.paciellogroup.com/2013/02/using-wai-
aria-landmarks-2013/

ARIA LANDMARKS

ARIA landmarks describe the purposes
of different areas of a page in a way
that Assistive Technologies (ATs) can
understand. They are intended as nav-
igational landmarks.

LIMITED ROLE CHOICES

Unlike the `class` and `id` attributes, the
caveat about using the ARIA `role` attribute is that its value is limited to
predetermined values.

HOOKING STYLES

Like the `class` and `id` attributes, the `role`
attribute will do nothing visually but can
be used as a styling "hook" for CSS.

In the document **03-role-attribute.html**,
you'll incorporate the `role` attribute into
your HTML elements.

ARIA LANDMARK: BANNER

The banner role value helps define a region that applies to the entire site—like the name of a company, a product, or a person (for a portfolio site).

STEP 6.5.1

In the **03-role-attribute.html** document, you have a div element containing an h1, an h2, and a list of items that will help visitors navigate your site. These elements should appear on each page of your site to help orient visitors to what site they're visiting. You simply need to add the role attribute with the banner value to the opening `<div>` tag.

```
<div role="banner">
<h1>Role Attributes</h1>
<h2>Examples in HTML and CSS</h2>
<ul>
  <li><a href="index.html">Home</a></li>
  <li><a href="about.html">About me</a></li>
  <li><a href="contact.html">Contact me</a></li>
</ul>
</div>
```

ARIA LANDMARK: NAVIGATION

The navigation role value defines the navigation section of your site. Since the navigation role is not "allowed" on the ul element, you can use the HTML5 nav element.

STEP 6.5.2

Below the h2 element, add the HTML5 nav element with the role attribute assigning the navigation landmark value to this region.

```
<div role="banner">
<h1>Role Attributes</h1>
<h2>Examples in HTML and CSS</h2>

<nav role="navigation">
<ul>
  <li><a href="index.html">Home</a></li>
  <li><a href="about.html">About me</a></li>
  <li><a href="contact.html">Contact me</a></li>
</ul>
</nav>
</div>
```

BANNER DAY FOR THE HEADER!

The HTML5 equivalent to the banner role would be the header element, and it's advised you use the two together. However, while it's possible to have more than one header element, you should not mark more than one element with the banner role.

```
<header role="banner">
...
</header>
```

W3C NAV SPECIFICATION

The nav element represents a section of a page that links to other pages or to parts within the page—a section with navigation links.

ARIA LANDMARK: MAIN

The `main` role value defines your main content area and should not be used more than once in the same document.

STEP 6.5.3

In the next empty `div` element, add the `role` attribute and assign the `main` landmark value.

```
<div role="main">
<h2>The Main Role</h2>
  <p>The <code>role="main"</code>
  refers to the main content of a
  document. This marks the content
  that is directly related to or
  expands upon the central topic of
  the document. Within any document
  or application, the author should
  mark no more than one element with
  the main role.</p>
</div>
```

ARIA LANDMARK: COMPLEMENTARY

The `complementary` role value defines the "supporting section" of the document that relates to the area defined as the `main` (see previous landmark) content in the document.

STEP 6.5.4

Add `role="complementary"` to the next section that is "complementary" to your main topic.

```
<div role="complementary">
    <p><strong>CSS:</strong> How do I use
    CSS to select the <code>role</code>
    attribute and value?</p>
</div>
```

ARIA LANDMARK: CONTENTINFO

The `contentinfo` landmark value normally resides at the end of your document and defines the area containing footnotes, copyrights, links to privacy statements, etc.

MAIN HTML5 EQUIVALENT?

The HTML5 equivalent to the `main` role would be the `<main>` tag; it's advised that you use the two together.

```
<main role="main">
...
</main>
```

IS IT RELATED?

If the text is completely unrelated to the main topic, do not use the `role="complementary"` attribute.

LIKE AN ASIDE?

The complementary role has some similarities to the HTML5 `<aside>` tag.

CONTENTINFO FOOTER?

While there is no specific HTML5 element equivalent to the contentinfo landmark, you could place it on a `<footer>` tag residing at the end of your document.

```
<footer role="contentinfo">
<p>Copyright &copy; 2013</p>
<p>Creative Commons License</p>
</footer>
```

HTML5 SOLUTION

If you used the HTML5 tags, the **03-role-html5.html** document shows you the completed version.

STEP 6.5.5

To the `div` that contains your copyright information, add `role="contentinfo"`.

```
<div role="contentinfo">
    <p>Copyright &copy; 2013</p>
    <p>Creative Commons License</p>
</div>
```

>>> ONCE IS ENOUGH

WITHIN ANY DOCUMENT, YOU SHOULD NOT APPLY role="contentinfo" *TO MORE THAN ONE ELEMENT.*

DOUBLE-CHECK YOUR WORK

The document **03-role-attribute.html**, in the **solutions** folder, has all this written out, so you can double-check your results.

>>> REMEMBER: VALIDATE YOURSELF

ALL ALONG THE WAY IT'S GOOD TO VALIDATE (SEE WEBSITE) YOUR CODE TO CATCH ANY ERRORS. THERE WILL BE LINKS ON THE WEBSITE TO HELP YOU IN THE USE OF THE role *ATTRIBUTE.*

WHAT IS THE RESULT?

Visually, your document looks no different than when you started, but you did define your document structure so assistive technologies can allow keyboard navigation from region to region (**Figure 6.11**).

Yes, there are other ARIA landmark values. You'll use `form` and `search` when you learn about the HTML `form` elements later in the book. For now, let's see how you can target attributes to style your page.

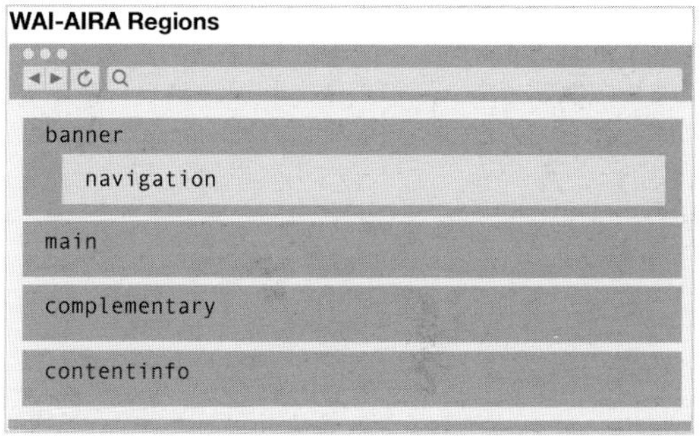

FIGURE 6.11
A visual outline of the layout using the ARIA landmark `role` attribute.

CSS: ATTRIBUTE SELECTORS

When you use CSS to select the `role` attribute, you have to use a different technique than you've seen thus far. In CSS, there is no symbol/sign to select the `role` attribute, so you need to create an attribute selector; do this by writing out the attribute name along with its value and wrapping them in [ ] brackets.

```
selector[attribute="value"]
```

STEP 6.6.1

Open the **03role.css** document (in the **css** folder).

Select the `div` element with the `role` attribute with a value of `banner`. In writing a CSS attribute selector, name the HTML element you're selecting and then place your attribute and value pair as it's written in HTML within square brackets [ ].

```
div[role="banner"] {
    background-color: lightblue;
}
```

So, the CSS attribute selector looks a little like HTML. When viewing your HTML document in a browser, you should now see a light blue background around the banner landmark region (**Figure 6.12**).

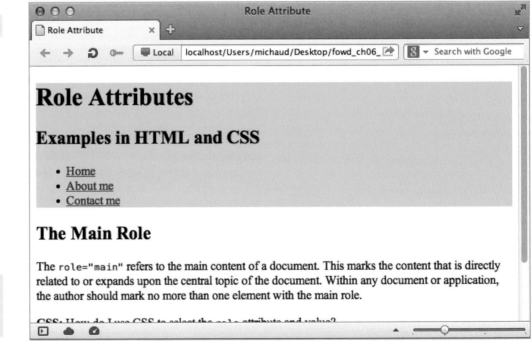

FIGURE 6.12
The CSS attribute selector allows you to use the `role` attribute as a hook for styling.

HTML5 SELECTOR

If you used the HTML5 header element, your CSS rule selector would be `header` and not `div`.

```
header[role="banner"] {
    background-color: lightblue;
}
```

⟫⟫ KEEP PLAYING!

YOU CAN PLAY AROUND BY ADDING OTHER BACKGROUND COLORS TO THE OTHER role *ATTRIBUTE AND VALUE PAIRS.*

*IF YOU OPEN **03-ROLE-ATTRIBUTE.HTML**, IN THE **SOLUTIONS** FOLDER, YOU'LL SEE HOW THE LAYOUT COULD LOOK USING CSS. IF YOU'RE REALLY UP FOR THE CHALLENGE, LOOK AT **03ROLE.CSS**, IN THE **SOLUTIONS/CSS** FOLDER, AND SEE THE RULES DEVELOPED FOR THIS LAYOUT. WHILE SOME THINGS WILL MAKE SENSE NOW, OTHER DECLARATIONS MAY TAKE A FEW MORE CHAPTERS TO UNDERSTAND.*

WRAPPING THINGS UP

So, those are the basics of using the id and class attributes and selectors—the most common attributes/selectors you'll use—in HTML and CSS. Also, you got a brief introduction to the useful and accessible ARIA role attribute. This attribute will help define regions (banner, navigation, main, complementary, contentinfo, form, and search) and structure your HTML document.

⟫⟫ *TIME FOR A BREAK, AND THEN WE'LL DELVE EVEN FURTHER INTO CSS TYPOGRAPHY! REMEMBER: MORE ON THE WEBSITE!*

⟫⟫ *MAKE SURE YOU CHECK OUT THE WEBSITE SECTION ON CHAPTER 6 TO LEARN MORE FROM OTHER RESOURCES AND FOR VIDEO TUTORIALS!*

{/}

CSS: STYLING TEXT

—

07

In this chapter, you'll begin the journey of delving deeper into using CSS to style the look and feel of your website. With some simple CSS rules, you can start to change the fonts you use and the look and color of your text.

There are a lot of things you can do with fonts in CSS, and I'm only going to cover a handful of basic but essential font and text rules you can use to transform text from the basic black-and-white serif text the browsers start with to something more uniquely your own.

FONT PROPERTIES

If you want to change the style (font family, size, style, weight, etc.) of a font, the following properties are some of the most common you'll use on any project. For the font property examples, open the **01-font.html** document in a browser and **01font.css** in your text editor.

FONT FAMILY

The `font-family` property allows you to modify the actual font family the user sees. By default, many browsers use a serif font like Times or Times New Roman (**Figure 7.1**).

So, let's talk about the `font-family` generic names and some of the "safe" fonts found on most computers.

SANS SERIF FONTS

Sans-serif fonts have a smooth look to them—they don't have the little end strokes you see on serif fonts. Some of the `font-family` values that you'll find associated with this family are `Arial`, `Helvetica`, `Impact`, `"Trebuchet MS"`, and `Verdana`.

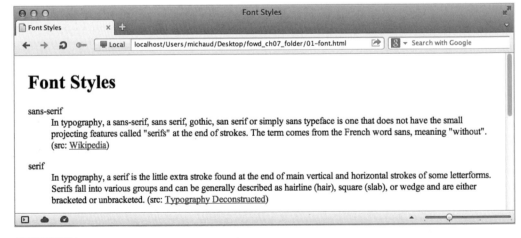

FIGURE 7.1
The default font in most browsers is a serif-style font.

STEP 7.1.1

In the **01font.css** document, add the following rule to the CSS for the ID (#) selector with the value of `sansFont` to apply the generic `sans-serif` value for the `font-family` property:

```
#sansFont {
  font-family: sans-serif;
}
```

The browser will search for a sans-serif font on your computer, and, depending upon your operating system, it could get anything from Arial (usually on Windows) to Helvetica (on a Mac) (**Figure 7.2**).

>>> *WINDOWS VS. MAC: IT'S INTERESTING TO NOTE THAT THIS GENERIC* sans-serif *VALUE MIGHT BE BETTER IF YOU WISH TO USE HELVETICA ON THE MAC AND ARIAL ON THE PC. ON EARLIER VERSIONS OF WINDOWS, HELVETICA USUALLY DID NOT RENDER AS WELL IN THE BROWSER AS ARIAL.*

STEP 7.1.2

When you add more fonts to your value, separate the font names with commas, adding in specific font choices before the generic name.

```
#sansFont {
  font-family: Verdana, sans-serif;
}
```

If you wish to add a font with multiple words in its name, you need to surround it with quotation marks (single 'font name' or double "font name").

```
#sansFont {
  font-family: "Trebuchet MS",
  Verdana, sans-serif;
}
```

Viewing your website again, you see a change from the default sans-serif font to something a little more unique (**Figure 7.3**).

---

sans-serif
In typography, a sans-serif, sans serif, gothic, san serif or simply sans typeface is one that does not have the small projecting features called "serifs" at the end of strokes. The term comes from the French word sans, meaning "without". (src: Wikipedia)

FIGURE 7.2
The default serif font is replaced by a default sans-serif font.

---

sans-serif
In typography, a sans-serif, sans serif, gothic, san serif or simply sans typeface is one that does not have the small projecting features called "serifs" at the end of strokes. The term comes from the French word sans, meaning "without". (src: Wikipedia)

FIGURE 7.3
Your font family now uses one of your named fonts.

 FONT STACKING

A font stack is a list of fonts declared in your CSS `font-family` property. It allows you to control the look of the fonts on your website. Fonts are listed in order of your preference. If the first font is not found on the user's system, the browser will go to your next option, and so on until it finds a font on the list or reaches the generic name.

SERIF FONTS

A serif font has those little curves on the ends of the glyphs—`serif` is also the default value for the `font-family` property for most (if not all) web browsers. The font family most often used is `Times` (or `"Times New Roman"`); other `serif` values include (but are not limited to) `Georgia` and `Palatino` (or `"Palatino Linotype"`).

STEP 7.1.3

Now add another CSS rule selecting the ID selector (#) with the value of `serifFont`, give the `font-family` property the value of `Georgia`, and close with `serif`.

```
#serifFont {
    font-family: Georgia, serif;
}
```

Returning to the browser, we only see a slight change from the default to Georgia—but it's a font that renders very well in the browser and is often a popular choice (**Figure 7.4**).

MONOSPACE FONTS

A `monospaced` value gives you a fixed-width font that looks similar to the text editor that you're typing code in.

HTML elements such as the `<pre></pre>` block element and `<code></code>` inline element give you a monospace font by default. Some system-safe values for the `font-family` include `"Andale Mono"`, `Courier`, `"Courier New"`, and `Monaco`.

GENERIC NAME NEEDED

Remember, it's always good to close with the default `font-family` value for the type of font you've chosen. If the font you've named is not on the user's computer, the generic value will find some font matching its criteria.

FIXED-WIDTH AND VARIABLE-WIDTH FONTS

Fixed-width fonts have letters and characters that occupy the same amount of horizontal space. Variable-width fonts have letters that differ in size from one another.

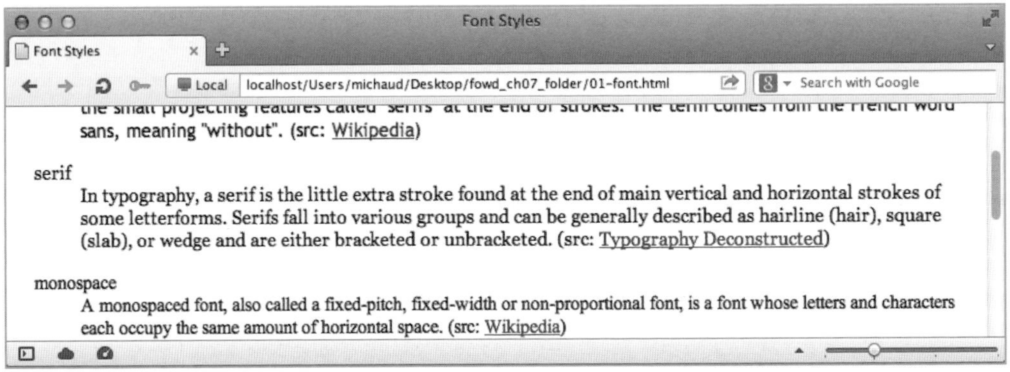

FIGURE 7.4
The serif Georgia font face has a sophisticated look and is easy on the eyes.

STEP 7.1.4

Add a new rule to select `#monoFont` that will apply `"Courier New"` to the `font-family` property—don't forget the generic name too.

```
#monoFont {
    font-family: "Courier New", monospace;
}
```

Now your "monospace" name and definition has a monospaced look (**Figure 7.5**).

```
monospace
    A monospaced font, also called a fixed-pitch, fixed-width or non-
    proportional font, is a font whose letters and characters each occupy the
    same amount of horizontal space. (src: Wikipedia)
```

FIGURE 7.5
Monospaced type looks like code or has a "typewriter" appearance.

cursive

Cursive, also known as script, joined-up writing, joint writing, linking, running writing, or handwriting is any style of penmanship in which the symbols of the language are written in a conjoined and/or flowing manner, generally for the purpose of making writing faster. (src: wikipedia)

FIGURE 7.6
How the generic cursive font is displayed on the Mac OS.

fantasy

Fantasy fonts often have a bold exaggerated style typical of poster display headings, sometimes with ornaments or quirky themes. Fantasy font faces include a wide variety of font style, which can have unpredictable results on the Web. Use the CSS font family name fantasy cautiously. (src: Code Style)

FIGURE 7.7
How the generic fantasy font is displayed on the Mac OS.

STEP 7.1.5

The next two values (`cursive` and `fantasy`) have very few fonts that are common among all computer operating systems. As a general rule, I strongly recommend staying away from using cursive or fantasy as a generic font, as you just don't know what the user will see. Here are the basic examples of what types of fonts you'd see using the generic family:

```
#cursiveFont {
    font-family: cursive;
}
```

On a Mac operating system, you'll often see the Apple Chancery font (**Figure 7.6**).

```
#fantasyFont {
    font-family: fantasy;
}
```

Also on a Mac operating system, you'll often see the font Papyrus (**Figure 7.7**)—it's certainly a font I always imagine when someone says "Think of a fantasy-style font."

So, here are some basic rules to follow when you style the `font-family` property value:

- You should always include the generic font family at the end of your list of font names.

- A font family that has more than one word in its name and has spaces needs to be within quotes (e.g., `"Trebuchet MS"` or `"Times New Roman"`).

- The font family name you use must be on the user's computer; otherwise, the generic font family will be used. However, on the website you'll find ways to use additional fonts that are not on the user's computer.

FONT SIZE

The `font-size` property allows you to increase and decrease the size of a font using a variety of measurements for the values.

When it comes to selecting what type of `font-size` value you want to use, you won't lack options:

- Common units including `px`, `%`, and `em`

- Keywords such as `xx-small`, `x-small`, `small`, `medium`, `large`, `x-large`, and `xx-large`

- Relative keywords such as `smaller` and `larger`

▶▶▶ *NOTE: FOR THE FOLLOWING EXAMPLES, YOU'LL STICK TO USING THE COMMON UNITS ONLY.*

COMMON UNITS: PIXELS

We'll keep it basic and use pixels for the unit of measurement to begin with. In CSS, the pixel unit is written as `px`. It gives you the most control (and is easiest to wrap your head around).

As a baseline size, most browsers set `font-size` to `16px` (**Figure 7.8**) or a keyword value of `normal`.

FIGURE 7.8
The default base font size for paragraphs, lists, and blockquotes is 16 pixels in height.

So, the size of the majority of HTML elements is set to a `16px` value. However, the `h1` thru `h6` elements' `font-size` is not set to a specific pixel size but to an `em` value (we'll look at that in just a moment). The `h1` usually calculates to `32px`, and the `h2` is usually `24px`. While you can choose any size you wish, it's best when starting out to keep it simple and not vary too much from the defaults.

STEP 7.2.1

Back in **01font.css**, write a rule to resize the `h1` element to a `font-size` of `72px` (**Figure 7.9**).

```
h1 {
    font-size: 72px;
}
```

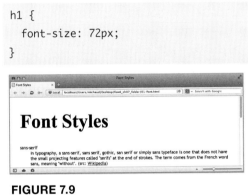

FIGURE 7.9
The words "Font Styles" have increased in size.

▶▶▶ *WEBSITE: CHECK OUT THE WEBSITE FOR LINKS TO LEARN MORE ABOUT TYPOGRAPHY.*

CONVERT PX TO %

STEP 7.2.2

To convert `72px` to a `%` (percentage), you need to use the following formula:

target ÷ context = result

So, take 72 (the target `font-size` value in pixels) and divide it by 16 (the contextual [browser] baseline). The result is 4.5.

72 ÷ 16 = 4.5

To get a percentage, move the decimal two places to the right to get 450%.

```
h1 {
    font-size: 450%;
}
```

When you reload the page, you'll notice no difference in the size of the words "Font Styles."

WHY CHANGE FROM PX TO % VALUE?

Great question. We'll discuss it further when we talk about fluid layouts in Chapter 10!

CONVERT PX TO EM

The em value (pronounced like saying the letter "M") is a bit different from either the px or %, as its base value (1em) is based upon the parent element's font size (in this case, it's the body element, which is set to 16px in the CSS).

>>> NOTE: *THERE ARE WHOLE CHAPTERS AND BLOG POSTS WRITTEN ON THE VALUE OF USING* em, *SO I'LL NOT DELVE INTO IT ANY DEEPER THAN HELPING YOU LEARN TO CONVERT* px *TO* em. *CHECK THE WEBSITE FOR INFORMATION.*

STEP 7.2.3

Again, take the h1 element you selected and use the formula

target ÷ context = result

You can plug in the numbers. The target size value is 72px, and you divide that by the context value of 16px, giving you a result of 4.5. Just leave the number as your result and add the em.

```
h1 {
    font-size: 4.5em;
}
```

Again, there's no change in the way the font size looks. While this might seem a bit complex, don't worry but keep trying different sizes (including em values that are less than 1, like .25em—but no negative values) and see what you get.

>>> ONLINE DEMOS: *THE WEBSITE HAS MORE DEMONSTRATIONS OF HOW TO USE % AND* em *VALUES FOR YOUR PROJECTS.*

FONT STYLE

The font-style property has three options for the value—normal, italic, and oblique—so it allows you to italicize fonts (or un-italicize a previously italicized font). Be careful, as not all fonts have an italicized font face. In that case, CSS simply slants the font (makes it oblique).

STEP 7.3.1

Style the h2 element with the italic value.

```
h2 {
    font-style: italic;
}
```

You can see the results in **Figure 7.10**.

FIGURE 7.10
The header font is displayed in italic font face.

FONT VARIANT

The `font-variant` property simply allows you to style text using the value of `small-caps`.

STEP 7.3.2

Set the `h2` element and apply the `font-variant` property with the value of `small-caps`.

Then view the result in the browser (**Figure 7.11**).

```
h2 {
  font-style: small-caps;
}
```

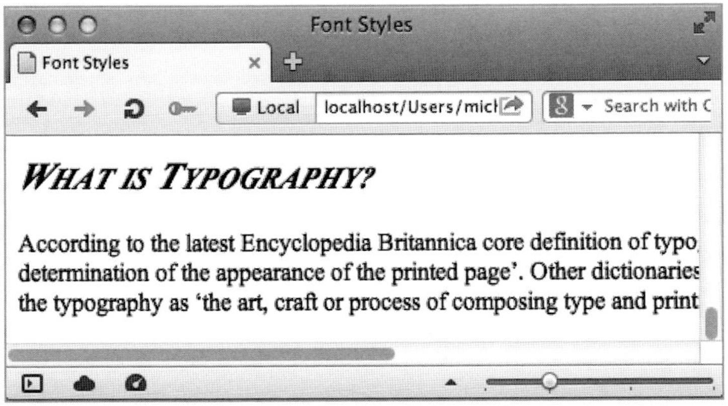

FONT WEIGHT

The `font-weight` property has a number of values you can choose from, but they do nearly the same thing: make your font `bold`, `bolder`, `normal`, or `lighter` in weight.

STEP 7.3.3

You can bold text that isn't bold by default.

```
dt {
  font-weight: bold;
}
```

And you can lighten text that is bold by default.

```
h2 {
  font-weight: lighter;
}
```

View the browser to see the changes in weight to the `dt` and `h2` elements (**Figure 7.12**).

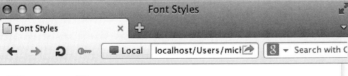

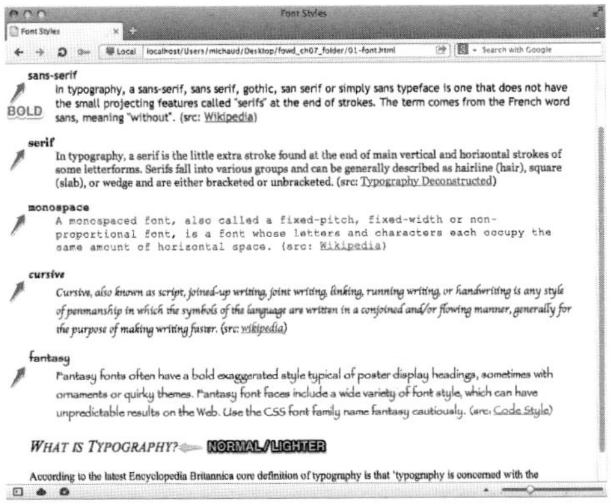

FIGURE 7.12
You can bold or lighten font weights.

FIGURE 7.11
The header font is displayed with small caps.

FONT PROPERTY SHORTHAND

The `font` property is a shorthand property that allows you to write all the previous property values into one space-separated value in this order:

```
font { [ font-style ]  [ font-
variant ]  [ font-weight ] [font-
size][ /line-height ] [font-family]
}
```

STEP 7.3.4

Say you wanted to select the `p` element that immediately follows the `h2` element and modify a few values (**Figure 7.13**):

```
h2 + p {
    font: italic 1.25em/1.4 Georgia,
serif;
}
```

>>> *NOTE: YOU DO NOT NEED TO ENTER A VALUE FOR ALL OPTIONS. IF A VALUE IS LEFT OUT FOR A PROPERTY, IT SIMPLY TAKES THE DEFAULT SETTING IF NO OTHER VALUE HAS BEEN SET PREVIOUSLY.*

TEXT PROPERTIES

The text properties `text-align`, `text-decoration`, `text-indent`, and `text-transform` normally deal with styling a whole block of text and not the font face style itself.

TEXT ALIGN

The `text-align` property is pretty self-explanatory, allowing the following values for alignment: `center`, `justify`, `left`, and `right`.

 LINE HEIGHT

The value written "/1.4" is for the `line-height` property and will be demonstrated later, but, in the `font` property, the `font-size` and `line-height` values are always written together and separated by the `/` symbol. In the `font` shorthand property, you can write the value for the `font-size` without the `line-height`, but you cannot write the value for the `line-height` without the value of the `font-size`.

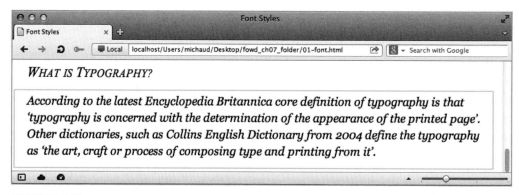

FIGURE 7.13
The paragraph that immediately follows the h2 now has multiple values applied.

STEP 7.4.1

Open **02text.css** (in the css folder) in the text editor. Write a new rule that selects the # (id) with the value of textAlign that has the dt, and set the text-align property to the right.

```
#textAlign dt {
    text-align: right;
}
```

View the **02-text.html** document in the browser to see the result (**Figure 7.14**).

>>> *COMPARE ALIGNMENTS: KEEP TESTING OUT EACH DIRECTION VALUE (*left, center, *AND BACK TO THE RIGHT ALIGNMENT BY USING THE VALUE* inherit*) AND REFRESHING THE BROWSER TO SEE THE RESULTS.*

STEP 7.4.2

One other value the text-align property permits is justify. Set the text-align to justify for the dd (definition description) of #textAlign.

```
#textAlign dd {
    text-align: justify;
}
```

Refresh the document in the browser to see the result (**Figure 7.15**).

You can see that the text now lines up on the left and right sides of your column (unlike the left-justified and ragged-right format that is most common).

USE CAUTION IN JUSTIFYING TEXT

Be careful when justifying text, as the typography controls in CSS are not as powerful as those in desktop publishing applications— it can produce some ugly spacing between words.

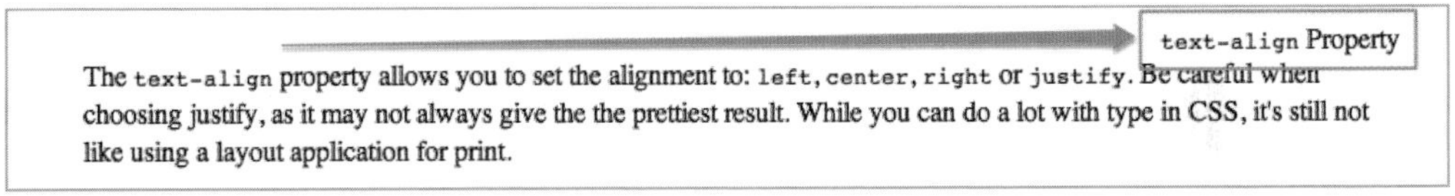

The text-align property allows you to set the alignment to: left, center, right or justify. Be careful when choosing justify, as it may not always give the the prettiest result. While you can do a lot with type in CSS, it's still not like using a layout application for print.

FIGURE 7.14
The definition title moves to the right.

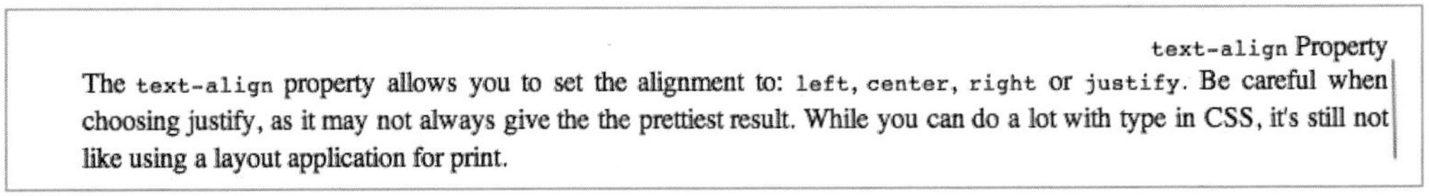

The text-align property allows you to set the alignment to: left, center, right or justify. Be careful when choosing justify, as it may not always give the the prettiest result. While you can do a lot with type in CSS, it's still not like using a layout application for print.

FIGURE 7.15
The description text left-aligned and right-justified.

TEXT DECORATION

The `text-decoration` property allows you to decorate text with (drumroll) … LINES! I know, exciting. Each value—`line-through`, `none`, `overline`, and `underline`—is pretty self-explanatory, so we'll simply look at the results of each value.

Open **02text.css** in a text editor. I've already set up the class attributes in the **02-text.html** document for the examples, so you just need to type out the CSS rules.

STEP 7.5.1

The `line-through` value can inform visitors that part of the text in your blog is out of date (**Figure 7.16**).

```
.throughText {
    text-decoration: line-through;
}
```

STEP 7.5.2

There are many designers who remove the underline from links by assigning the value `none` to anchor (`a`) elements (**Figure 7.17**).

```
.underTextNone a {
    text-decoration: none;
}
```

REMOVING UNDERLINES FROM LINKS

Normally I avoid removing the underline from links—it's a good visual reference. However, if it's something you choose to do, make sure visitors can visually differentiate between regular text and a link.

STEP 7.5.3

The `overline` value could be useful in adding lines above headers (`h1`, `h2`, `h3`, `dt`, etc.) to help visually separate sections (**Figure 7.18**).

```
.overText {
    text-decoration: overline;
}
```

»» *LIMITED USEFULNESS: THE* overline *STYLE IS NOT THE BEST OPTION. THE* border-top *PROPERTY (DISCUSSED IN CHAPTER 8) IS A BETTER SOLUTION AND CAN BE STYLED WITH CSS.*

• Add a `line-through` text (like you're saying "~~this text is no longer needed~~")

FIGURE 7.16
A line through text may indicate text that is out of date.

• Remove the `underline` from a link

FIGURE 7.17
Removing underlines from links is a common practice.

• Add an overline to a text block

FIGURE 7.18
A line over text could help to visually separate it from text above it.

STEP 7.5.4

The `underline` value may help with citations of book titles, when an underline is required (**Figure 7.19**).

```
.underText {
    text-decoration: underline;
}
```

> • Add an underline to a text block

FIGURE 7.19
A line under text can help with book title citations or highlight a thought.

TEXT INDENT

The `text-indent` property indents the first line in a block of text—unlike `margin`, which moves the entire element.

```
#textIndent dd {
  text-indent: 20px;
}
```

When you refresh your browser, you'll see the first lines of each `dd` element are indented 20 pixels (**Figure 7.20**).

TEXT TRANSFORM

The `text-transform` property allows you to capitalize text, transform uppercase text to lowercase, and change lowercase text to uppercase.

STEP 7.6.1

The `capitalize` value capitalizes the first letter of each word in the text block (**Figure 7.21**).

```
.textCapital {
    text-transform: capitalize;
}
```

This is helpful for titles (headers) where you want all the words to begin with a capital letter.

STEP 7.6.2

Add another rule to transform the text to all `uppercase` (**Figure 7.22**).

```
.textUpper {
    text-transform: uppercase;
}
```

> • To Capitalize All First Letters In A Text Block

FIGURE 7.21
The first letter in each word is capitalized.

> • TO SET OUR TEXT IN ALL UPPERCASE.

FIGURE 7.22
All text is transformed to uppercase text.

---

text-indent Property

➡ The text-indent property allows you to, well, indent text. However, unlike margin, the text-indent property *only* moves the first line of text in an element and *not* the whole block.

➡ The indent value can be positive, to move the text to the right, or negative, to move the text to the left. Many web designers use a negative text value (text-indent: -9999px;) to hide text when using images to replace text. However, according to Jeffery Zeldman, there is a method that could be better.

FIGURE 7.20
The first line of text is indented.

STEP 7.6.3

Finally, use the `lowercase` value to transform all uppercase and capitalized text to lowercase (**Figure 7.23**).

```
.textLower {
    text-transform: lowercase;
}
```

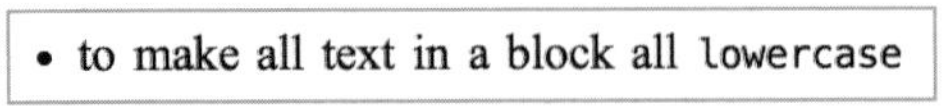

- to make all text in a block all lowercase

FIGURE 7.23
All uppercase text is transformed
to lowercase.

SPACING PROPERTIES

Transforming text is not all you can do with CSS; there are a few more controls for spacing between letters, words, and lines of text, and for vertical alignment.

LINE-HEIGHT

The `line-height` property allows you to control the spacing between lines of text. In traditional typographic terms, this was known as leading. A common spacing between lines of text in a paragraph equals the font size (which you know is, by default, set to `16px` or `normal`) multiplied by the value of 1.5. If you multiply 16 (pixels) by 1.5, you'll get the value of 24 (pixels).

STEP 7.7.1

In **03spacing.css**, set your paragraph (`p`), within the `blockquote`, to have a `line-height` value of `24px`.

```
blockquote p {
    line-height: 24px;
}
```

View the **03-spacing.html** document in a browser, and notice the paragraph in the blockquote has more space between lines than the paragraph above it (**Figure 7.24**).

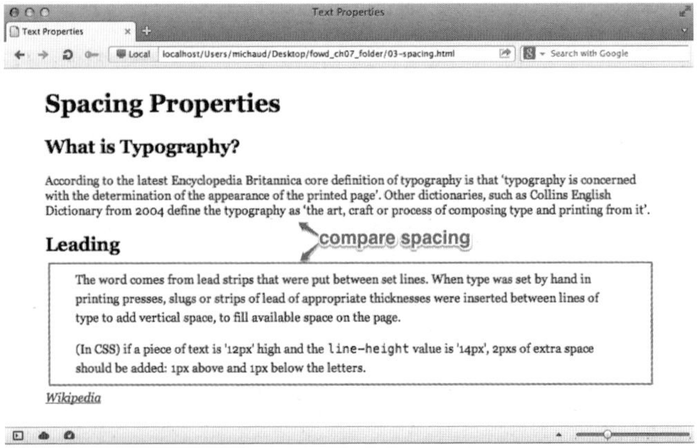

BROWSER DEFAULT LINE-HEIGHT

The first paragraph has the browser's default `line-height` setting (which is approximately 1.1875 times the default font size—so, for 16px font, the line height is 19px).

FIGURE 7.24
Spacing has increased only in
the blockquote text.

Spacing Properties

What is Typography?

According to the latest Encyclopedia Britannica core definition of typography is that 'typography is concerned with the determination of the appearance of the printed page'. Other dictionaries, such as Collins English Dictionary from 2004 define the typography as 'the art, craft or process of composing type and printing from it'.

Leading   compare spacing

The word comes from lead strips that were put between set lines. When type was set by hand in printing presses, slugs or strips of lead of appropriate thicknesses were inserted between lines of type to add vertical space, to fill available space on the page.

(In CSS) if a piece of text is '12px' high and the line-height value is '14px', 2pxs of extra space should be added: 1px above and 1px below the letters.

Wikipedia

FIXED VS. RELATIVE LEADING

What if you wanted to set a larger font size? You would have to recalculate the line height. Ugh! That would get tedious. However, there's a simple solution: Change the `line-height` value from a fixed `px` value to a relative `em` value. Then, if you change the `font-size` value in the `body` (or if the user changes his or her browser font size) to be larger or smaller than `16px`, the `line-height` value will automatically be calculated!

- Font size: `14px` * line height: 1.5 = 21px of space between lines of text

- Font size: `18px` * line height: 1.5 = 27px of space between lines of text

STEP 7.7.2

Change the `24px` fixed value to the relative `1.5em` value for the `line-height`.

```
blockquote p {
    line-height: 1.5;
}
```

⟫ *NOTE: WHEN SETTING THE LINE-HEIGHT TO AN EM VALUE, YOU ARE NOT REQUIRED TO PLACE THE "EM" AFTER THE NUMBER.*

No change occurs in the spacing, but you have more flexibility if the `font-size` ever changes.

CHALLENGE

Change the `font-size` for the `blockquote p` from `16px` to `18px`, and see if the line spacing changes. Then remove the `blockquote` selector so you're selecting only the `p` (paragraph) element. You should see the same spacing for the text within the `blockquote` paragraph and the text within the paragraph above it.

WEBSITE RESOURCES ON FONT STYLES

There are other typographical controls that are demonstrated on the website:

- `letter-spacing`

- `vertical-align`

- `white-space`

- `word-spacing`

There is much, much more to learn about font spacing, sizing, and families, so I suggest you check out the website resources for Chapter 7. I'll provide links to articles and demonstrations of web typography design practices.

COLOR

CSS gives you a lot of options when choosing colors for your website, and it gives you options for how to express the values of those colors (some easier to understand than others). Since we're still in the chapter dealing with text, we'll look at the CSS property that targets your text color … called, well, `color`!

NAME VALUE CHALLENGE

Can you write out additional CSS rules for the selectors .blue, .green, .olive, and .gray, with their keyword names, to match **Figure 7.25**? If you get stuck, view **04color.css** in the **solutions** folder.

>>> *NOTE: IN THE FUTURE, DON'T MAKE IT A HABIT TO USE PRESENTATIONAL NAMES AS CSS CLASS SELECTOR NAMES.*

COLOR PROPERTY

The CSS color property is used to set the **foreground** color of an element's text content.

COLOR VALUE: NAMES

By default, browsers set the text to "black."

You can use CSS to change the color of your text simply by typing one of the 147 accepted named color values, like red, blue, green, etc.

For these examples, you'll apply your CSS rules in **04color.css**.

STEP 7.8.1

In your CSS document, change your font color to the value red (**Figure 7.25**).

```
.red {
    color: red;
}
```

 MAKE A STICKY NOTE

There is no property called font-color! And to get a color behind the text, you cannot use the color property—it only works on the "foreground" color of an element's text.

> LOTS OF NAMES

There are 147 names you can choose from. A great resource to view the names—and their color swatches—is 147 Colors (http://bit.ly/SkR58G). Simply mouse over a swatch to reveal the name value.

Color Name Values

- Black
- Red = red
- Green = green
- Blue = blue
- Olive = olivedrab
- Gray / Grey = gray or grey

FIGURE 7.25
Color names can be easy to remember.

COLOR VALUE: HEXADECIMAL (HEX)

The hex value starts with a hash symbol (#) and is composed of a six-character combination of numbers and letters (ranging from 0-9 and a-f). Each pair of characters corresponds to one of the three primary additive colors: red, green, and blue (**Figure 7.26**). You can mix different combinations to get around 16 million colors.*

 I BELIEVE THAT'S MORE THAN THE HUMAN EYE CAN ACTUALLY DISTINGUISH.

For more complex colors, it's sometimes best to use an application to help get the hex value (**Figure 7.27**).

SHORTEN THE HEX VALUE

Did you notice, in the illustration, that you can write a shorthand value if the characters within the pairs repeat?

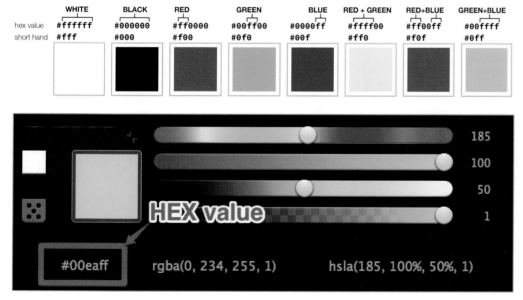

	WHITE	BLACK	RED	GREEN	BLUE	RED + GREEN	RED+BLUE	GREEN+BLUE
hex value	#ffffff	#000000	#ff0000	#00ff00	#0000ff	#ffff00	#ff00ff	#00ffff
short hand	#fff	#000	#f00	#0f0	#00f	#ff0	#f0f	#0ff

FIGURE 7.26
An illustration of the basic hex colors.

#00eaff   rgba(0, 234, 255, 1)   hsla(185, 100%, 50%, 1)

FIGURE 7.27
The HSL Color Picker (http://hslpicker.com/) is a great online application!

HEX VALUE CHALLENGE

Using the color combinations already shown, can you write additional CSS rules for the hex values of green, blue, yellow, magenta, and cyan? Selectors should be similar to the one you used for red: `#hex .red` ... (**hint:** green's selector would be `#hex .green`). If you get stuck, view **04color.css** in the solutions folder.

STEP 7.8.2

In **04color.css**, create a rule using the hex value for red (`#ff0000`) to change the `color` (**Figure 7.28**). Your selector will be the `#` (`id` attribute) with a value of `hex` and a descendant selector of `.` (`class` attribute) with the value of `red`.

```
#hex .red {
    color: #ff0000;
}
```

STEP 7.8.3

Since each paired value repeats—`ff`, `00`, and `00`—you can write a single value for each pair:

```
#hex .red {
    color: #f00;
}
```

COLOR VALUE: RGB

The `rgb()` value uses numbers between `0` (black or no color) and `255` (light or full color). The value must start with `rgb` (red, green, blue), and the numbers must be separated by commas and within parentheses: `(0,0,0)`.

Hex Color Values

- Red #ff0000
- Green #00ff00
- Blue #0000ff
- Red + Green = Yellow #ffff00
- Red + Blue = Magenta #ff00ff
- Green + Blue = Cyan #00ffff

FIGURE 7.28
Hex values can be a little difficult to learn, but they increase the color choice selection.

STEP 7.8.4

Writing a CSS rule for an `rgb(255,0,0)` value changes your text to red (**Figure 7.29**).

```
#rgb .red {
  color: rgb(255, 0, 0);
}
```

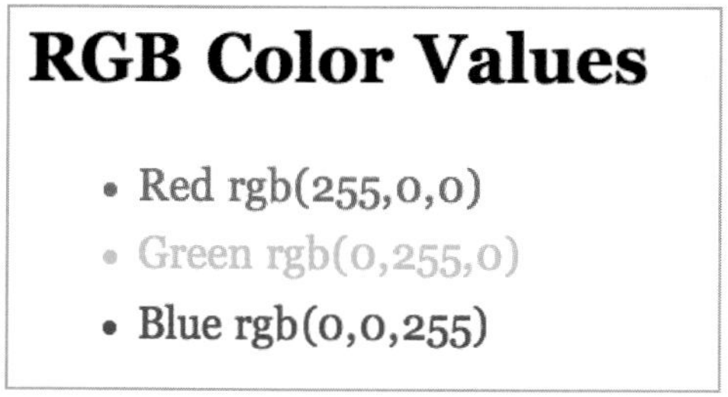

⟫ NOTE: *THE RGB COLOR MODEL WORKS IN BASICALLY THE SAME WAY AS HEX VALUES, BUT YOU ARE WRITING YOUR VALUE FOR EACH COLOR CHANNEL IN INTEGER VALUES OF 0-255, RATHER THAN TWO HEX VALUES OF 0-F.*

RGB Color Values

- Red rgb(255,0,0)
- Green rgb(0,255,0)
- Blue rgb(0,0,255)

FIGURE 7.29
Your text colors changed using the `rgb()` value.

WRAPPING THINGS UP

Wow! You're on your way to becoming a web typography master! Actually, you've only scratched the surface on this topic. But you can now start to take your font-styling knowledge beyond the browser defaults.

Next, we'll delve deeper into CSS and talk about the legendary "Box Model."

⟫ DOWNLOAD REMINDER: *THERE IS BONUS CONTENT TO DOWNLOAD FOR ADDITIONAL CSS FONT AND TEXT PROPERTIES AND AN ASSIGNMENT TO TEST YOUR SKILLS!*

THE BOX MODEL

—

08

All HTML elements displayed in the browser are drawn in a "box" shape. While the shape isn't always a perfect square, it does have four sides—top, right, bottom, and left—and a central content area surrounded by an area of padding, then a border, then an outer margin area (**Figure 8.1**). CSS can target these sides to manipulate elements in various ways; for example, by adding padding, margins, and borders to the different sides, or by adding images and color inside the content, padding, and border areas.

BOX DIMENSIONS

The **content** could be a paragraph, list, text header, or object (like an image or video).

The **padding** is the space between the content and the border. The default `padding` value is the initial value of the individual HTML element.

The **border** is the box's outer edge. By default, the `border-style` is set to `none`, which means the border will not display and which sets the `border-width` to "0". If there is no padding, the border sits at the outer edge of the content.

The **margin** is the space outside of the box. The default `margin` value is the initial value of the individual HTML element.

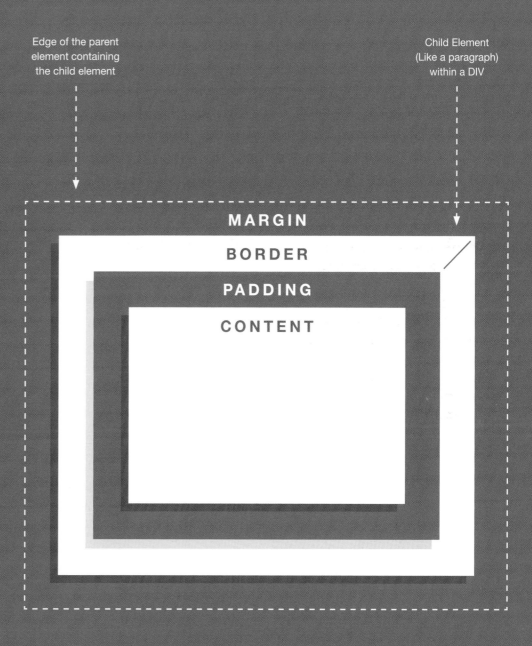

Edge of the parent element containing the child element

Child Element (Like a paragraph) within a DIV

MARGIN

BORDER

PADDING

CONTENT

FIGURE 8.1

Two-dimensional illustration of the box model.

WORKING WITH THE BOX

While this description offers a visual idea of the box, getting into the code and viewing it in the browser will clearly demonstrate the box's properties and their values. The document **01-box-model.html**, in the **fowd_ch08_folder**, has the following HTML code:

```
<div class="container">
  <p class="box">Lorem ipsum dolor sit
  amet, consectetur adipiscing elit. Ut
  quis fermentum magna. Integer suscipit
  tellus laoreet augue imperdiet in
  porttitor eros ultricies. Maecenas
  cursus odio at augue congue sed
  scelerisque eros sodales. Curabitur
  vestibulum blandit mauris, eu
  malesuada dolor dignissim et.</p>
</div> <!-- end .container -->
```

The **child** `<p>…</p>` element, with the `class` attribute with the value of `box`, is contained within the **parent** `<div>…</div>` element that has the `class` attribute with the value of `container`.

CONTENT

The text of the `<p>…</p>` element is your content—the inside of the box (**Figure 8.2**). Since "content" is not a CSS property, you could use (as one option) an element type selector (p) to apply styles to your content.

FIGURE 8.2
The content is the text of the paragraph element.

CHILD AND PARENT ELEMENTS

```
<div>
    <p>...</p>
</div>
```

When an element (`<p>…</p>`) is within another element (`<div>...</div>`), it's considered the **child**. Thus the element that contains another element is called the **parent.**

ARE THERE SIBLINGS?

```
<h1>...</h1>
```

```
<p>...</p>
```

When there is an element (`<h1>...</h1>`) above another element (`<p>...</p>`), the second (p) element is a sibling of the previous (h1) element.

The CSS document you'll use to style your HTML, which is linked to **01-box-model.html**, can be found in the **css** folder under the name **box-model.css**.

NOTE THE PRE-CODED CODE

In some examples, you'll notice the CSS document has some rules already applied. This simply helps to center the demonstrations in the browser.

```
.container {
    width: 50%;
    margin: 10% auto;
}
```

Always take time to study the code, even if you don't know what it does. Usually you'll understand by the end of the chapter.

BORDER

Before talking about the padding, let's move to the border—the area between the padding and margin.

BORDER STYLE

Since its default style value is none, we cannot see any border. To create a visible border, you need to use the border-style property. Remember, there are four sides to your element: top, right, bottom, and left.

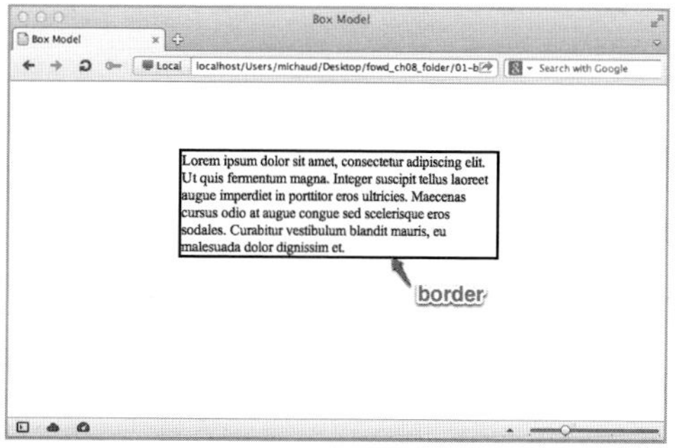

STEP 8.1.1

The first rule set will apply a solid line to all four sides.

```
.box {
    border-top-style: solid;
    border-right-style: solid;
    border-bottom-style: solid;
    border-left-style: solid;
}
```

>>> REMEMBER: *SAVE AFTER CHANGES. SELECT FROM THE MENU:*
FILE > SAVE.
AFTER YOU MAKE A CHANGE TO YOUR CSS DOCUMENT, SAVE YOUR WORK! THEN REFRESH THE BROWSER TO SEE CHANGES.

The content now has a solid black border around its edge (**Figure 8.3**).

FIGURE 8.3
The content now has a border.

STEP 8.1.2

The shorthand version of the border style can be written without the locations by applying space-separated values.

```
.box{
    border-style: solid solid solid solid;
}
```

STEP 8.1.3

If all four sides are the same value, simply write the value one time.

```
.box{
    border-style: solid;
}
```

BORDER COLOR

Did you notice that the color black was automatically applied to your border? By default, the border color takes on the color of the content. In this case, the text color is using the browser default of black, so the border will be black.

STEP 8.1.4

When you change the font color to red, the border becomes red (**Figure 8.4**).

```
.box{
    color: red;
    border-style: solid;
}
```

FIGURE 8.4
If the border color is not specified, the border takes on the color of the text.

 STYLIN' BORDERS

Including the values that will remove border styles (none and hidden), there are a number of visual values to choose from:

```
dotted | dashed | solid |
double | groove | ridge |
inset | outset
```

Play around with all of them to see what they look like. You can also apply different values to each of the four sides.

STYLIN' BORDERS — SPACE-SEPARATED VALUES

Space-separated values start with the top and work clockwise: top right bottom left. Some web designers use the mnemonic **TR**ou**BL**e to remember the order.

SHORTHAND BORDER COLOR

You can apply different colors to all four sides by specifying locations:

```
border-top-color: blue;
border-right-color: red;
border-bottom-color: green;
border-left-color: gray;
```

You can also use the shorthand version and set the four locations (starting with the top location and working clockwise).

```
border-color: blue red green gray;
```

BORDER WIDTH SHORTHAND

Establish a different border width for each side by using specific locations:

```
border-top-width: 5px;
border-right-width: 10px;
border-bottom-width: 5px;
border-left-width: 10px;
```

Or, use the shorthand with multiple values:

```
border-width: 5px 10px 5px 10px;
```

FIGURE 8.5
Applying a color to the border allows you to set the border apart from the text color.

STEP 8.1.5

If you don't want the text color to determine the color of the border, try adjusting the color of the border by using the `border-color` property (**Figure 8.5**).

```
.box{
    color: red;
    border-style: solid;
    border-color: gray;
}
```

Border color values, like those for the `color` property, can use predefined color names, hexadecimal colors, RGB colors, RGBa colors, HSL colors, and HSLa colors.

BORDER WIDTH

To establish the width, use the `border-width` property. The width value can be set as a numerical value (pixels, ems, rems, cm, etc.) or with a keyword (`medium`, `thick`, and `thin`).

STEP 8.1.6

By default, the width is set to medium, but you'll set the `border-width` to be a heavy `10px` (**Figure 8.6**).

```
.box{
    color: red;
    border-style: solid;
    border-color: gray;
    border-width: 10px;
}
```

FIGURE 8.6
You now have a nice, chunky border.

BORDER SHORTHAND

If you style the border with one value each for the `-width`, `-style`, and `-color` properties, the shorthand `border` property can be used rather than the three individual properties. The order of the space-separated values must be `border-width` value, `border-style` value, and `border-color` value.

STEP 8.1.7

Merge the border width, style, and color into the shorthand `border` property.

```
.box{
    color: red;
    border: 10px solid gray;
    /* replaces individual properties*/
}
```

PADDING

The `padding` property allows you to add space between the outer edge of the content box and the inner edge of its border. Like the properties for the border, you can apply values to all four sides.

STEP 8.1.8

```
.box{
    color: red;
    border: 10px solid gray;
    padding-top: 10%;
    padding-right: 10%;
    padding-bottom: 10%;
    padding-left: 10%;
}
```

When viewing the document, you see space between the content and its border (**Figure 8.7**).

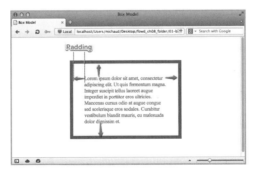

FIGURE 8.7
Padding allows some breathing room between the content and border.

 BORDER WITHOUT VALUES

Since the border property has three values, it's best to apply three values. If, by chance, you don't apply a value to a given style, this is what happens:

Leaving out the value for `border-width` will cause it to revert to the `medium` value.

Leaving out the value for the `border-color` will cause the border to revert to the default value of "black" or whatever value the property color is set to.

```
.box{
    color: red;
    border: solid gray;
}
```

Leaving out the `border-width` value will cause the border to be set to none—and to be no longer visible.

WHAT ABOUT THREE VALUES?

While the examples have shown margin and padding with one, two, and four values, you can also have three values.

```
margin: 5% 10% 5%;
```

The top is set to the first value, the left and right are set to the second, and the bottom is set to the third.

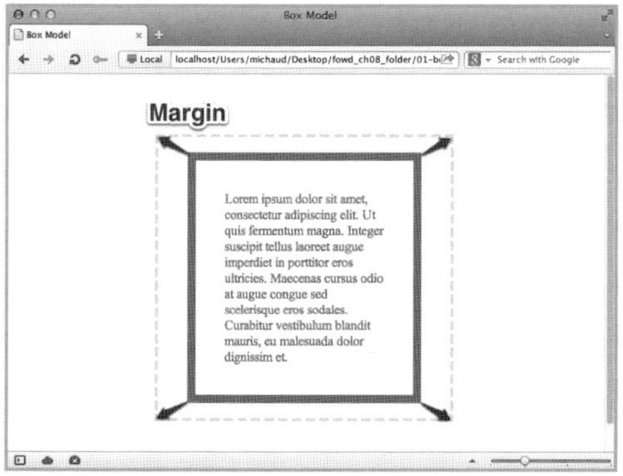

FIGURE 8.8
You now have margins extending beyond the element's border!

STEP 8.1.9

Since all four sides have the same value of 10%, you can use the shorthand `padding` property.

```
.box{
    color: red;
    border: 10px solid gray;
    padding: 10%;
}
```

MARGIN

The `margin` property allows you to add space between the outside edge of the border and the inner edge of the parent element. In this case, the `div` element, which surrounds the `p` element, is the parent element.

STEP 8.1.10

In order to see the transparent margin of your content `p` element, you first need to apply a `border` to the `<div class="container">` element.

```
.container{
    border: 4px dashed lightblue;
}
```

STEP 8.1.11

You can now apply the `margin` property to each side for your `.box` class selector—which applies a margin to your `p` element (**Figure 8.8**).

```
.box{
    color: red;
    border: 10px solid gray;
    padding: 10%;
    margin-top: 5%;
    margin-right: 10%;
    margin-bottom: 5%;
    margin-left: 10%;
}
```

While the margin values are not the same, you can still use the shorthand margin property. If you give two values, the first value will be applied to the top and bottom and the second value to the right and left.

STEP 8.1.12

```
.box{
    color: red;
    border: 10px solid gray;
    padding: 10%;
    margin: 5% 10%
}
```

BACKGROUND COLOR

Thus far, the boxes you've created are actually transparent (yes, there is a `transparent` color value). The white color you see is the default white background color of the browser application. You can apply a background color to any HTML element by using the `background-color` property.

STEP 8.2.1

In the example document **02-width-height. html**, you'll notice there is some content on a white background (**Figure 8.9**).

FIGURE 8.9
Your content box on a white background (the browser).

Looking at the HTML, you have a parent element.

```
<div class="container">
    <p class="box">content</p>
</div>
```

The parent element contains the child element (your content).

```
<div class="container">
    <p class="box">Imagine you...</p>
</div>
```

STEP 8.2.2

In the CSS document **width-height. css**, the linked style sheet for your HTML document, add the `background-color` to the parent.

```
.container {
    width:500px;
    margin: 50px 0;
    background-color: lightblue;
}
```

The parent element now has a light blue background (**Figure 8.10**).

Looking at the result onscreen doesn't tell the whole story. Let's view the box model in 3D (**Figure 8.11**).

Notice how the transparent child content box allows the parent box element's background color to show behind the text.

STEP 8.2.3

You can also apply a `background-color` property to the child element.

```
.box{
    background-color: gold;
}
```

However, the background color for the content box has just made the background color for the parent element disappear (**Figure 8.12**)!

What happened to the light blue color? Since the child element sits atop the parent element in the stacking order (more on this in Chapter 9), the child's background color covers the parent (**Figure 8.13**).

If you don't set a width to a child element, the child takes on the width of the parent element. We'll look at controlling the width in the next section.

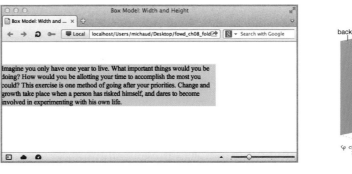

FIGURE 8.10
Your box model now has a light blue background color.

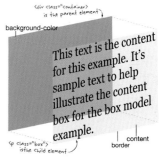

FIGURE 8.11
Three-dimensional box model showing the parent's background color and the transparent background of the content.

FIGURE 8.12
The content box color covers up the parent box color.

FIGURE 8.13
The child sits atop the parent in the stacking order of elements.

WIDTH, HEIGHT, AND OVERFLOW

Let's keep things simple while getting to understand the `width` and `height` properties of the box model, and just deal with pixel values (for now).

If the child element's `width` property is not set, it takes on the parent's width. If the `width` property of the parent element is set to `500px`, the width of the child element also becomes 500px (**Figure 8.14**).

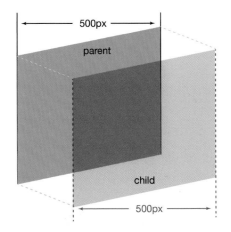

FIGURE 8.14
If the child element doesn't have a width, it inherits the parent's width.

(Figure 8.14 labels: 500px, parent, child, 500px)

STEP 8.2.4

If you define the child's `width` value as half of the parent element, you'll see both background colors (**Figure 8.15**).

```
.box{
    background-color: gold;
    width: 250px;
}
```

Did you notice the child box and parent box got taller when you narrowed the child element's width? As long as the parent element's `height` is not specifically set, it will always extend with its child element.

STEP 8.2.5

If you set the `height` property on the child element, the parent element will extend to meet that height too (**Figure 8.16**).

```
.box{
    background-color: gold;
    width: 250px;
    height: 225px;
}
```

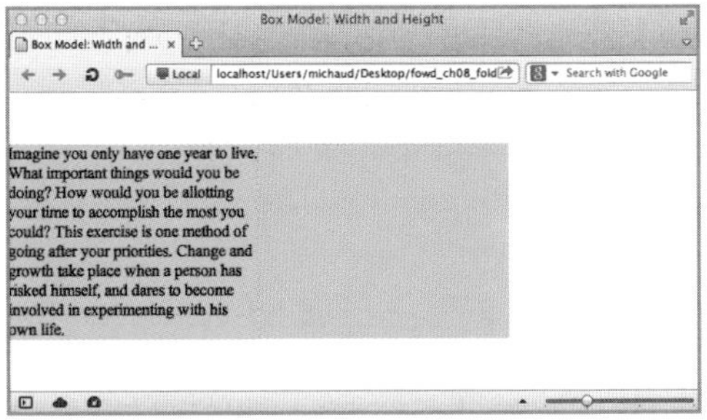

FIGURE 8.15
The child element is half the width of the parent.

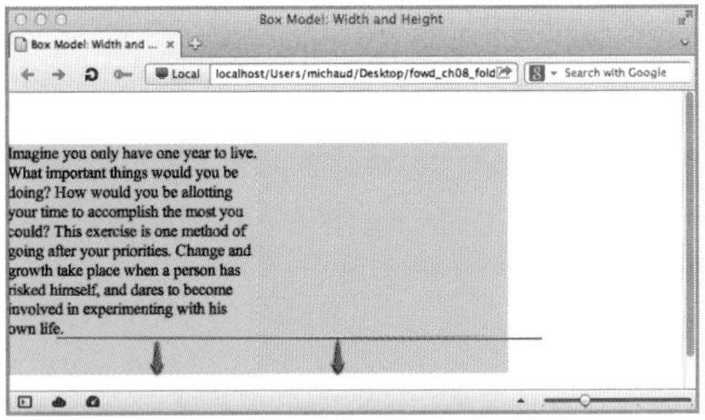

FIGURE 8.16
The parent extends to meet the height set for the child.

STEP 8.2.6

But what happens if you set a fixed height on the parent element so the child content extends past the `height` value you have established? By default, the content will **overflow** the boundaries of the box (**Figure 8.17**).

```
.box{
    background-color: gold;
    width: 250px;
    height: 150px;
}
```

Normally it's best to not set a `height` value on an element and to just let the box

naturally extend based on the content. However, some designs may warrant the element's box having an established height. So, how can you get the content to stay within the box?

STEP 8.2.7

The `overflow` property gives you some options. You have a choice of setting the value to `auto`, `hidden`, `scroll`, or `visible`.

```
.box{
    background-color: gold;
    width: 250px;
    height: 150px;
    overflow: auto;
}
```

Start with `auto` on the `overflow` and then try switching the values to see their results (**Figure 8.18**).

FIGURE 8.17
The content overflows beyond the height of the box.

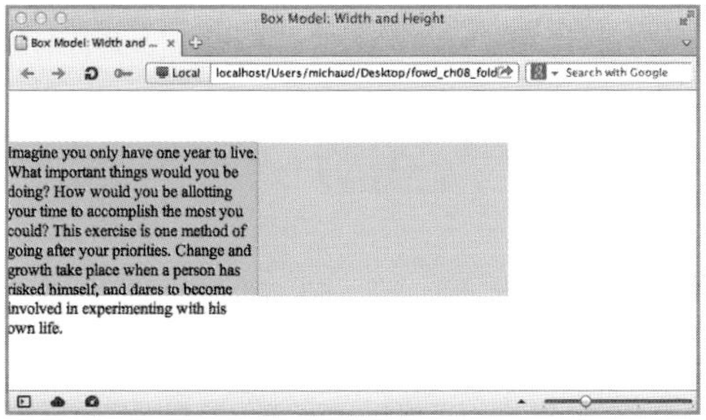

FIGURE 8.18
Examples of the `overflow` values (clockwise from top left): `auto`, `hidden`, `visible`, and `scroll`.

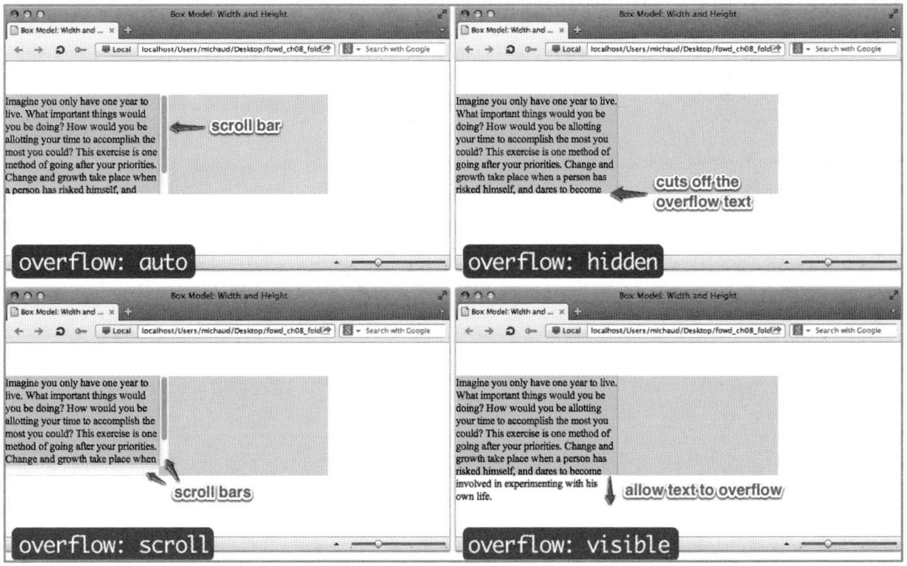

BOX SIZING

While it's easy enough with background colors to visualize an element's width and height, the `padding` and `border` properties also play a role.

Looking at **03-box-sizing.html** in the browser, you can see that the paragraph (content) element's `width` property has been given a value of `400px` (**Figure 8.19**).

STEP 8.3.1

In the CSS document **css/box-sizing.css**, let's see what happens when you add a `25px` value to the `border` and a `50px` value to the `padding` property for the `.box` class selector (**Figure 8.20**).

```
.box{
    background-color: gold;
    width: 400px;
    border: 25px solid black;
    padding: 50px;
}
```

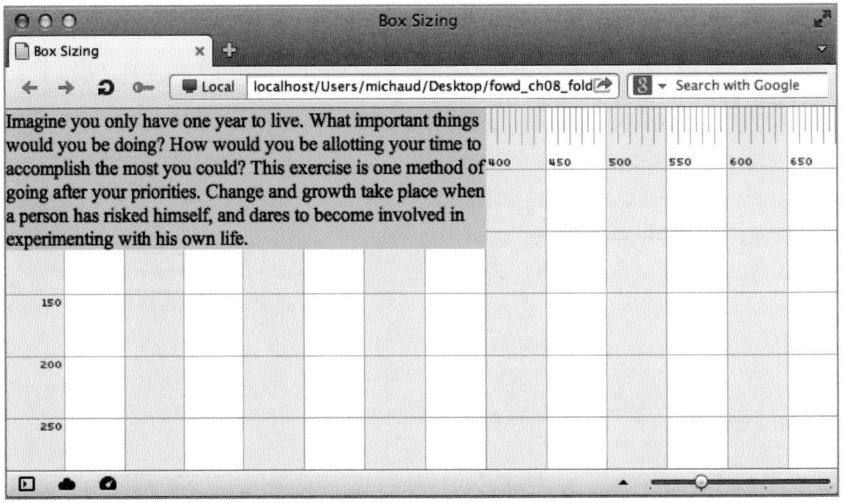

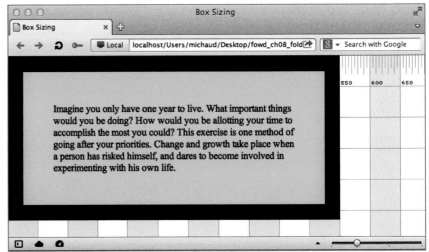

FIGURE 8.19
A background image grid helps you see the size of your box.

FIGURE 8.20
The box grew wider and taller.

HOW ABOUT HEIGHT?

Since you don't have a fixed height, you can't determine the exact height of the box by simple math (as you don't know the height of your content), but browsers have tools to help determine the height. **Figure 8.21** shows a browser "inspectors tool" that will show you the size of the box (including the height of your content)—in this case you add:

108px (content height) + 50px (padding top) + 50px (padding bottom) + 25px (border top) + 25px (border bottom) = 258 (total height)

Access the video on Web Developer Tools on the website to learn more.

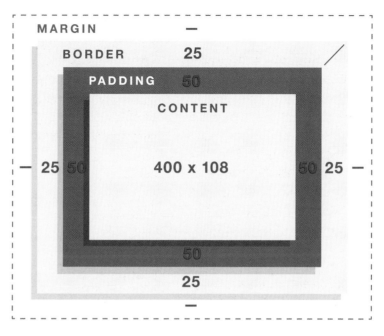

FIGURE 8.21
How your computed styles look to the box model.

The `padding` and `border` properties actually add to your element's visual width and height!

Since you know the value of your width, you can apply the formula:

content width + padding-right + padding-left + border-right + border-left = total rendered width of box

So, if you plug in your values, you can determine the box's visual width (**Figure 8.21**).

400px (content width) **+ 50px** (padding right) **+ 50px** (padding left) **+ 25px** (border right) **+ 25px** (border left) **= 550px** (total width)

BOX-SIZING CAUTION

The `*{box-sizing: border-box}` can be hazardous to use when retrofitting it to an existing project or a project where you are using lots of third-party code, because it might have unexpected adverse effects on what is already there. So, it might be better to just use it on the layout elements that need it, rather than everything on the site.

BOX-SIZING BOX SIZING

Remembering to add all those properties together just to determine an element's width could get a little daunting. Wouldn't it be easier if you could just set the width on an element and know that was going to be the width?

STEP 8.3.2

The CSS property `box-sizing` allows the element width to stay as it is and causes the width to include the border and padding. By adding a universal selector (*), with the `box-sizing` property with a value of `border-box`, you can change the way the browser renders the element's box size (**Figure 8.22**).

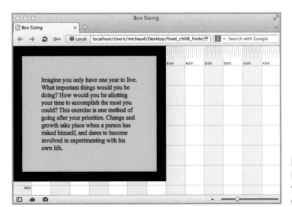

VENDOR PREFIX

As of this writing, Firefox still needs the `-moz-` prefix, and iOS4 (and earlier), Android 2.3 (and earlier) need the `-webkit-` prefix.

Paul Irish has a great blog post on the subject of using box-sizing (http://paulirish.com/2012/box-sizing-border-box-ftw/).

```
* {
-moz-box-sizing: border-box;
/*vendor prefix for firefox */
-webkit-box-sizing: border-box;
/*vendor prefix for webkit */
box-sizing: border-box;
}

.box{
background-color: gold;
width: 400px;
border: 25px solid black;
padding: 50px;
}
```

FIGURE 8.22
Box-sizing returns our element to the original width of 400px but increases the height based on the needs of the content.

As you can see from your result (**Figure 8.22**) and the browser's inspection tool (**Figure 8.23**), the overall width has returned to the value (400) you set in your CSS. Instead of the padding and the border width adding to the total width, they move inward.

BOX-SIZING BOX WIDTH

So, the formula for your element's box is:

250px (content width) + **50px** (padding right) + **50px** (padding left) + **25px** (border right) + **25px** (border left) = **400px** (total width)

BOX-SIZING BOX HEIGHT

The padding and border have reduced the space the content takes up on the inside of the box. Since the content narrows, it increases its length.

180px (content height) + **50px** (padding top) + **50px** (padding bottom) + **25px** (border top) + **25px** (border bottom) = **258px** (total height)

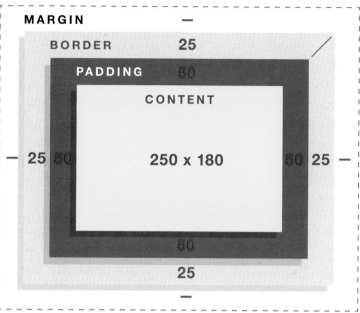

FIGURE 8.23
The browser's inspection tool informs you that the content is now 250px wide.

BROWSER DEFAULT MARGIN & PADDING

One last topic needs to be addressed on the box model. By default, the browser adds some values to the `margin` and `padding` of some HTML elements. In the example **04-default.html** document, I've added a `border` and `background-color` (view the document: **css/default.css**) around each block-level text element. This shows the spacing between elements (margin) and within an element (padding in the unordered list) (**Figure 8.24**).

>>> *WHY DO BROWSERS ADD DEFAULT MARGINS AND PADDINGS? SIMPLY TO MAKE UNSTYLED HTML LEGIBLE.*

FIGURE 8.24
Spaces between and within elements show the browser's default settings for margins and padding on some text elements.

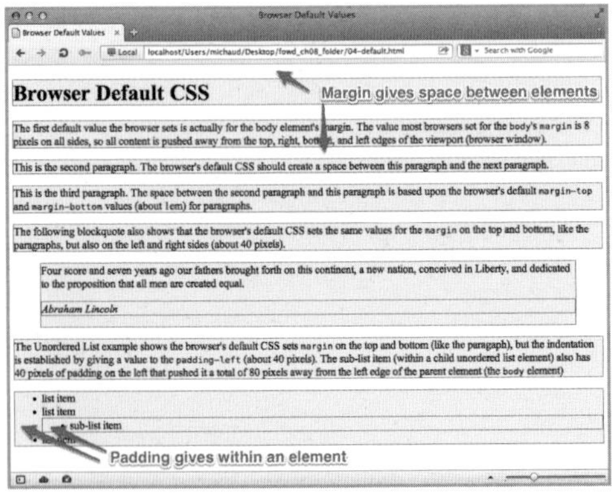

RESETTING THE DEFAULT

You can easily override (reset) the browser defaults using your own CSS. The **05-reset.html** document has the text from the previous example, but the new CSS document (**css/reset.css**) adds the universal selector (*)—that selects all HTML elements—and the rules setting the `margin` and `padding` properties to a value of 0.

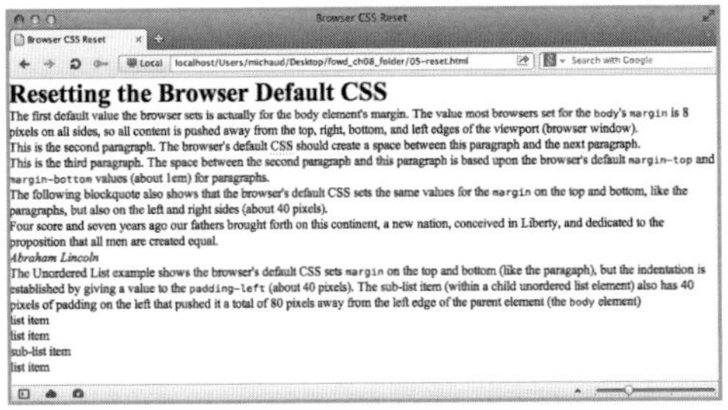

When you remove the `border` and `background-color` styles, it becomes more difficult to distinguish between paragraphs, blockquotes, and lists. So why would anyone want to remove the browser defaults? It's easier to start from ground zero and not worry what the browser has or has not set.

```
* {
    margin: 0;
    padding: 0;
}
```

Notice that the margins and paddings have all been removed (**Figure 8.25**).

FIGURE 8.25
A simple reset removes margins and padding from HTML elements.

Just know this: simply resetting the defaults and adding in your own CSS rules will not guarantee that your website will look the same in all browsers. While developers have worked to create robust reset stylesheets, browsers still have varied support of some CSS rules.

A BEGINNER'S OPTION FOR RESET

Developers have created a number of CSS reset options that remove all or some of the browser defaults.

SOME CSS RESETS REMOVE MOST OF THE BROWSER DEFAULT SETTINGS AND ADD IN SOME BASIC RULES (SEE ERIC MEYER'S RESET: HTTP://MEYERWEB.COM/ERIC/TOOLS/CSS/RESET/). THESE TYPES OF RESETS ARE BETTER RESERVED FOR THOSE WHO ARE MORE COMFORTABLE STARTING AT GROUND ZERO.

Others reset some properties but add in some styles—providing a less intimidating starting point (see Normalize by Nicolas Gallagher & Jonathan Neal: http://necolas.github.io/normalize.css/). These types of resets are easier to start with for beginners—as well as experienced coders.

The example **06-normalize.html** (**Figure 8.26**) uses the Normalize reset document (**css/normalize.css**).

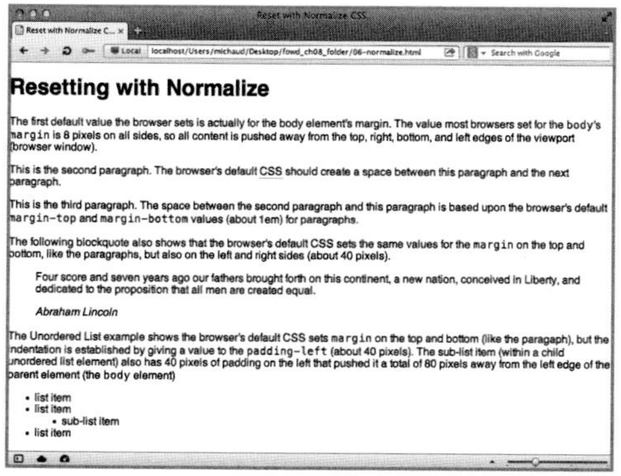

FIGURE 8.26
The normalize.css allows for a less intimidating "reset."

WRAPPING THINGS UP

While I've tried to present the box model in simple terms, it takes time to really grasp how the content, padding, margin, border, width, height, etc. all play together. The box-sizing property and CSS resets try to get the majority of browsers on a level playing field, but you'll come to find that your site will still display slightly differently among various browsers—and that's OK!

In coming chapters, we'll continue to expand your knowledge of the box model and get into some serious work laying out a website!

≫ DOWNLOAD REMINDER

THERE IS BONUS CONTENT TO DOWNLOAD FOR ADDITIONAL MARKUP FOR THE BOX MODEL AND AN ASSIGNMENT TO TEST YOUR SKILLS!

PART
—
03

LAYOUT & INTERACTIVITY

◯

▣	**LAYOUT PROPERTIES**
▤	**PAGE LAYOUT**
☰	**NAVIGATION**
☑	**FORMS**

LAYOUT PROPERTIES

—

09

THE CODE EXAMPLES FOR THIS CHAPTER CAN BE DOWNLOADED FROM THE WEBSITE (HTTP://FOUNDATIONSOFWEBDESIGN.COM).

To control the position, behavior, and visibility of the document's box elements, you'll use the `float`, `position`, and `display` properties.

BOX ELEMENT REVIEW

Remember, CSS sees each HTML element as a box. These boxes will either be block-level boxes or inline boxes.

BLOCK ELEMENTS

Block-level elements are those elements of an HTML document that are formatted visually as blocks (e.g., `<h1></h1>`, `<div></div>`, `<p></p>`, `<table></table>`). They begin on new lines. If no width is set, they will expand naturally to fill their parent containers. While they can contain inline-level elements, some can also contain other block elements (**Figure 9.1**).

INLINE ELEMENTS

Inline-level elements are contained within block-level elements and do not begin a new line (**Figure 9.2**). They may contain only data and other inline elements (e.g., `<em></em>`, `</strong></strong>`, `<span></span>`).

WILD CARD BOX: REPLACED ELEMENTS

Replaced elements are HTML elements that have a predetermined width and height without benefit of CSS. Their appearance and dimensions are defined by an external resource (e.g., `<img>`, `<br>`, `<hr>`, `<object>`). Like inline elements, they can be within other block elements; like block-level elements, they can stand on their own (**Figure 9.3**).

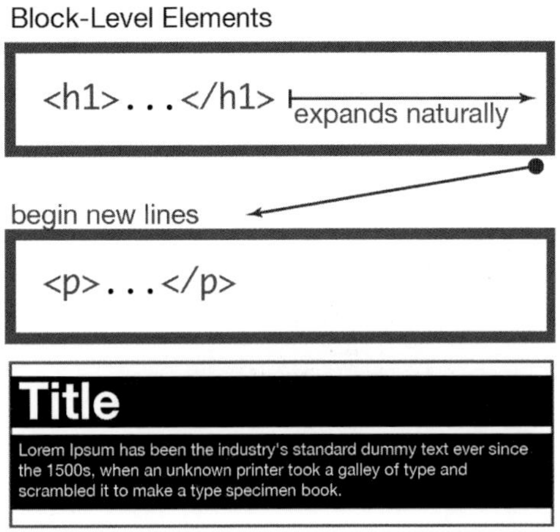

FIGURE 9.1
Block-level element illustration.

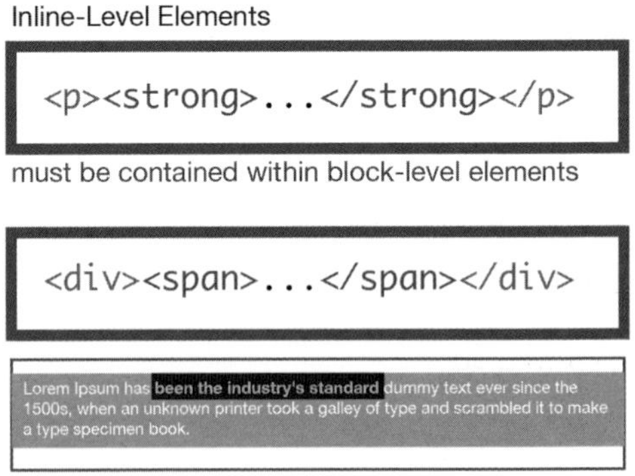

FIGURE 9.2
Inline-level element illustration.

FLOAT

You're probably familiar with magazines, books, and other printed material that have images on a page and text flowing around them. The designer places the images in the layout and sets the image to allow the boxes containing text to "wrap" around them (**Figure 9.4**).

In web design, you can do something similar by using the CSS `float` property to allow blocks of text to flow around your images (**Figure 9.5**).

The `float` property specifies whether or not a block-level element should float and, if so, whether it should float to the `left`, to the `right`, or not at all (`none`). A floating element is shifted to the left or to the right as far as it can go, and non-floating content in the normal flow will flow around it on the opposite side.

If you view the **01-float.html** document in a browser, you'll see "boxes" (`div` elements) stacked on top of each other that contain other box elements (`div`, `h1`, `h2`, `p`, `img`) which hold the content (**Figure 9.6A** and **Figure 9.6B**).

PRINT AND WEB ARE DIFFERENT

While there are properties to help you lay out your design for the web, the options you have for web layout are much more limited than for print.

Replaced Elements

FIGURE 9.3
Replaced element illustration.

PRINT LAYOUT

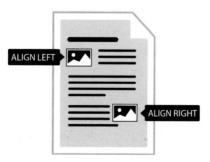

FIGURE 9.4
Illustration of text wrapping around images on a print document.

WEB LAYOUT

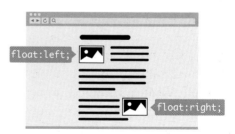

FIGURE 9.5
Illustration of text flowing around images on a website.

STACKED BOX ORDER

Elements at the beginning of the source order will appear above elements later in the source order.

CONTAINING BOXES

A box may be nested within other box elements, and the containing box is the direct parent of a nested box.

RESPONSIVE DESIGN

Responsive design is an important concept that you'll need to learn before long. It is an approach aimed at crafting sites to provide an optimal viewing experience across a wide range of devices—enabling easy reading and navigation with a minimum of resizing, panning, and scrolling. While the basics of responsive design will be covered in Chapter 10, it's beyond the scope of this book to cover the topic in-depth. Refer to the website for additional resources.

FLOAT: NONE

STEP 9.1.1

By default, elements do not have a float property applied (refer to **Figure 9.5**). In the **float-image.css** document, add the following rule:

```
img {
    float: none;
}
```

The none value is only needed when you want to remove a float value from an element that already has—or inherited—a float value of right, left, or inherit set. When would such an opportunity arise? Responsive Web Design layouts use the none value to remove a float from an image or element to create a single-column layout (**Figure 9.7**).

FLOAT: LEFT

To float the first img element within the <div class="main"> box to the left, simply use the class selector for the class attribute value of .main and a descendant selector for the img:

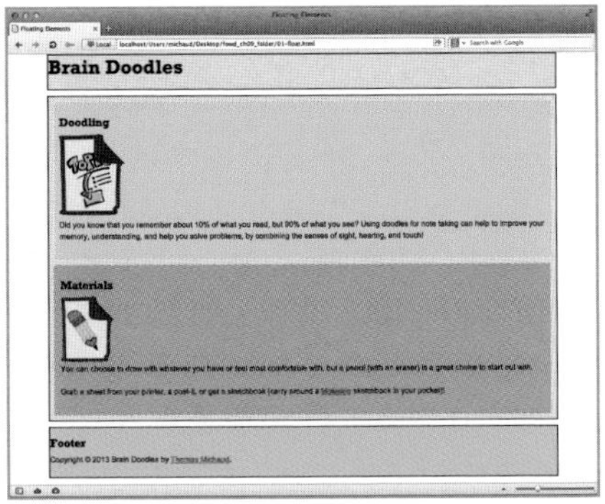

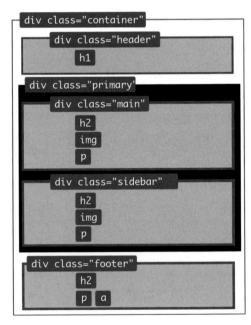

FIGURE 9.6A
The default stacked box layout.

FIGURE 9.6B
Illustration of stacked and containing boxes.

STEP 9.1.2

```
.main img {
    float: left;
}
```

After saving the document and refreshing your browser, you'll see the image has stayed on the left, but the text flows to the right of the image (**Figure 9.8**).

>>> REMEMBER FLOATS AND FLOW

WHEN AN ELEMENT IS FLOATED, WE'RE TAKING IT OUT OF THE NORMAL FLOW AND ALLOWING ALL THE CONTENT (REMEMBER THE BOX MODEL?) THAT COMES AFTER IT TO WRAP AROUND THE FLOATED ELEMENT.

Notice the box collapses to the height of the content (since it ignores the floated element) while still expanding to the width of the parent element (behind the image). The content in the next box—below the floated image—also moves up and the content (h2 text) flows to the right of the image.

FLOAT: RIGHT

Now, float the second img element in the <div class="sidebar"> to the right.

STEP 9.1.3

```
.sidebar img {
    float: right;
}
```

Going back to the browser, you now see the image floating right with the content flowing to the left (**Figure 9.9**).

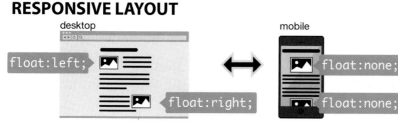

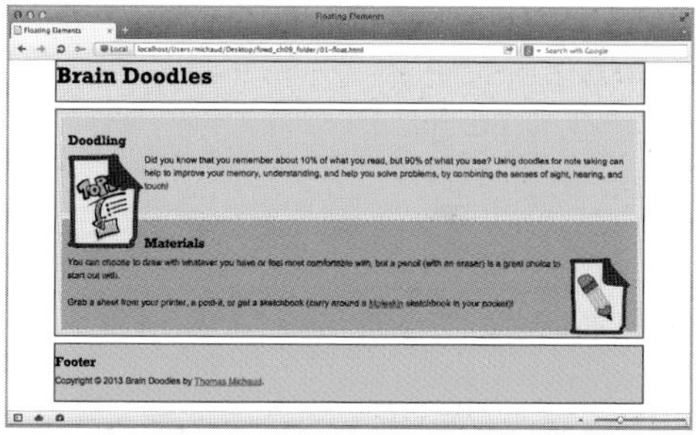

FIGURE 9.8
An element floated left will move left, with the non-floated content flowing on the right side.

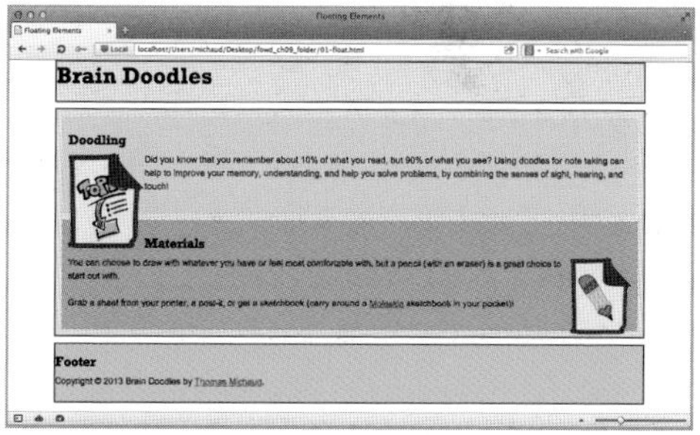

FIGURE 9.9
An element floated right will move right, with the non-floated content flowing on the left-hand side.

RESPONSIVE LAYOUT

desktop

float:left;

float:right;

mobile

float:none;

float:none;

FIGURE 9.7
An illustration of a responsive layout going from a desktop layout to a mobile layout.

FLOAT: INHERIT

The `inherit` value specifies that the value of the `float` property should be inherited from the parent element.

STEP 9.1.4

Now, float the parent `.main` element left so the child `img` element can inherit its value, then add a `width` of `620px`.

```
.main {
    float: left;
    width: 620px;
}
.main img{
    float: inherit;/*changed from: left*/
}
```

FIGURE 9.10
The image inherits the paragraph element's *float* value, and the description list extends to the header element.

When you view the result, there's a lot that's changed (**Figure 9.10**).

When you float the containing `<div class="main">` box element

- The `<img>` (child) element inherits the parent element's `float` value of `left`.

- The sibling `<div class="sidebar">` box element ignores both floated box elements and extends up to reach the containing box element—`<div class="primary">`—which is not floated (**Figure 9.11**).

STEP 9.1.5

Now add another rule for the `.sidebar` class selector and float it right with a width of `290px` (**Figure 9.12**).

```
.sidebar {
    float: right;
    width: 290px
}
```

INHERITANCE
HAS LIMITS

The value `inherit`, which can be applied to nearly any CSS property, does not work in Internet Explorer versions up to and including 7.

REMEMBER THE
RELATIONSHIP:

The parent element (<div class="main">...</div>) contains a child (<img>) element

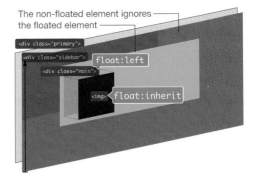

FIGURE 9.11
An illustration of the sibling element ignoring the floated sibling box above it.

When all of the nested elements within the containing `<div class="primary">` are floated

- The containing element collapses, as the nested boxes are no longer in the "flow" of the containing element.

- The `<div class="footer">` fills the space behind the two floated `div`s, with the content flowing to the left of the right-floated box (**Figure 9.13**).

The next objectives will be to move the `<div class="footer">` below both floated divs and to uncollapse the containing `<div class="primary">` box.

CLEAR FLOATS

The `clear` property specifies the sides of an element where other floating elements are not allowed. It lets you "clear" floated elements from the `left` side, `right` side, or `both` sides of an element.

STEP 9.1.6

To allow the `<div class="footer">` to clear

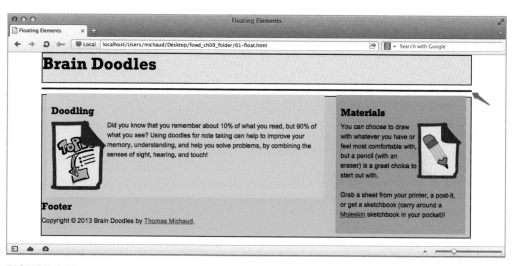

FIGURE 9.12
The containing block collapses when all nested elements are floated.

the `left` floated box element, simply write the rule:

```
.footer {
    clear: left;
}
```

The footer box now clears (or moves below) any floated elements that would be on its left side, creating space between the two elements once again (**Figure 9.14**).

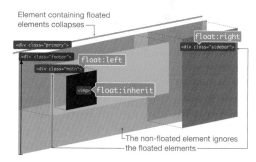

FIGURE 9.13
An illustration of the collapsing containing box with nested boxes floated.

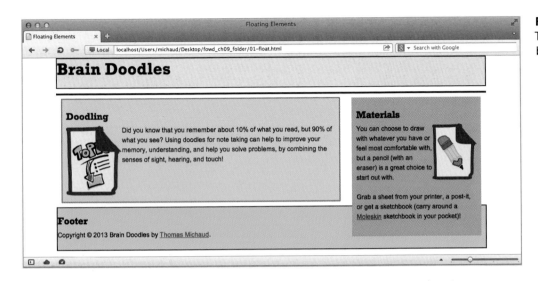

FIGURE 9.14
The footer div moves back
below the left-floated div.

The footer is now set to clear any floated
box above it in the future.

FIXING THE COLLAPSE

There are a few methods to uncollapse
a parent container of floated elements.
Each has its own positives and
negatives—this book will discuss two.

CLEARFIX

The "clearfix" method uses the pseudo-
element :after with a class selector to
place in empty content after the nested
elements, display it as a block-level
element, and clear both left- and right-
floated elements.

Most designers add a class name to
a containing element's class attribute,
signifying it contains a **"group"** of
elements (which may or may not be
floated). So, any time you have a "group"
of nested elements, you could apply a
"clearfix" rule to prevent any box collapse
(**Figure 9.17**).

STEP 9.1.7

To make the footer clear the right-
floated div, change the clear value
from left to right .

```
.footer {
    clear: right;
}
```

Since the sidebar div on the right is
longer, the footer div moves below both
the right- and left-floated divs above it
(**Figure 9.15**).

However, what if the <div class="main">
box added more content and became
longer than the <div class="sidebar">
box (**Figure 9.16**)?

STEP 9.1.8

If you set the .footer class selector's
float property to the value of both, it will
clear any right- or left-floated element.

```
.footer {
    clear: both;
}
```

STEP 9.1.10

In the HTML, we'll use the opening `<div class="primary group">` tag that has the necessary `group` class applied.

In your CSS, add the following rule:

```
.group:after {
    content: " ";
    display: block;
    clear: both;
}
```

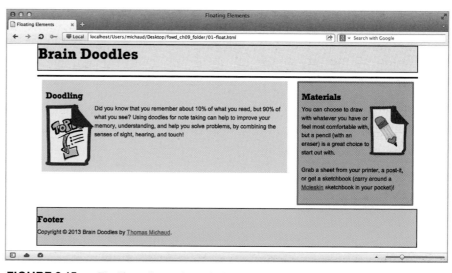

FIGURE 9.15   The "footer" now clears the longer box floated right.

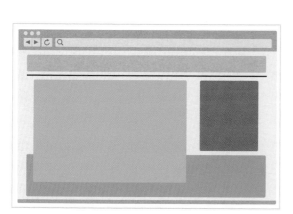

FIGURE 9.16

If the left (main) box increased in length, it would overlap the footer box, which is only set to clear box elements floated to the right.

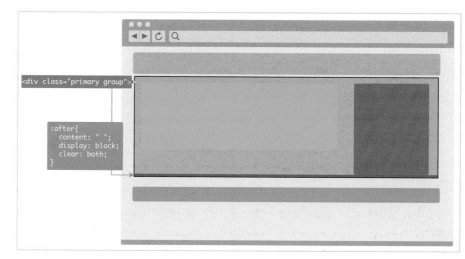

FIGURE 9.17

An empty (no-height) block element is placed under the bottom of the parent element and is able to clear floated elements.

CLEARFIX FOR OLDER BROWSERS

For older-version browsers, the clearfix method requires additional rules and modifications:

```
.group:before, .group:after {
    content: " ";
    display: table;
}
```

>>> *NOTE*: *THE USE OF* table *RATHER THAN* block *IS ONLY NECESSARY IF USING* :before *TO CONTAIN THE TOP MARGINS OF CHILD ELEMENTS.*

```
.group:after {
    clear: both;
}
.group {
    *zoom: 1; /*For IE 6/7 only*/
}
```

>>> *KNOWN SUPPORT: FIREFOX 3.5+, SAFARI 4+, CHROME, OPERA 9+, IE 6+*

By Nicolas Gallagher (http://bit.ly/evOPw5).

OVERFLOW CLEAR

STEP 9.1.11

Another method is to use the `overflow` property on the containing parent element.

```
.primary {
    overflow: auto;
    width: 100%;
}
```

If the containing element's `overflow` is set to `auto` or `hidden`, it will expand to include the floated boxes (**Figure 9.18**).

FIGURE 9.18
With the clearfix method or the overflow method, the parent element will expand to include the nested elements that are floated.

>>> *CAUTION: BE CAREFUL WITH* overflow: auto *AND* overflow: hidden, *AS THERE CAN BE TIMES WHERE UNWANTED SCROLLBARS SHOW UP OR CONTENT IS INADVERTENTLY HIDDEN.*

While on the topic of overflow, it's a good idea to look at a few additional examples that work with scrolling and hidden content.

OVERFLOW

Open the **02-overflow.html** document and notice the two floated boxes of content nested within a containing element (**Figure 9.19**). There are two possible values for `overflow`: `scroll` and `hidden`.

```
<div class="characters group">
<div class="box batman">
    <img>
    <p>...</p>
</div> <!-- close box batman -->
<div class="box robin">
    <img>
    <p>...</p>
</div> <!-- close box robin -->
</div> <!-- close characters -->
```

What if the intention is to have the nested elements be the same height, so the layout has a balanced look?

STEP 9.2.1

Use the class selector for `.box` and set its `height` at `300px`.

```
.box {
    height: 300px;
}
```

When you refresh the page, you'll see the content—which is longer than 300px—overflowing the boxes (**Figure 9.20**).

SCROLL

The `scroll` value tucks the content within its containing element and adds a scrollbar to the box so users can scroll to see the hidden content (**Figure 9.21**).

Add a new rule, using the `.batman` class selector, to `scroll` the `overflow` content.

```
batman {
    overflow: scroll;
}
```

Notice the `scroll` value adds a horizontal scrollbar path whether it's needed or not.

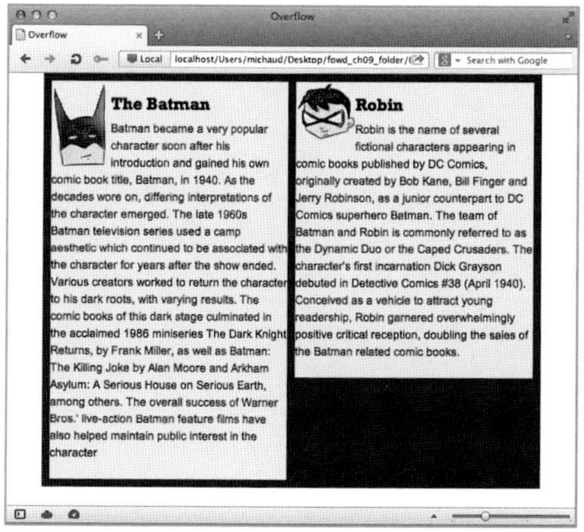

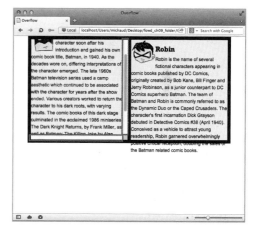

FIGURE 9.19
A containing element holds two nested boxes of varying heights.

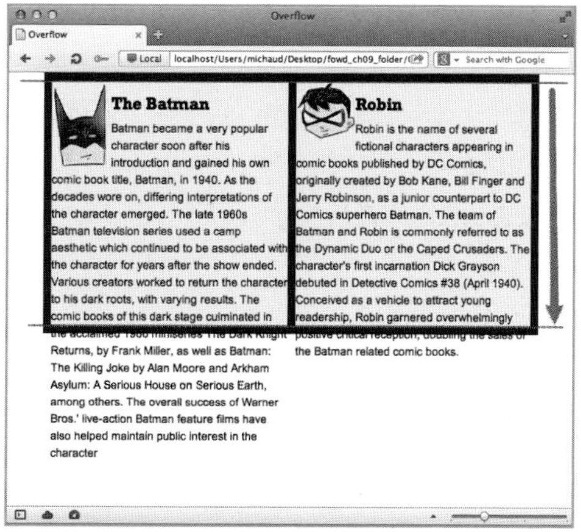

FIGURE 9.20
The lengthy content overflows the set height of its containing element.

FIGURE 9.21
A scrollbar is added to allow users to see the hidden content.

HORIZONTAL SCROLLBAR

When using the value auto, if the image is wider than the containing element, the horizontal scrollbar will be added to allow the user to scroll left and right to see the image (**Figure 9.23**).

STEP 9.2.3

By switching the value from scroll to auto, you can clean up the look (**Figure 9.22**).

```
.batman {
    overflow: auto;
}
```

HIDDEN

The hidden value simply hides any extra content that does not fit in the containing box (**Figure 9.24**).

STEP 9.2.4

Add a new rule, using the .robin class selector, and apply the overflow property with the value of hidden.

```
.robin {
    overflow: hidden;
}
```

On to positioning and moving the box elements all over the place!

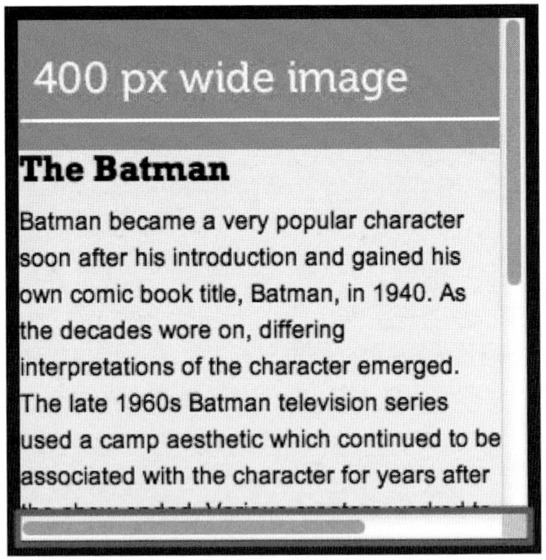

FIGURE 9.23
The auto value will automatically add a horizontal scrollbar only if needed.

FIGURE 9.22
The auto value removes the unnecessary horizontal scrollbar path.

FIGURE 9.24
The extra content is clipped off at the bottom of the containing element.

POSITION

The `float` property is not the only way to move elements about. The `position` property defines the type of positioning method used for an element. Possible values are `static`, `relative`, `absolute`, or `fixed`. You can then use the `top`, `right`, `bottom`, and `left` properties to specify the element's position.

>>> *FOR THE POSITIONING DEMONSTRATION, VIEW THE **03-POSITIONING.HTML** DOCUMENT IN YOUR BROWSER AND ADD YOUR CSS RULES TO POSITION.CSS (IN THE CSS FOLDER).*

POSITION: STATIC

The `static` position is the default way an element will appear in the normal flow of your HTML file if no position is specified at all.

>>> *THE `top`, `right`, `bottom`, AND `left` PROPERTIES HAVE NO EFFECT ON A STATI-CALLY POSITIONED ELEMENT.*

STEP 9.3.1

Apply `position: static` to the `.first` box element and view the result (**Figure 9.25**).

```
.first {
    position: static;
    /* the default position = no changes */
}
```

POSITION: RELATIVE

Positioning an element with the `relative` value keeps the element (and the space it occupies) in the normal flow of your HTML file. You can then move the element by some amount using the properties `left`, `right`, `top`, and `bottom`. However, this may cause the element to overlap other elements that are on the page—which may or may not be the effect that you want.

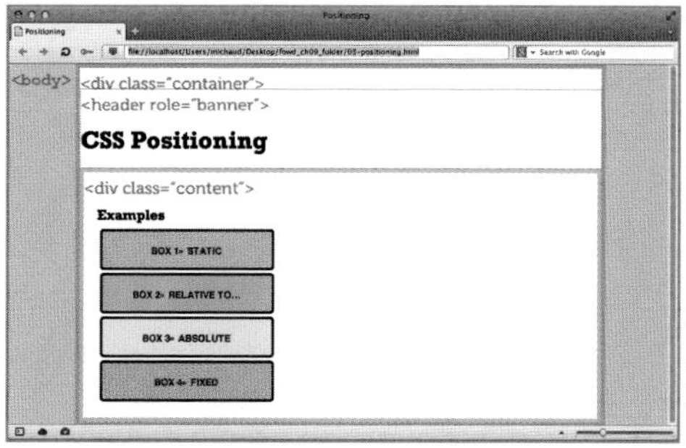

FIGURE 9.25
The default layout doesn't change when applying `static` positioning to any element.

WHY USE STATIC?

Like `float:none`, use `position: static` when you want to remove one of the other values (`relative`, `absolute`, or `fixed`) that have previously been set on an element.

151

Add a new rule to apply `position: relative` to the `.second` box element. To "pull" the element up from its current position, use the `top` property with a value of `-20px`. Then, "push" the element to the right using the `left` property, with a value of `50px`. View the result (**Figure 9.26**).

```
.second {
    position: relative;
    /* move it from its normal position */
    top: -20px;
    /* use negative value to pull it up */
    left: 50px;
    /* move away from the left (50px to
    the right) */
}
```

FIGURE 9.26
A relatively positioned element can move from its spot, but the space it occupied remains.

The result shows the relatively positioned `div` element moved from its original position up (using a negative value) and to the right. However, notice two additional results:

- The space the `div` element originally occupied still remains—the element below doesn't come up to fill the vacated spot.

- The first `div` element is now being overlapped by the second `div` element—more on this in a moment.

POSITION: ABSOLUTE

Applying the `absolute` position value to an element removes it from the normal flow. When you move the `absolute` positioned element, its reference point is the top/left of its nearest containing element that has a position declared other than `static`—also called its nearest positioning context. So, if no containing element with a position other than `static` exists, then it will be positioned from the top-left corner of the `body` element.

Write a new rule applying the `absolute` value to the `position` property for the `.third` box element. Then set its `top` and `left` properties to `30px` each (**Figure 9.27**).

```
.third {
    position: absolute;
    top: 30px;
    /* add spacing to the top */
    left: 30px;
    /* add spacing to the left */
}
```

Since the two containing `div` elements (with `class="content"` and `class="container"` attributes) are set to `static` (by the browser's default CSS), the element is absolutely positioned relative to the `body` element.

If one of the containing `div` elements is set to a `relative` position, the absolutely positioned element's `top` and `left` values will be applied to the relatively positioned element.

STEP 9.3.4

Set the `.container` selector to have a `position` value of `relative`.

```
.container{
    position: relative;
    /* relative containing element */
}
```

Setting a `relative` position to a containing element gives the absolutely positioned element a new reference point (**Figure 9.28**).

POSITION: FIXED

Positioning an element with the `fixed` value is the same as using the `absolute` value, except the containing element is always the browser window.

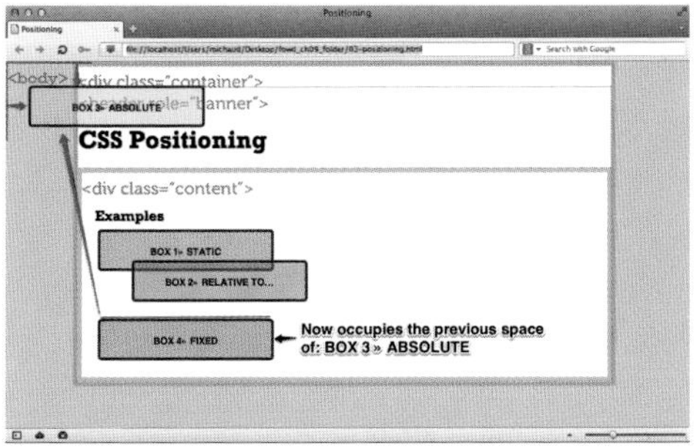

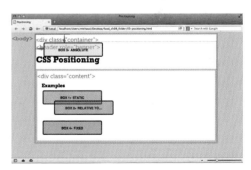

FIGURE 9.27
Absolute positioning of a box element.

STEP 9.3.5

Write a new rule for `.fourth` box to apply the `fixed` value to the `position` property, with a `top` value of 0, a `left` value of 300px, and a `margin` of 0.

```
.fourth{
    position: fixed;
    top: 0;
    /* no spacing added to the top */
    left: 300px;
    /* adds spacing on the left side */
    margin: 0;
    /* removes margin set earlier in the
    css */
}
```

The element is removed from the flow of the content—the bottom of the containing `div` collapses to the relatively positioned element—and fixed at the top of the `body` element (**Figure 9.29**).

Furthermore, an element that is positioned with a fixed value will not scroll with the document. It will remain in its position regardless of the scroll position of the page.

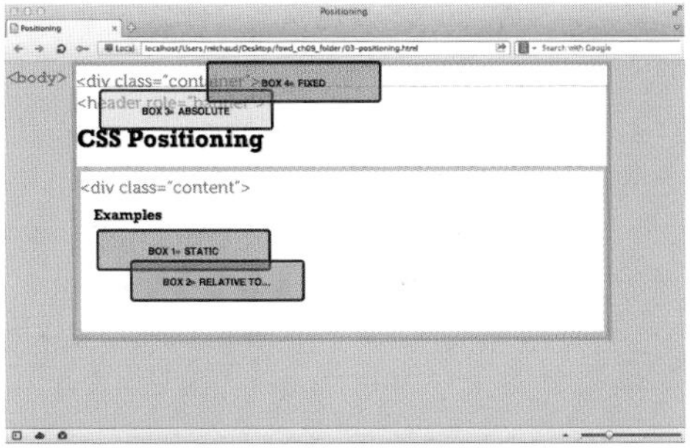

FIGURE 9.28
A containing element needs to have a value other than `static` to be the reference point for absolutely positioned elements.

FIGURE 9.29
A fixed element's reference point, in terms of positioning, is the `body` element.

STEP 9.3.6

So you can see the fixed element in action (staying put), add a new rule to the `body` element that sets the `min-height` property to a value of `800px`.

```
body {
    min-height: 800px;
}
```

When you review the result in the browser, resize your browser height if needed until you see a scrollbar on the right side (**Figure 9.30**).

You've seen fixed elements before on websites that fix navigation to the top (or even the bottom) of the page (**Figure 9.31**).

FIGURE 9.31
The website http://foundcolor.com uses a fixed element for navigation, allowing content to scroll underneath.

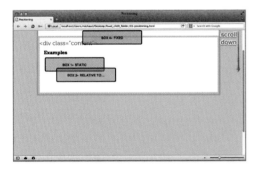

FIGURE 9.30
A fixed element will not scroll with the rest of the content.

Now, on to the topic of the stacking order of positioned elements.

Z-INDEX

There's one more property to cover that works in conjunction with the `position` property. The `z-index` property sets the stack order of an element. An element with greater stack order value is always in front (on top) of another element with lower stack order value. By default, elements later in the source order will appear on top of elements earlier in the source order. The `z-index` property allows you to alter this default stacking order.

Values for the z-index—which can be negative—set the order of the stack level. By default, elements have a value of `auto`, which sets the stack order equal to their parent elements.

REMEMBER THE BROWSER DEFAULTS

The browser's computed default value for position is `static` and the `z-index` is auto, thus the elements stack vertically (**Figure 9.33**).

ELEMENT ORDER

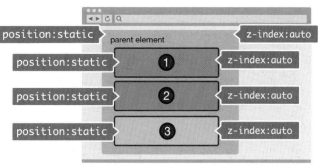

FIGURE 9.33
Illustration of the default browser values for `position` and `z-index`.

>>> **NOTE:** z-index *ONLY WORKS ON POSI-TIONED ELEMENTS (OTHER THAN* static*)*.

Looking at **04-z-index.html** in a browser, you'll see a normal stacking order—with the default `z-index` value of `auto` and a `position` value of `static` (**Figure 9.32**).

When you open the **z-index.css** document in a text editor, you'll see the default values for each element:

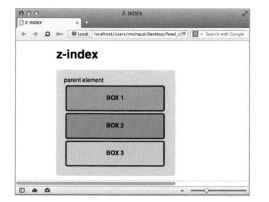

FIGURE 9.32
Normal stacking order of elements.

```
.content {
    position: static;
    /* browser default */
    z-index: auto;
    /* browser default */
}
.first {
    position: static;
    /* browser default */
    z-index: auto;
    /* browser default */
}
.second {
    position: static;
    /* browser default */
    z-index: auto;
    /* browser default */
}
.third {
    position: static;
    /* browser default */
    z-index: auto;
    /* browser default */
}
```

While these values are defaults, it's important to see what you'll be changing.

STEP 9.4.1

First, change the `static` value to `relative` for the `.content` and `.first` class selectors, and then change `static` to `absolute` for the `.second` and `.third` class selectors.

```
.content {
    position: relative;
    z-index: auto;
    /* browser default */
}
.first {
    position: relative;
    z-index: auto;
    /* browser default */
}
.second {
    position: absolute;
    z-index: auto;
    /* browser default */
}
.third {
    position: absolute;
    z-index: auto;
    /* browser default */
}
```

STEP 9.4.2

Next, add `top` and `left` values for the `.second` and `.third` class selectors.

```
.second {
    position: absolute;
    top: 0px;
    left: 40px;
    z-index: auto;
    /* browser default */
}
.third {
    position: absolute;
    top: 20px;
    left: 200px;
    z-index: auto;
    /* browser default */
}
```

The result shows a stacking order that is more three-dimensional (**Figure 9.34**).

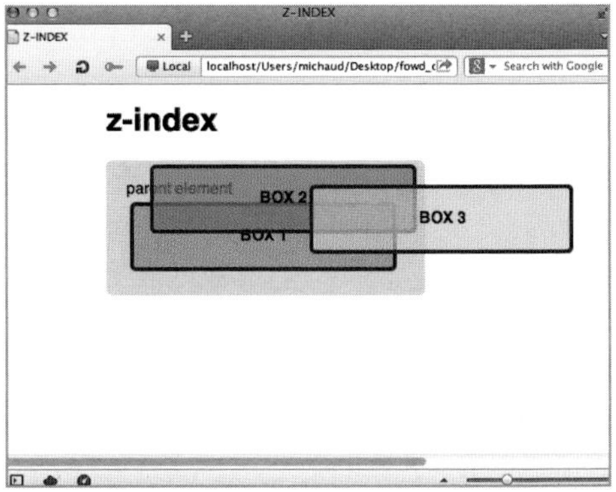

FIGURE 9.34
The default stacking order of positioned elements.

By default, the first HTML element (`<div class="container">`) is farther back and the last element (`<div class="box third">`) is on top (**Figure 9.35**).

FIGURE 9.35
An illustration showing the visual stacking order.

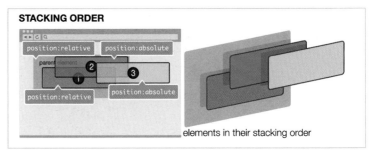

STEP 9.4.3

If you change the z-index value from auto to 1 for the .first class selector, a change in the stacking order will occur (**Figure 9.36**).

```
.first {
    position: relative;
    z-index: 1;
}
```

While the first box was originally below the two other boxes, simply adding a value of 1 sends the element to the top of the other elements (**Figure 9.37**).

However, elements can also be moved down (or farther away) in the stacking order with negative values.

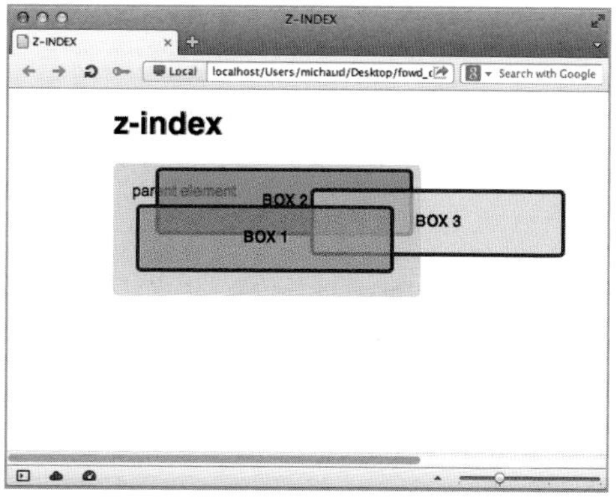

FIGURE 9.36
By increasing the z-index value, you can bring elements closer (on top of other elements).

FIGURE 9.37
The stacking order changes when the value is changed from auto to an integer.

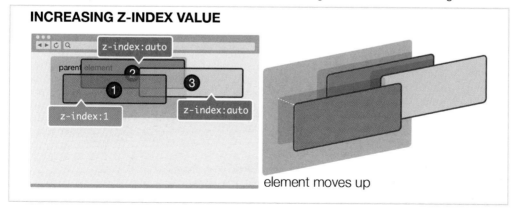

VIDEO TUTORIALS

Remember, at any time, you can view video demonstrations of the topics you're learning. For some, it's easier to see things happening onscreen (or in person) than through text—and sometimes it's good to just learn the same thing through a slightly different medium to reinforce the subject!

STEP 9.4.4

Change the `.third` class selector's `z-index` value from `auto` to `-1`.

```
.third {
    position: absolute;
    top: 20px;
    left: 200px;
    z-index: -1;
}
```

Since two other elements have a value of `auto` for their `z-index`, the negative value will cause the element to be displayed behind them (**Figure 9.38**).

With two elements that have the default `z-index` value of `auto`, an element with an integer value (positive or negative) will automatically bypass them and move in front (with a positive value) or behind (with a negative value) (**Figure 9.39**).

Wow! Now you have the foundations of positioning and stacking order (of positioned elements) with the `z-index` property! There is one last layout property to review.

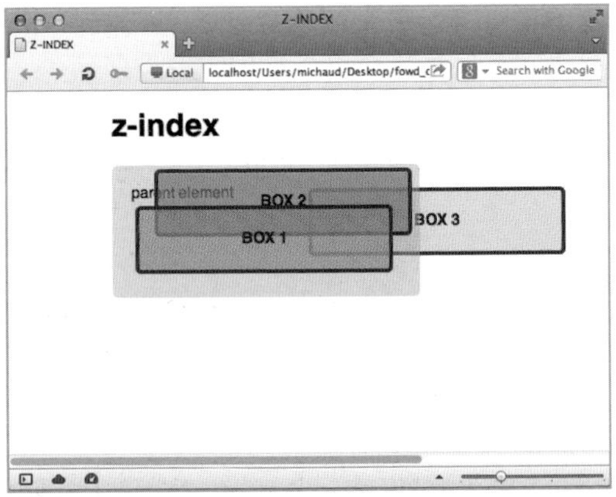

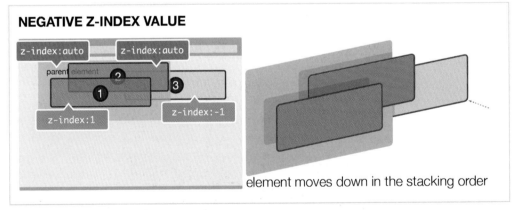

FIGURE 9.38
A negative value places elements farther away (or behind elements).

FIGURE 9.39
Elements with a `z-index` value of auto are bypassed (forward or backward) by elements that have a `z-index` with an integer value.

DISPLAY

The `display` property controls the type of box an element generates. You know there are block-level elements (`p`, `h1`, `blockquote`, `ul`, etc.), inline elements (`span`, `strong`, `em`, etc.), and even replaced elements (`img`, `br`, `hr`, `object`). Well, you can cause a block-level element to display like an `inline` element or an inline element to display as a `block` element. There's even an option to have them render as an `inline-block` (two blocks in one)!

First, open **05-display.html** in a browser. You'll see a page with one section that has text surrounded by an inline (`<em>…</em>`) element (**Figure 9.40A**) and another section containing block-level (`<dl>…</dl>`) elements (**Figure 9.40B**).

Now, in a text editor, open the **display.css** document to work through the examples that follow.

FIGURE 9.40B
Each block-level element creates a new line and (if a width is not set) spans the length of the containing element.

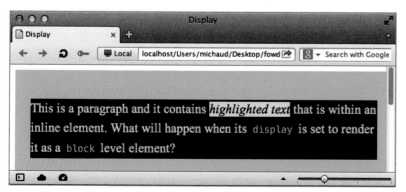

FIGURE 9.40A
Inline elements stay within the flow of the text.

> ### ELEMENTAL REVIEW OF BLOCK-LEVEL ELEMENTS
>
> Block-level elements are those elements of an HTML document that are formatted visually as blocks. They begin on new lines. If no width is set, they will expand naturally to fill their parent containers. While they can contain inline-level elements, some can also contain other block elements.

> ### INLINE ELEMENTS
>
> Inline-level elements are contained within block-level elements and do not begin a new line. They can contain only data and other inline elements, and cannot have a width or height set.

> ### AREN'T THERE MORE DISPLAY PROPERTIES?
>
> Yes, there are about 15 different values you can apply to the display property! However, the examples in the book will touch briefly on block, inline, and inline-block. Many of the additional display values are shown in video tutorials on the website.

DISPLAY: BLOCK

The block value causes an element to generate a block box. When rendering an inline element as a block, the element no longer sits inline but on a new line, and it spans the width of the containing element.

STEP 9.5.1

Enter in the properties and values for margin, padding, text-align, and line-height for the inline em element selector.

```
/* inline to block */
em {
  margin: 20px 10px 20px 0;
  /* inline: only left and right margins */
  padding: 10px;
  /* inline: accepts padding */
  text-align: right;
  /* inline: no text-align */
  line-height: 2.5em;
  /* inline: no line-height */
}
```

When viewing the changes, notice the properties that affect horizontal spacing but not vertical (top/bottom) spacing are applied (**Figure 9.41**).

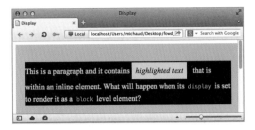

FIGURE 9.41
An inline element accepts horizontal style values but not vertical.

>>> NOTE: THE WIDTH PROPERTY CANNOT BE APPLIED TO INLINE ELEMENTS.

STEP 9.5.2

Now add the display property with the block value.

```
/* inline to block */
em {
  margin: 20px 10px 20px 0;
  /* inline: only left and right margins */
  padding: 10px;
  /* inline: accepts padding */
  text-align: right;
  /* inline: no text-align */
  line-height: 2.5em;
  /* inline: no line-height */
  display: block;
}
```

The browser now renders the inline element as if it were a block-level element (**Figure 9.42**).

With the inline element rendered as a block

- The inline element renders a new block box—creating a new line, like a block element.

- The margin values for top and bottom will now apply.

- The element will expand to the width of the containing element—NOTE: The margin of 10px on the right is adding space between the em element and p element.

- The line-height property now applies.

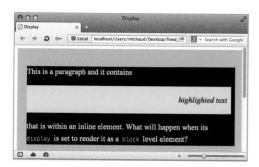

FIGURE 9.42
The inline element rendered as a block element now accepts horizontal and vertical values.

DISPLAY: INLINE

The `inline` value causes an element to generate one or more inline boxes. An inline element accepts margin and padding but will only push other elements horizontally, not vertically. When the block element is rendered as an inline element, it no longer breaks the flow of text but sits within the line.

For your block `dd` element selector, the following code is already provided:

```
/* block to inline */
dd {
  border-radius: 3px;
  background: white;
  padding: 5px;
  /* block elements apply padding */
  margin: 10px 2px 10px 2px;
  /* block elements apply margin on all
  sides */
  height: 50px;
  /* block elements can have height */
}
```

STEP 9.5.3

Now simply add in the `display` property with the value of `inline`.

```
/* inline to block */
dd {
  border-radius: 3px;
  background: white;
  padding: 5px; /* block elements apply
padding */
  margin: 10px 2px 10px 2px; /* block
elements apply margin on all sides */
  height: 50px; /* block elements can
have height */
  display: inline;
}
```

When viewing the result, the block elements now render as inline elements (**Figure 9.43**).

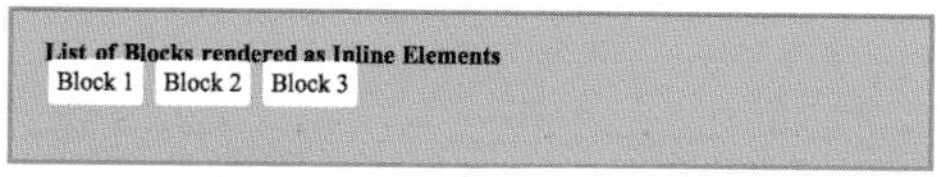

List of Blocks rendered as Inline Elements
Block 1   Block 2   Block 3

FIGURE 9.43
Block elements are rendered as inline elements (like a horizontal navigation bar).

NAVIGATION STYLES

When designers want to create horizontal navigation, the inline value for `display` has often been applied to `li` elements that contain links (`a` element). More on navigation styles in Chapter 12!

OVERRIDE PREVIOUS RULES

You can override previous declaration settings. Remember the cascade effect discussed in Chapter 5?

Once the block-level element is rendered as an inline element

- The block element will display inline (not on its own line).

- Margin will no longer be applied to the top and bottom.

- The element will expand only to the width of its content (plus any applied padding).

DISPLAY: INLINE-BLOCK

The `inline-block` value makes the element generate one or more inline boxes and generate a block box that's laid out as if it were an inline box. So, an inline-block has some characteristics of an inline element and some characteristics of a block-level element.

- **Inline quality**: Elements remain in the flow of text.

- **Block quality**: Elements accept vertical values—e.g., `margin` (top and bottom included), `height`, and `line-height`.

STEP 9.5.4

Finally, add a new rule that applies the `inline-block` value for the `display` property for both the `em` and `dd` selectors.

```
/*display: inline-block */
em,dd {
    display: inline-block;
    /* overrides previous settings */
}
```

When refreshing the browser, notice the changes to both the rendered block-level element (the highlighted text) and the rendered inline elements (white boxes) (**Figure 9.44**).

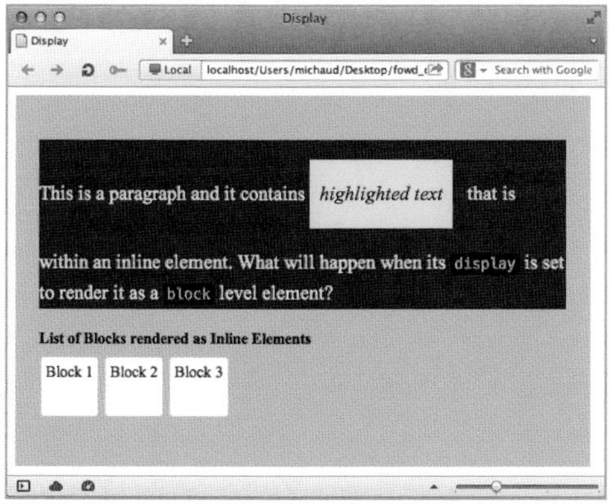

FIGURE 9.44
The transformation of an inline-level element to an inline-block element.

The inside of an inline-block is formatted as a block box, and the element itself is formatted as an inline-level box.

- **Inline quality**: The element stays on the same line.

- **Block quality**: Vertical spacing values (e.g., `margin` top and bottom) are allowed.

A pretty powerful and useful property/value combination! However, as with any good thing in web design, there are "gotchas" to be had with this value. Check out the website for links to articles concerning the `inline-block` value.

OTHER DISPLAY VALUES

As mentioned, there are a number of other display values (about 14 more—including `inherit` and `none`) at your disposal. Check out the website for video tutorials and resources.

WRAPPING THINGS UP

You made it through the basics of the display properties—`float`, `position`, and `display`—in CSS, along with some of their associated properties—`clear`, `overflow`, and `z-index`. In the next couple of chapters, you're going to use these properties to learn how web designers develop layouts for websites—as well as some new CSS3 layout options!

>>> *DOWNLOAD REMINDER: ON THE WEBSITE, THERE ARE ADDITIONAL RESOURCES AND VIDEO TUTORIALS ON THE LAYOUT PROPERTY—AND AN ASSIGNMENT TO TEST YOUR SKILLS!*

PAGE LAYOUT

—

10

>>> CHAPTER CODE

THE CODE EXAMPLES FOR THIS CHAPTER CAN BE DOWNLOADED FROM THE WEBSITE (HTTP://FOUNDATIONSOFWEBDESIGN.COM).

Just when web design seemed to be getting pretty predictable and familiar, Ethan Marcotte's article, "Responsive Web Design," posted on A List Apart in May of 2010 (http://alistapart.com/article/responsive-web-design), inspired people to reconsider the way they approached web page layout. The growth of the mobile market caused a fundamental shift in terms of web design as well as content management.

This chapter will provide an overview of how layout was done in the past (which for many is still the norm), what's currently the "standard," and what is coming up for layout in the near future.

FIXED-WIDTH LAYOUTS

A fixed layout is one that does not change sizes as the browser width widens or narrows—much like a layout on a printed page (**Figure 10.2**). The units web designers most often use for fixed-layout design are pixels.

WHAT IS THE WEB?

People now have more options than ever for how and when they'll connect to a website. Desktop computers are no longer the "norm," as smartphones and tablets have become more prevalent (**Figure 10.1**). Additionally, users can view websites on large-screen televisions, refrigerators, cars, and (soon) glasses.

FIGURE 10.1
Websites are no longer just viewed on desktops or laptops.

DETERMINE THE AUDIENCE

You need to determine who your audience is and what types of devices they will be using to view your website. Since a good number of visitors to websites today use mobile devices, fixed-width-only designs are becoming less prevalent.

DETERMINE BROWSERS

Another question you will need to ask yourself—or your client—is what browser versions will the site support? What is the oldest version of Internet Explorer (a main concern among most web designers)? Microsoft no longer supports version 6, but some companies may need their sites to support it.

The demonstrations provided in this chapter primarily support Internet Explorer 8 and above, and the modern versions of Chrome, Firefox, and Safari.

WHY USE A FIXED DESIGN?

- Layout of elements will behave the same at different browser window/device widths, so you only need to worry about one layout.

- Fixed-width layouts are the same for every browser, so there is less hassle with adjusting content or objects for different browsers.

- Controlling typography (size and line-height) is easier.

WHY AVOID A FIXED DESIGN?

- A fixed design may create excessive white space for users with larger screen resolutions.

- Smaller screens may require a horizontal scrollbar; the design may appear extremely small on mobile devices.

- If a user increases her font size, text may no longer fit into its defined (fixed-pixel) space.

For print designers learning to lay out a website, starting with a fixed-width layout can be helpful, since dealing with pixel values is similar to using inches, points, or centimeters in a print layout.

In the folder for this chapter (**fowd_ch10_folder**) find the **01-layout.html** document, and open it in your browser. Notice how the sections of content are stacked on top of each other (**Figure 10.3**).

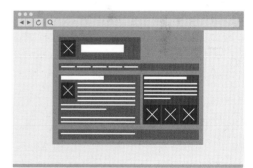

FIGURE 10.2
Fixed-width designs stay the same width when the browser width expands or contracts.

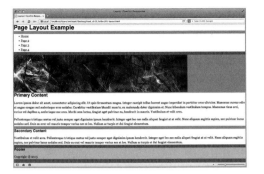

FIGURE 10.3
Without structure, content
is simply stacked vertically.

Before working on your design, it's best
to form some idea of your plan of action
for your CSS rules by sketching out your
layout (**Figure 10.4**).

Knowing the pixel dimensions of the
outer website container (960px), the
dimensions for each box, and how some
boxes will be placed next to each other
gives you an idea of how the CSS rules
should be written.

When you view the **01-layout.html**
document in your text editor, notice the
elements containing your content:

FIGURE 10.4
A sketch provides a plan of
action for your CSS rules.

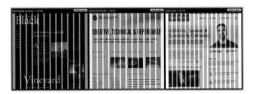

FIGURE 10.5
Grid systems can provide a great basis
for your design—for both symmetrical
and asymmetrical layouts.

WORKFLOW OF A DESIGNER

The workflow of a web designer
ranges from research, to sketching,
to coding, and will be covered in
more detail in Chapter 13.

GRID LAYOUT

Using a grid to lay out a design
(for web or print) allows you
to align content and visualize
proportions, and provides visual
comfort. You might feel confined
using a structured grid, but the
design doesn't always have to be
symmetrical. A great grid system
to help you get your feet wet in
layout is the 960 Grid System by
Nathan Smith (http://960.gs). On
the front page there are examples
of how designers use 12- and
16-column layouts (**Figure 10.5**).

PRINTABLE GRIDS ON THE WEBSITE

The website has more resources
for grid layouts along with printable
grids for sketching.

```
<div class="content">
  <div role="banner">
    <div class="container">
      <div class="group">
        <div class="header">
        <h1>Page Layout Example</h1>
        </div><!-- end .header -->
        <nav role="navigation"
class="navbar">
        <ul>
        <li><a href="#">Home</a></li>
        <li><a href="#">Page 2</a></li>
        <li><a href="#">Page 3</a></li>
        <li><a href="#">Page 4</a></li>
        </ul>
        </nav><!-- end .navbar-->
      </div><!-- end .group -->
    </div><!-- end .container -->
  </div><!-- end banner -->
  <div role="main">
    <div class="container">
      <img src="http://lorempixel.
com/960/200/abstract/1" alt="">
      <div class="group">
        <div class="primary">
        <h2>Primary Content</h2>
        <p>...</p>
        <p>...</p>
        </div><!-- end .primary -->
```

```
        <div class="secondary">
        <h3>Secondary Content</h3>
        <p>...</p>
        </div><!-- end .secondary -->
      </div><!-- end .group -->
    </div><!-- end .container -->
  </div><!-- end main -->
  <div role="contentinfo">
    <div class="container">
      <div class="footer">
      <h3>Footer</h3>
      <p>Copyright &copy; 2013</p>
      </div><!-- end .footer -->
    </div><!-- end .container -->
  </div><!-- end contentinfo-->
</div> <!-- end .content -->
```

BREAKING DOWN THE STRUCTURE

While this may seem like a lot to take in, you can break it down into three regions: top, middle, and bottom.

The top (**Figure 10.6**) is where you have the site name and navigation.

The middle (**Figure 10.7**) contains the primary and secondary content for your page.

The bottom (**Figure 10.8**) contains the copyright information.

While there might be further elements and content added in the future, they should be added to one of these three sections to keep the overall structure.

FIGURE 10.6
Top section of the website's content.

```
<div role="banner">
  <div class="container">
    <div class="group">
      <div class="header">
        <h1>...</h1>
      </div><!-- end .header -->
      <nav role="navigation" class="navbar">
        <ul>...</ul>
      </nav><!-- end .navbar-->
    </div><!-- end .group -->
  </div><!-- end .container -->
</div><!-- end banner -->
```

FIGURE 10.7
Main section of the website's content.

```
<div role="contentinfo">
  <div class="container">
    <div class="footer">
      <h3>...</h3>
      <p>...</p>
    </div><!-- end .footer -->
  </div><!-- end .container -->
</div><!-- end contentinfo-->
```

FIGURE 10.8
The bottom section of the website's content.

EXTRA DIVS

You might wonder why there are div elements with the class attribute with the values of container and group. While they might not always be necessary, they can provide hooks for CSS for clearing floats or adding additional styling.

GOSPEL USAGE OF DIV ELEMENTS

By no means is this example the only way to structure a website or to name divs. You can (and will) find other methods for structuring a website and other class attribute values for the div element. I'm just showing you one way that works, to give you guidance and inspiration.

CODING CSS FIXED RULES

Now open **layout.css** to add CSS rules for the layout.

First, notice one of the divs that repeats in each area:

```
<div class="container">
```

STEP 10.1.1

Use the class selector .container to establish the width for this containing element and margin to center the content.

```
.container {
    width: 960px;
    margin: 0px auto;
    /* centers content on screen */
}
```

Viewing the page in the browser, you'll see the design now has a fixed width and is centered within the browser window (**Figure 10.9**).

AUTO MARGIN

When you specify a width for the object to which you have applied margin: 0 auto, the object will sit centrally within its parent container. Specifying auto as the second parameter tells the browser to automatically determine the left and right margins, which it does by setting them equally, to half the available horizontal space inside the parent container. The first parameter, 0, indicates that no margin will be applied to the top and bottom of the element.

FIGURE 10.9
A fixed-width layout that is centered on screen.

STEP 10.1.2

Now that the parent (`.container`) element's width is set, it's time to move to the first set of child elements.

The top section has two elements:

```
<div class="header">
<nav role="navigation" class="navbar">
```

The plan is for the boxes to appear side by side and to have the same specific width (**Figure 10.10**).

Use the class selector for each element to set its `width`, `margin`, and `float` properties:

```
.header {
    width: 460px;
    margin: 0 10px;
    float: left;
}
.navbar {
    width: 460px;
    margin: 0 10px;
    float: left;
}
```

The rules first tell the `.header` and `.navbar` each to only take up `480px` of space (`width` + `margin-right` + `margin-left`) and to `float` `left`, allowing the `.navbar` to move up and fill the space to the right of the `.header` (**Figure 10.11**).

In the middle section, since the image (`<img>`) is the width it needs to be (960px), the focus is on the website's "primary" and "secondary" content.

```
<div class="primary">
<div class="secondary">
```

This section also needs to have a two-column look, but with slightly different dimensions (**Figure 10.12**).

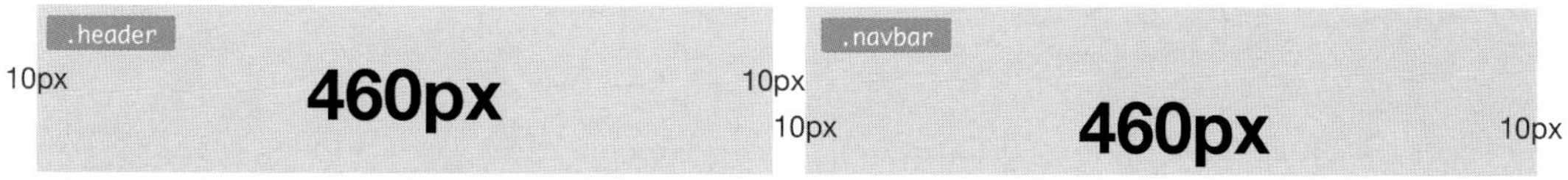

FIGURE 10.10
Illustrated plan of layout.

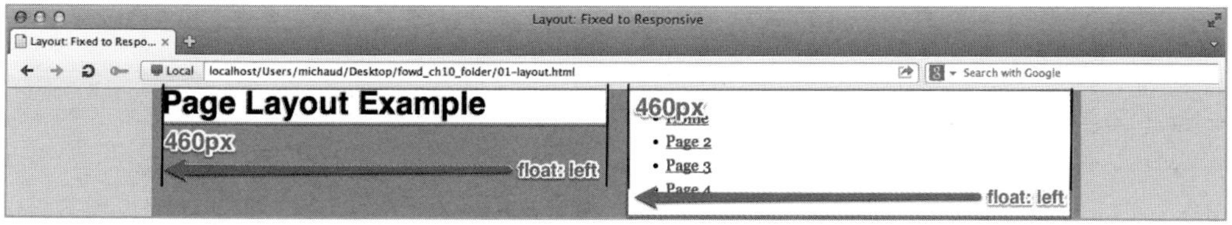

FIGURE 10.11
Two nested floated elements within a parent container create a two-column look.

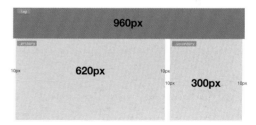

FIGURE 10.12
Columns can be asymmetrical in balance.

STEP 10.1.3

Just like the top section, use the class selector for each box and set its `width`, `margin`, and `float` properties:

```
.primary {
    width: 620px;
    margin: 0 10px;
    float: left;
}
.secondary {
    width: 300px;
    margin: 0 10px;
    float: left;
}
```

Can you start to see a pattern for creating a two-column layout? Again, if you take the `width` of the elements (620px and 300px) and add them to the `left` and `right` margin (10px x 4), you'll get the width (960px) of the parent container (**Figure 10.13**).

FIGURE 10.13
The middle section now has an asymmetrical two-column layout.

The bottom box (`<div class="footer">`) is simple, since it is only one column with margins on the left and right (**Figure 10.14**).

STEP 10.1.4

While the `.footer` class selector, like the other selectors, sets the `width` and `margin`, it also needs to use the `clear` property to ensure that it doesn't move up into the empty space below the floated elements above it.

```
.footer {
    width: 940px;
    margin: 0 10px;
    clear: both; /*use this value to
    clear floats above container */
}
```

The bottom box is now in place (**Figure 10.15**).

REMEMBER WHAT ADDS TO BOX SIZING

Be careful: If you add `padding` or `border`, you add to the box's width, unless you apply the `box-sizing: border-box;` property (Chapter 8).

```
* {
    -moz-box-sizing: border-box
    -webkit-box-sizing: border-
    box;
    box-sizing: border-box;
}
```

However, this property only works in Internet Explorer 8+. There are other ways to help IE7 on the website.

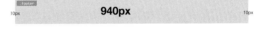

FIGURE 10.14
The footer is a single box with margins on the right and left.

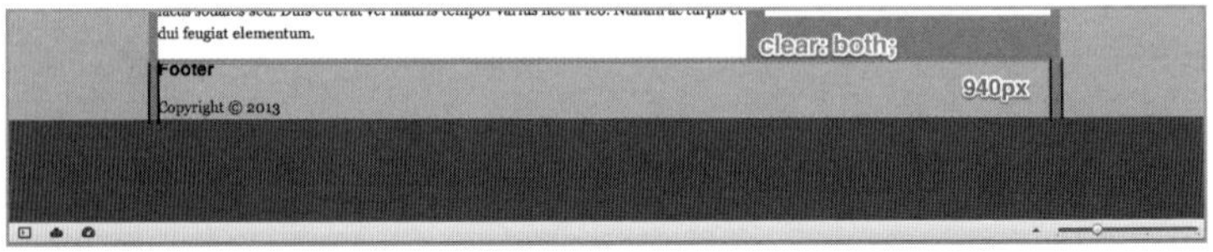

FIGURE 10.15
The footer at the bottom of the layout clears floated elements above it.

>>> *WHILE* clear: left *WOULD HAVE CLEARED BOTH BOXES (SET TO* float: left;*) ABOVE THE FOOTER, ONE (OR BOTH) OF THE ELEMENTS ABOVE COULD BE SET TO* float: right. clear: both *ALLOWS YOU TO "FUTURE-PROOF" AGAINST A FLOAT IN EITHER DIRECTION.*

The final step in the layout is to uncollapse the collapsed containing box elements of the nested floated elements (**Figure 10.16**).

Do you remember the two options for clearing floats that are nested within a containing parent element that were mentioned in Chapter 9?

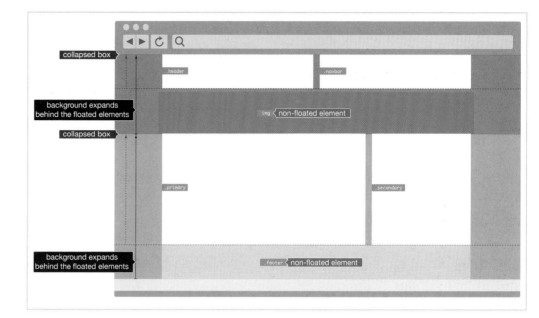

FIGURE 10.16
Containing elements with floated elements collapse.

There is a div (<div class="group">) element surrounding the group of elements floated in each parent element.

```
<div role="banner">
  <div class="container">
    <div class="group">
    <!-- floated .header -->
    <!-- floated .navbar -->
    </div><!-- end .group -->
  </div>
</div>
```

```
<div role="main">
  <div class="container">
    <div class="group">
    <!-- floated .primary -->
    <!-- floated .secondary -->
    </div><!-- end .group -->
  </div>
</div>
```

STEP 10.1.5

Use the `.group` class selector to either apply the `overflow` property:

```
.group {
    overflow: auto;
    width: 100%;
}
```

FIGURE 10.17
The containing parent elements uncollapse.

or

Use the `:after` pseudo class selector to apply the "clearfix" method:

```
.group:after {
    content: " ";
    display: block;
    clear: both;
}
```

CHALLENGE

Take what you've learned and create a three-column section in **layout-challenge.css** for **layout-challenge.html**.

Remember, always start with a plan (a sketch or diagram) to determine the width and margins needed to accomplish the task (**Figure 10.18**).

>>> *WHILE YOU CAN KEEP BOTH RULES IN YOUR CSS FOR THIS DEMONSTRATION, IT'S BEST TO CHOOSE ONE METHOD AND REMOVE THE OTHER.*

While both methods will give the same result, expanding the containing parent element (**Figure 10.17**), each has its positives and negatives (refer to Chapter 9 and the website for a review).

Congratulations—you have developed your fixed-width layout!

This is just one way to accomplish a layout; you can play around with the code and change it to your heart's content.

You have the HTML and CSS starting point (**Figure 10.19**); you just need to write one new CSS rule set to finish the challenge (**Figure 10.20**).

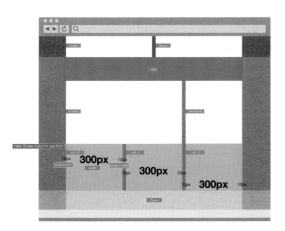

FIGURE 10.18
Diagramming the layout before
you code helps you determine
the width and margins needed.

FLUID LAYOUTS

Fluid layouts resize as the user increases
or decreases the width of the browser
(**Figure 10.21**).

This layout style has its advantages:

- Content expands to help fill the
  browser window.

- Content can resize to smaller layouts if
  the user has a smaller browser window.

▶▶▶ *REMEMBER: IF YOU GET STUCK, THE*
***SOLUTIONS** FOLDER HOLDS THE ANSWER KEY.*

FIGURE 10.20
The finished layout with three new columns.

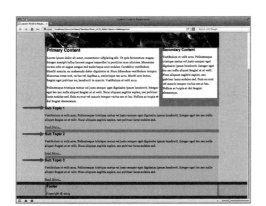

FIGURE 10.19
Layout before the new CSS rules.

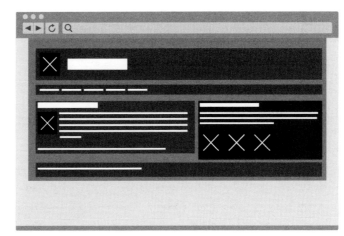

FIGURE 10.21
Fluid layouts expand and contract as the browser resizes.

It also has disadvantages:

- For beginners, layouts can be more difficult to plan.

- At larger screen sizes, lack of content may create excess whitespace and create a less-than-appealing look. Increased line length of paragraphs can also cause problems with readability.

- Nested fixed-width elements can cause problems in the layout and can overflow their containing boxes.

In order to accomplish going from a fixed, pixel-based design to a fluid design, you'll need percentage values.

FIXED GRID TO FLUID GRID

How do you transform a fixed layout into a fluid layout? With a little math.

This will mostly consist of converting fixed-width containers to percentage widths. First, take the pixel width of the box you are trying to convert from fixed-width to percentage and divide it by the overall width of the parent container.

target ÷ context = result

In the case of the website you've developed (**Figure 10.22**)

The target = any nested element with pixel values for width and margin

The context = the parent element, with the established width of 960px

When you divide 460 (pixel width of the .header) by 960 (pixel width of the .container), the result is a long string of numbers: .479166667.

Move the decimal two places to the right to get the percent value.

Do not round the number (.479166667 should not be 48 percent).

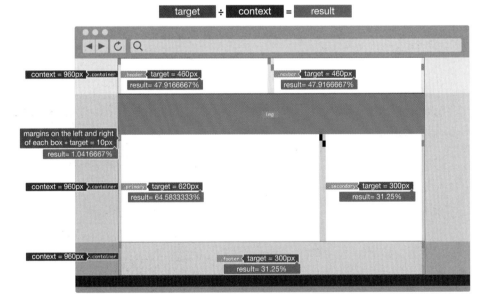

FIGURE 10.22
Formula for conversion from pixel values to percentages.

STEP 10.2.1

In your document, take each pixel value for the `width` and `margin` properties and divide it by 960 to get the percentage (remember to move the decimal two places to the right). Replace the `px` value with the `%` value.

If you do this for each child element of the `.container`, you end up with

```
.header {
    width: 47.9166667%; /* 460px ÷ 960 */
    margin: 0 1.0416667%; /* 10px ÷ 960 */
    float: left;
}
.navbar {
    width: 47.9166667%; /* 460px ÷ 960 */
    margin: 0 1.0416667%; /* 10px ÷ 960 */
    float: left;
}
.primary {
    width: 64.5833333%; /* 620px ÷ 960px */
    margin: 0 1.0416667%; /* 10px ÷ 960*/
    float: left;
}
```

```
.secondary {
    width: 31.25%; /* 300px ÷ 60 */
    margin: 0 1.0416667%; /* 10px ÷ 960*/
    float: left;
}
.footer {
    width: 97.9166667%; /* 940px ÷ 960 */
    margin: 0 1.0416667%; /* 10px ÷ 960*/
    clear: both;
}
```

However, if you view the website in a browser and resize the browser, you'll see no change to the layout (**Figure 10.23**).

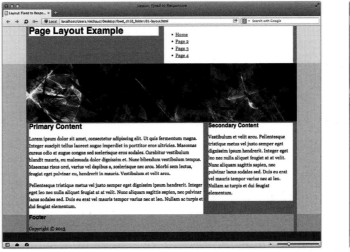

FIGURE 10.23
The nested elements do not resize (yet) with the resizing of the browser.

177

STEP 10.2.2

To make the `.container` fluid, we need to make its pixel width a percentage as well. While the `width` could simply be set to `100%`, the layout would stretch to the very edges of the browser window. To give the layout a little space to the left and right, the value could be set to `90%`. There's nothing magical about that number; it's simply an arbitrary value.

```
.container {
    width: 90%;
    /* arbitrary starting point for 960px */
    margin: 0 auto; /*center layout */
}
```

While the layout is now "fluid," it's not looking great beyond 960px or when the browser is narrowed (**Figure 10.24**).

STEP 10.2.3

To help control the layout, the `.container` can have a maximum width (`max-width`) of `960px` and the `body` element can be set to have a minimum width (`min-width`) of `320px`.

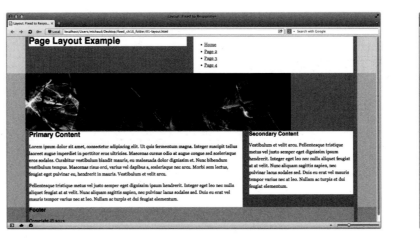

FIGURE 10.24
Expanding and narrowing the browser shows an adverse effect on the layout.

```
body {
    margin: 0;
    min-width: 320px;
    /*minimum width the layout will narrow
    to*/
}
.container {
    width:90%;
    /* arbitrary starting point for 960px
    */
    max-width: 960px;
    margin: 0 auto; /*center layout */
}
```

While the layout is fine as the browser widens, the image overflows the container as the browser narrows (**Figure 10.25**).

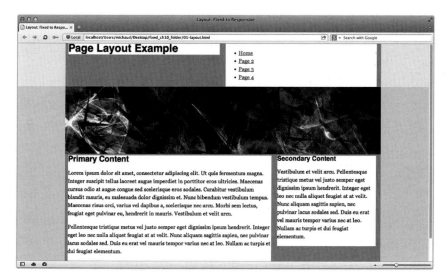 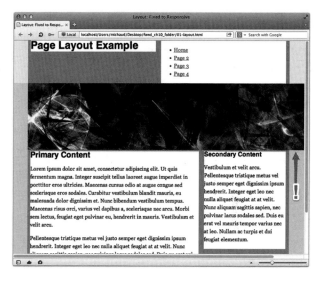

FIGURE 10.25
The fixed-width image overflows the containing box as the browser narrows.

STEP 10.2.4

To make the image fluid, the `img` selector simply needs a `max-width` set to `100%`.

```
body {
    ...
}
.container {
    ...
}
/* add in for fluid image */
img {
    max-width: 100%;
}
```

>>> THE `max-width` *ATTRIBUTE WILL NOT WORK ON INTERNET EXPLORER 7 AND BELOW, SO YOU CAN SET ANOTHER RULE FOR THE* `img` *TO HAVE A WIDTH OF 100%:*

```
img {
    width: 100%;
}
```

Now the whole layout, including the image, is fluid (**Figure 10.26**) when the browser is narrowed below 960 pixels (the maximum width it will expand to).

FIGURE 10.26
The image now resizes as the browser width is narrowed.

RESPONSIVE LAYOUTS

The final transformation for the layout is to become **responsive**. At certain points in the layout, the content becomes squished and difficult to read. Additionally, if the website is going to be viewed on devices (especially mobile) with different screen resolutions, presentation and content can both provide a less-than-ideal experience. Enter, as coined by Ethan Marcotte, "Responsive Web Design."

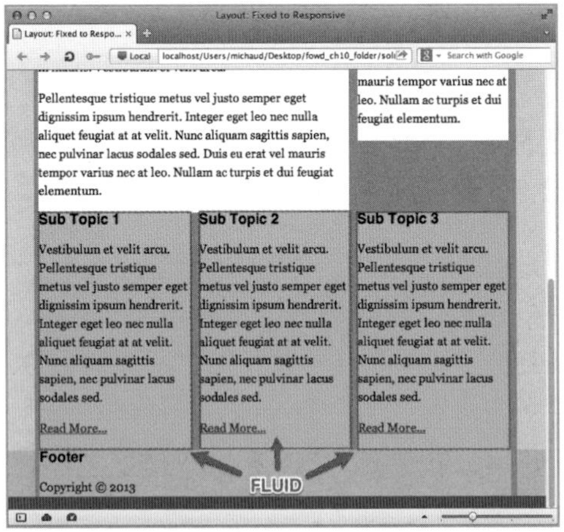

> *Rather than tailoring disconnected designs to each of an ever-increasing number of web devices, we can treat them as facets of the same experience. We can design for an optimal viewing experience, but embed standards-based technologies into our designs to make them not only more flexible, but more adaptive to the media that renders them.*

Ethan Marcotte

Responsive Web Design

A List Apart, May 25, 2010

While, as a designer, you want a design that can adapt to specific sizes, the devices users can access your website on are not limited to a specific brand of laptop, tablet, and phone (**Figure 10.28**).

CHALLENGE

From what you've just learned, make the CSS rules for **layout-challenge.css** percentages—including the `.col-3` class selector (**Figure 10.27**).

FIGURE 10.27
Make the challenge layout fluid.

FIGURE 10.28
While design should be responsive, don't limit your design to one specific brand of device.

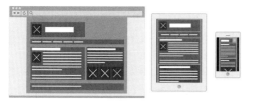

The determining factor in how the design changes shouldn't be the device, but how the content (such as typography, hierarchy, navigation) changes appearance as one increases or decreases the size of the browser.

To determine where the design needs to change, a basic test is to resize the browser and note where a change in layout should occur.

MOBILE FIRST WOULD BE BEST...

Once content is structured, the first context to pipe the content into is the mobile web. Why start here and not the desktop? The mobile web is far more restrictive, eclectic and unstable than other contexts... In short, if you can support the mobile web, you can support anything.

Brad Frost

Mobile-First Responsive Web Design
http://bradfrostweb.com/blog/web/mobile-first-responsive-web-design/

CHECKING DESIGN DIMENSIONS

The website has resources and video tutorials on various "responsive" design tools, but here are some you may already have:

Use the "inspector" that comes built-in with most browsers—quickly found in the contextual menu when you right-click with your mouse or Control+click in the browser window (**Figure 10.29**).

From the Web Developer Toolbar (see the website on how to install the Web Developer Toolbar in Firefox and Chrome), you can choose Display Div Dimensions (**Figure 10.30**).

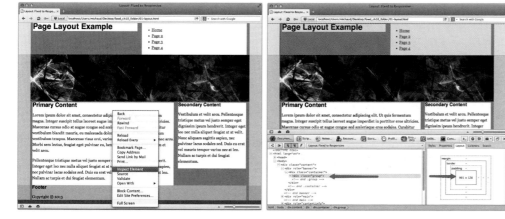

FIGURE 10.29
Web browsers have a built-in inspector that can show you the box dimension for any element.

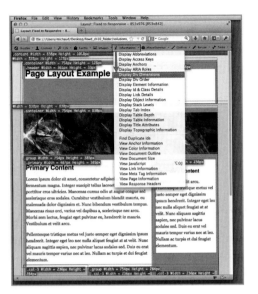

FIGURE 10.30
The Web Developer Toolbar for
Firefox and Chrome can display
all `div` element dimensions.

While it's normally best to start with the narrowest view (mobile) first to focus on core content and functionality, your site started as a 960px-wide layout—hey, sometimes you'll be asked to make a fixed design into a responsive design.

》》》 *THE WEBSITE HAS RESOURCES TO HELP YOU DELVE FURTHER INTO THE WORLD OF RESPONSIVE WEB DESIGN.*

FIXED TO RESPONSIVE

In your **01-layout.html** document, change the CSS document name, in the `link` element, to `layout-responsive.css`.

```
<link rel="stylesheet" href="css/layout-
responsive.css">
```

This new CSS document brings you back to the fixed-width starting point, but you'll add the fluid grid back in—with conditions.

@MEDIA

The `@media` rule prevents the CSS nested inside it from being applied to the HTML unless the browser meets certain conditions.

For example, if you wanted to write a `@media` rule making the `body` element's `background` color `black` and the `color` of the text `white` when the browser is 400 pixels wide or narrower, you'd write

```
@media screen and (max-width: 400px) {
  body {
    background: black;
    color: white;
  }
}
```

However, once the browser width is greater than 400px, the `body` element reverts to the default transparent background and black text color.

With CSS2 media types, you could have one layout for `screen` and another for `print`. In CSS3, you can add additional conditions for screen: `orientation`, `max-width`, `min-width`, `device-width`, and `color`.

ADDING MEDIA TYPES

You could add in the conditions in your HTML within the `link` element:

```
<link rel="stylesheet" href="css/layout-
responsive.css" media="screen and (max-
width: 960px)">
```

You could add them in your CSS document:

```
@media screen and (max-width: 960px) {
/* conditional rules go between curly
brackets */
}
```

The great thing about the `@media` query is that you can add multiple queries in a single CSS document:

```
@media screen and (max-width: 960px) {
/* conditional rules go between curly
brackets */
}
@media screen and (max-width: 600px) {
/* conditional rules go between curly
brackets */
}
@media screen and (max-width: 320px) {
/* conditional rules go between curly
brackets */
}
```

The breakdown of the media query is simple:

- `@media screen` = use this rule only for screen devices (not for print, etc.)

- `and (max-width: 960)` = and activate the CSS rules up to a width of 960 pixels

STEP 10.3.1

The first media query you'll add is for the `max-width` of `960px`. Since your fixed-width design is 960 pixels, anytime the browser is smaller than `960px` the fluid design will take over.

After the fixed rules, starting around line 55, add the following media query:

```
@media screen and (max-width 960px) {
/* fluid grid goes here */
}
```

KEEPING OPTIONS BASIC

The `max-width` and `min-width` are the two most commonly used properties and the easiest to get started with.

There are other logical operators (besides `and`) by which you can establish a query, including `not` and `only`.

Check the website for links to examples and online resources.

STEP 10.3.2

Now place the following fluid rules—which you can copy from the **layout.css** document—between the curly brackets {...} of the @media rule:

```css
@media screen and (max-width:960px) {
 /* fluid grid goes here */
 img {
   max-width: 100%;
 }
 .container {
 width: 90%;/* arbitrary starting
point for 960px */
 }
 .header {
 width: 47.9166667%; /* 460px ÷ 960 */
 margin: 0 1.0416667%; /* 10px ÷ 960 */
 }
 .navbar {
 width: 47.9166667%; /* 460px ÷ 960 */
 margin: 0 1.0416667%; /* 10px ÷ 960 */
 }
 .primary {
 width: 64.5833333%; /* 620px ÷ 960px */
 margin: 0 1.0416667%; /* 10px ÷ 960*/
 background: lightblue; /* change
background for fun*/
 }
```

```css
 .secondary {
 width: 31.25%; /* 300px ÷ 60 */
 margin: 0 1.0416667%; /* 10px ÷ 960*/
 background: lightsalmon; /* change
background for fun*/
 }
 .footer {
 width: 97.9166667%; /* 940px ÷ 960 */
 margin: 0 1.0416667%; /* 10px ÷ 960*/
 }
}
```

▶▶▶ *DID YOU NOTICE THE ADDITION TO THE CSS RULES? SINCE YOU CAN TELL THE ELEMENTS TO ADD OR REMOVE STYLES, TWO ELEMENTS ADDED A DIFFERENT BACKGROUND COLOR—A* lightblue *COLOR FOR THE* .primary *CLASS SELECTOR AND A* lightsalmon *COLOR FOR THE* .secondary *CLASS SELECTOR.*

INHERITANCE KICKS IN

Since your fixed-width rules established which elements floated and cleared floats, those declarations can be deleted in the fluid layout, as the elements inherit those properties and values.

When viewing the **layout.html** document in a browser, with the new style sheet attached, you'll see a change as you narrow the width of the browser (**Figure 10.31**).

FIGURE 10.31
The fixed-width layout becomes fluid and the background colors change for the .primary and .secondary boxes.

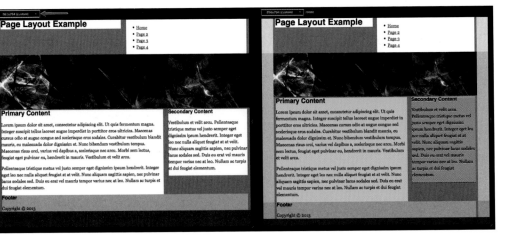

Figure 10.31 shows the layout using the Firefox built-in Responsive Design View tool (**Figure 10.32**).

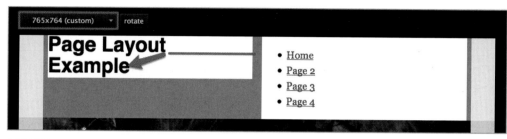

FIGURE 10.33
The box width can no longer contain the text on one line as the viewport narrows further.

FIGURE 10.32
Firefox has a built-in Responsive Design View tool.

The next break in the design comes when the site name breaks and spills into a second line when the browser's viewport is 765 pixels wide (**Figure 10.33**).

A new rule could be set up for a max-width of 765px, but

- Some tablet screens (depending upon their orientation) have a maximum width of 800 pixels.

- Space could be given on the box's right side before actually hitting the text.

So, 800px could be a good breakpoint. However, it's your choice if you want a breakpoint value of 765, 800, or some other value in-between.

STEP 10.3.3

So, write a new @media rule (after the previous @media rule closes) for a screen with a max-width of 800px, where the .header and .navbar auto expand their width to the containing parent element and have a float of none.

```
@media screen and (max-width:800px) {
  .header {
    width: auto;
    float: none;
  }
  .navbar {
    width: auto;
    float: none;
  }
  .navbar ul {
    margin-bottom: 0;
  }
}
```

>>> *MAKE SURE THE NEW @media RULE IS NOT WITHIN (AND COMES AFTER) THE PREVIOUS @media RULE.*

When the two elements no longer float, there's a margin on the bottom of the navigation box that causes an ugly gap between it and the image (**Figure 10.34**).

STEP 10.3.4

To remove that space, add a rule to remove the `margin-bottom` from the `ul` selector of the `.navbar` class selector.

```
@media screen and (max-width:800px) {
  .header {
    width: auto;
    float: none;
    padding-bottom: 1.25%;
  }
  .navbar {
    width: auto;
    float: none;
  }
  .navbar ul {
    margin-bottom: 0;
  }
}
```

Now the design looks better (**Figure 10.35**).

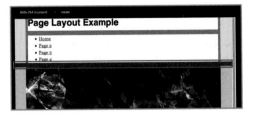

FIGURE 10.34
An ugly gap occurs because of a margin being applied to the bottom of the navigation element.

STEP 10.3.5

The next concern comes with the primary and secondary content boxes getting a little too narrow. Depending upon the text you have, you may require a different breakpoint, but for this demonstration, establish a new media query at 700px after the previous media query closes (about line 102 in the text editor).

```
@media screen and (max-width:700px) {
}
```

FIGURE 10.35
The gap no longer appears between the navigation element and the image.

STEP 10.3.6

In this rule, for the `.primary` and `.secondary` class selectors, set the `float` to `none` and the `width` to `auto`:

```
@media screen and (max-width:700px) {
  .primary {
    width: auto;
    float: none;
  }
  .secondary {
    width: auto;
    float: none;
  }
}
```

Now that all the floats are gone, the bottom paragraph margin creates a gap before the footer (**Figure 10.36**).

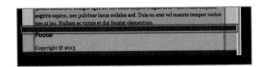

FIGURE 10.36
A gap occurs because of the clearfix rule on the `.group` class selector—with the `:after` pseudo class—used to clear floats.

WHY AUTO WIDTH?

The initial value of a block-level element is `auto`. By setting the value of `auto`, the element contained within the parent can expand to occupy all available space within its containing block. More on this can be found in a short article entitled "The Difference Between width: auto and width: 100%," by Roger Johansson at 456 Berea Street. (http://bit.ly/1bO7FHE).

MOBILE NAVIGATION CONCERNS

Mobile navigation layout will be discussed in Chapter 11.

STEP 10.3.7

In order to fill in the gap, simply apply the `overflow` property with the value of `auto` to the `.secondary` class selector.

```
@media screen and (max-width:700px) {
  .primary {
    width: auto;
    float: none;
  }
  .secondary {
    width: auto;
    float: none;
    overflow: auto;
  }
}
```

The footer looks much better and is nearly complete (**Figure 10.37**).

The last check will be for mobile devices that have a width of less than 480 pixels (**Figure 10.38**).

When considering mobile devices, there might be a need to remove an element that is not absolutely necessary—such as an image that gets too small to be useful (see sidebar note).

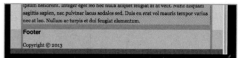

FIGURE 10.37
The gap between the two box elements is removed.

⟫ *IS THERE ANY BENEFIT TO NOT DISPLAYING THE IMAGE BUT ALLOWING THE HTML TO LOAD? WHILE THE IMAGE MAY NOT BE USEFUL FOR VISUAL REQUIREMENTS, SCREEN READERS CAN STILL DETECT THE IMAGE AND RELAY ITS CONTENT TO THOSE WHO ARE VISUALLY IMPAIRED.*

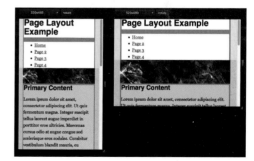

FIGURE 10.38
The layout shown with the viewport at 320 pixels wide in portrait and 480 pixels wide in landscape.

CONDITIONAL LOADING

While hiding content is simple with CSS, you should do so with caution, as the browser still loads the HTML that is requested. It's best to use scripting techniques that load content based upon "conditions"—e.g., if the screen is less than 480 pixels, then don't show the image. Resources for these methods can be found on the website.

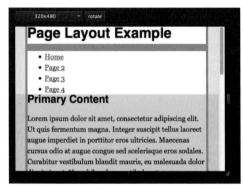

FIGURE 10.39
While the HTML still loads the content, CSS can hide it from view.

STEP 10.3.8

To hide an element for screen sizes below 480 pixels, simply add a media query (below the previous media query—around line 118) that applies the `display` property with the value of `none` for an `img` element:

```
@media screen and (max-width:480px) {
  img {
    display: none;
  }
}
```

>>> NOTE: *USE OF* `display:none;` *SHOULD BE LIMITED AND NEVER TO HIDE CONTENT FROM MOBILE USERS.*

When the page is resized to 480 pixels and below, the image no longer appears (**Figure 10.39**).

CONVERT PIXELS TO EMS

In the media queries you just created, all the values were in fixed pixels (px); however, you can easily convert them all to the relative measurement: em .

Why em? The short answer: to allow your design to scale if users happen to increase the browser font setting. The conversion is simple:

Take the value of the screen size of the media query—use 960, since it's the first media query.

Divide the screen size by 16px—the font size (remember Chapter 7, "CSS: Typography"?).

$960 \div 16 = 60em$

Do the same for the remaining values.

$800 \div 16 = 50em$

$700 \div 16 = 43.75em$

$480 \div 16 = 30em$

STEP 10.3.9

Now replace your px value with the new em value for each media query:

```
/* for 960 or less or 60em */
@media screen and (max-width:60em) {
  ...
}
/* for 800 or less or 50em */
@media screen and (max-width:50em) {
  ...
}
/* for 700px (43.75em) or less*/
@media screen and (max-width:43.75em) {
  ...
}
/* for 480  (or 30em) or less*/
@media screen and (max-width:30em) {
  ...
}
```

You may not see any immediate change in your website layout, but your site is now scalable if the user increases his font size (uses the "zoom" feature on his browser)!

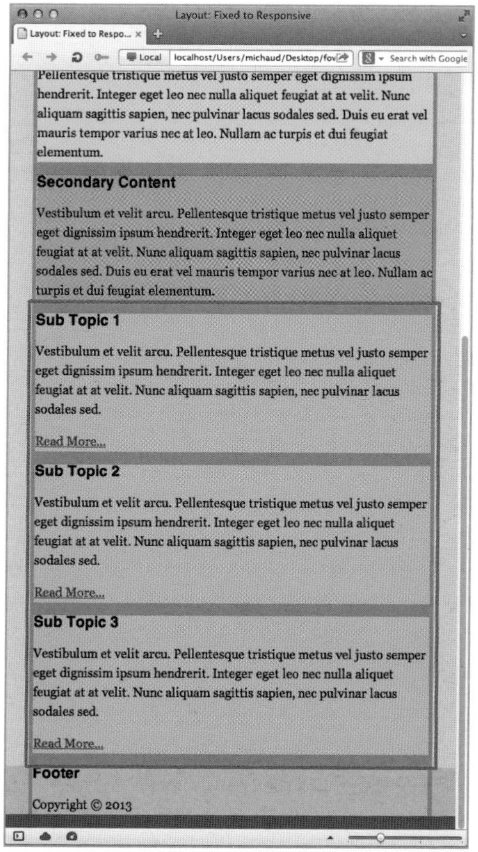

FIGURE 10.40
The three-column sub-topic boxes now become single columns when the browser is narrowed to 700 pixels or less.

The longer answer (a must-read) is well documented in a blog post called "The EMs have it: Proportional Media Queries FTW!" by Liz Gardner at Cloud Four (http://blog.cloudfour.com/the-ems-have-it-proportional-media-queries-ftw/).

CHALLENGE

Return to the **layout-challenge. css** document. From what you've just learned, create a rule within the media query for screens 700 pixels and smaller to make the .col-3 class selector's width automatically expand to the width of the parent container and no longer float (**Figure 10.40**).

While the basic CSS foundation is complete, there is one last concern that needs to be addressed for mobile devices—their viewport scaling.

VIEWPORT

While the responsive design has been working great in your desktop browser—as you resize the browser or use one of the responsive design tools—if you were to view the site on a mobile device, you would see a different story (**Figure 10.41**).

Not really "responsive" is it? Why?

The mobile device is not putting the media queries into action, but instead showing a tiny zoomed-out version of the desktop layout. Why? Mobile devices lie, and use a larger assumed viewport width to render sites at, the result of which is then shrunk to fit on the screen.

In order for the @media queries to work on mobile devices, you'll need to use the meta tag with the name attribute with the value viewport (a.k.a. the viewport meta tag).

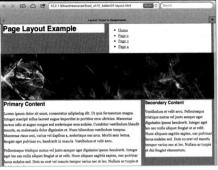
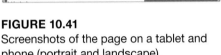
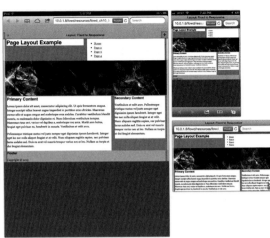

FIGURE 10.41
Screenshots of the page on a tablet and phone (portrait and landscape).

STEP 10.3.10

Return to your **01-layout.html** document; add the viewport meta tag after the title element.

```
<head>
<meta charset="utf-8">
<title>Layout: Fixed to Responsive</title>
<meta name="viewport" content=" ">
<link rel="stylesheet" href="css/normalize.css">
<link rel="stylesheet" href="css/demo-master.css">
<link rel="stylesheet" href="css/layout-responsive.css">
</head>
```

STEP 10.3.11

Within the content attribute there are a number of values you could add, but you just need to detect the width of the device.

```
<meta name="viewport"
content="width=device-width">
```

OPTIONAL SCALE SETTING

Since the media queries have been optimized for different screen sizes, you can (if you wish) prevent the user from scaling the web page.

```
<meta name="viewport"
content="width=device-width,
initial-scale=1.0, user-
scalable=no">
```

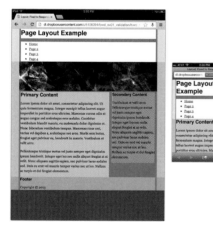

FIGURE 10.42
Screenshot of tablet and phone with the viewport meta tag at work.

STEP 10.3.12

Then, add another value (separated by a comma) where the initial scale sets the web page to fit within the visible area.

```
<meta name="viewport"
content="width=device-width, initial-
scale=1.0">
```

⟫ *THE VALUE OF 1.0 MEANS NO INITIAL ZOOM BUT TELLS THE BROWSER TO SET THE VIEWPORT TO THE WIDTH OF THE DEVICE WITH AN INITIAL SCALE OF 1. IT ALSO ALLOWS THE USER TO ZOOM.*

⟫ *THE* user-scalable *PROPERTY SETS WHETHER THE USER CAN ZOOM IN AND OUT OF A WEB PAGE. IT CAN BE SET TO* yes *OR* no.

⟫ *HOWEVER, IT'S HIGHLY ADVISED, FOR BEST ACCESSIBILITY, TO ALLOW USERS TO SCALE.*

That's it! Now the site renders properly on mobile devices (**Figure 10.42**).

You've now changed your fixed layout into a responsive layout, but there's plenty more to learn. While resources are listed on the website, make sure you bookmark the Responsive Resources website by Brad Frost: http://bradfrost.github.io/this-is-responsive/resources.html.

WRAPPING THINGS UP

You've developed a fixed layout using floats and transformed it into a fluid layout that is mobile-ready. Remember, when planning a new site, it's best to lay out the mobile version first—to help you plan your content strategy for mobile layout and for progressive design (as you get more and more real estate). Certainly there's more to learn, but you have a solid foundation to create a layout for any site. However, there's one part of the layout that isn't complete: the navigation.

In the upcoming chapter, we'll focus on styling navigation. There's a lot to consider when styling your navigation:

- Should it be horizontal?
- Should it be vertical?
- How will it display on a mobile device

When you're ready, head over to Chapter 11 and get started!

⟫ *DOWNLOAD REMINDER: THERE IS BONUS CONTENT TO DOWNLOAD FOR ADDITIONAL WORK ON LAYOUTS AND AN ASSIGNMENT TO TEST YOUR SKILLS!*

NAVIGATION

11

CHAPTER CODE

>>> *THE CODE EXAMPLES FOR THIS CHAPTER CAN BE DOWNLOADED FROM THE WEBSITE (HTTP://FOUNDATIONSOFWEBDESIGN.COM).*

When traveling to an area that's unfamiliar to you, it's helpful to have a map to navigate around with. When visitors navigate around a website, it's good to have areas clearly marked where they can find the content they want. Navigation is an essential concern as you work on the layout of your (or your client's) website. Here are some questions you should ask when developing your website's navigation design:

- How many pages will your site have?

- What will the pages be called?

- Will there be sub-pages to a parent page?

- What kind of navigation would work best—a standard list of links, a site map, a search form, or multiple types?

- Will you need breadcrumb navigation?

- Will it be located on the top, bottom, right, or left?

- Will the navigation menus be vertical, horizontal, or a combination?

- How will it look on mobile devices?

In this chapter, you'll learn how to code and style some of these navigation types.

THE HTML OF NAVIGATION

Before getting into the CSS of navigation, it's best to consider some patterns in HTML for navigation content.

UNORDERED LISTS

The most common HTML navigation pattern is the unordered list:

```
<nav role="navigation">
<ul>
  <li><a href="#">Home</a></li>
  <li><a href="#">About</a></li>
  <li><a href="#">Portfolio</a></li>
</ul>
</nav>
```

This pattern results in a vertical, bulleted display of links (**Figure 11.1**).

- Home
- About
- Portfolio

FIGURE 11.1
A navigation menu with block-level elements displays vertically.

Why an unordered list? Many will say it's similar to a table of contents in a book (listing the numbered chapters). However, the listing of the pages in your site doesn't mean the user will select the navigation in a specific (sequential) order—hence an unordered list rather than an ordered list.

>>> *MOST (IF NOT ALL) CONTENT MANAGEMENT SYSTEMS AUTOMATICALLY OUTPUT PAGE LISTS AS UNORDERED LISTS BY DEFAULT.*

THE NAV ELEMENT

The HTML5 nav element will be used extensively throughout this chapter, as it's a useful way to define the section of your site dealing with navigation (no matter what type of navigation you're using).

Some suggest, although the HTML5 specification is a little fuzzy, only using the nav element around the primary site-navigation links.

The nav element, versus writing <div class="nav">, helps to provide more structural meaning. While this may someday help screen readers, the ARIA role="navigation" is well supported by screen readers.

ORDERED LISTS

Could there ever be a time to use an ordered list? Maybe, if the site is built like an instruction manual or a storybook where sequential order is essential—to guide the user from Step 1 to Step 2 and so forth, sequentially:

```
<nav role="navigation">
<ol>
  <li>
    <a href="">Step 1: Beginning</a>
  </li>
  <li>
    <a href="">Step 2: Middle</a>
  </li>
  <li>
    <a href="">Step 3: End</a>
  </li>
</ol>
</nav>
```

This results in a vertical, sequentially numbered display of links (**Figure 11.2**).

1. Step 1: Beginning
2. Step 2: Middle
3. Step 3: End

FIGURE 11.2
Sequential navigation could be appropriate for a website that requires the user to visit pages in a specific order.

Home
Description about the page

About
Description about the page

Portfolio
Description about the page

FIGURE 11.3
A description list for navigation could provide useful descriptions for pages.

DESCRIPTION LISTS

However, one could make an argument for using a description list—where the title is the page link and a description gives a brief note about the page.

```
<nav role="navigation">
<dl>
  <dt>
    <a href="">Home</a>
  </dt>
  <dd>Description about the page</dd>
  <dt>
    <a href="">About</a>
  </dt>
  <dd>Description about the page</dd>
  <dt>
    <a href="">Portfolio</a>
  </dt>
  <dd>Description about the page</dd>
</dl>
</nav>
```

The result creates a vertical display of links with a description below each (**Figure 11.3**).

While this could be done with an unordered list (along with a generic span element), it really wouldn't be as semantically correct as using a description list.

```
<nav role="navigation">
<ul>
  <li><a href="">Home</a>
    <span>
    Description about the page
    </span>
  </li>
  <li><a href="">About</a>
    <span>
    Description about the page
    </span>
  </li>
  <li><a href="">Portfolio</a>
    <span>
    Description about the page
    </span>
  </li>
</ul>
</nav>
```

With a little styling, you can display the page name on one line and the description on another (**Figure 11.4**).

Home	About	Portfolio
Description about the page	Description about the page	Description about the page

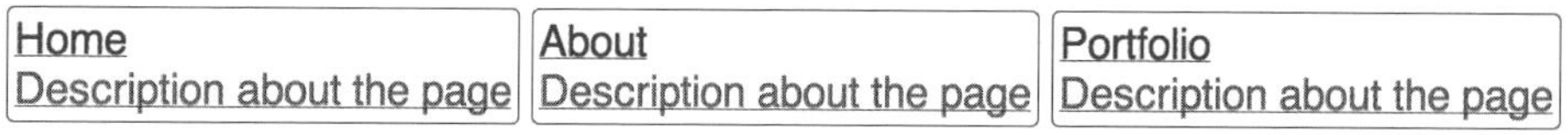

FIGURE 11.4
Descriptions can be added to unordered lists with the addition of inline elements.

NO LISTS

Finally, there are even some web designers who have discussed doing away with lists altogether:

```
<nav role="navigation" class="navbar">
  <a href="#">Home</a>
  <a href="#">About</a>
  <a href="#">Portfolio</a>
</nav>
```

>>> NOTE: *THE PAGE NAME AND DESCRIPTION ARE BOTH PART OF THE LINK— THIS MAY OR MAY NOT BE THE DESIRED OUTCOME YOU DESIRE.*

This results in a horizontal display of links (**Figure 11.5**).

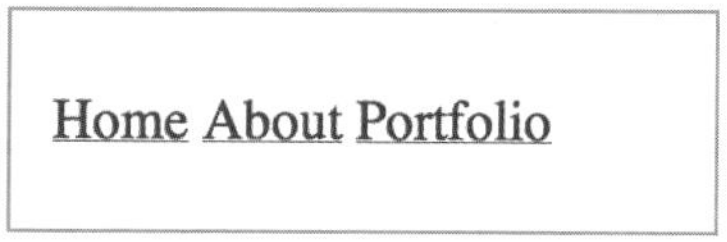

Home About Portfolio

FIGURE 11.5
A navigation menu without block-level elements displays horizontally.

While this option offers a few positives for a smaller site, they may not be enough to break the established pattern of using lists inside links for structure (because lists can provide an easier method for defining hierarchical structure for sub-menus).

>>> *EXAMPLES IN THIS CHAPTER WILL BE USING UNORDERED LISTS TO STRUCTURE NAVIGATION.*

TYPES OF NAVIGATION

Basically, there are two types of traditional navigation menus: vertical and horizontal. While there are other atypical/artistic navigation patterns, it's good to start with fundamentals.

VERTICAL NAVIGATION

Links, as you now know, structured with the block-level unordered list element display vertically. Sites use vertical navigation when displaying long lists of departments, teams, or other selections (**Figure 11.6**).

FIGURE 11.6
Zappos and Amazon use vertical lists to display long lists of different departments.

Open the folder for this chapter, and in the **01-nav-vertical.html** document, you'll see your navigation list ready to go:

```
<nav role="navigation">
<ul class="primary">
  <li><a href="#">Home</a></li>
  <li><a href="#">Electronics</a></li>
  <li><a href="#">Books</a></li>
  <li><a href="#">Home &amp; Garden
    </a></li>
  <li><a href="#">Toys</a></li>
  <li><a href="#">Sports</a></li>
  <li><a href="#">Automotive</a></li>
</ul>
</nav>
```

The website shows the list displayed vertically, as expected (**Figure 11.7**).

FIGURE 11.7
The default vertical navigation list currently stacks between the site title and the content.

Now, the first objective is to bring the list to the left side of the content. From the previous chapter, you know the commonly used method to create a two-column look is to set the width on both elements and float them.

STEP 11.1.1

To add the CSS rules for your navigation, open the **nav-vertical.css** document in the css folder.

Using the role attribute selector and class selector for the .primary content, set the width and float it to the left.

```
div[role="main"] .primary {
  width:78.3333333%;
  /* 940px ÷ 1200px */
  float:left;
}
```

STEP 11.1.2

Using the `role` attribute selector again, with the descendant `ul` element selector, select the unordered list and

- Set the width.

- float the unordered list left.

- Remove any padding.

- Remove the bullet list-style, padding, and top margin.

- Add margin-right and -left and a border-right.

WHAT HAPPENED TO 960PX?

In the last chapter, you used 960 pixels (for the parent element) to determine the percentages for the fluid width of child elements. However, not every client will want her design to be 960 pixels, so it's good practice to try different values.

```
nav[role="navigation"] ul {
  width: 18.3333333%;
  /* 220px ÷ 1200px */
  float: left;
  list-style: none;
  /* removes the bullets */
  padding: 0;
  /* removes the padding that
  indents the li elements */
  margin-top: 0;
  margin-right: .8333333%;
  /* 10 ÷ 1200 */
  margin-left: .8333333%;
  /* 10 ÷ 1200 */
  border-right: 1px solid #aaa;
}
```

Now you'll find the navigation menu is to the left of the website's primary content (**Figure 11.8**).

STEP 11.1.3

FIGURE 11.8
The navigation list has moved to the left and the content to the right.

The second objective is to add more clickable (or touchable, for mobile) space around the links—currently, the user will have to tap right on the word to activate the link.

In the new rule, you'll still use the `role` attribute selector, but using the descendant selector, you'll move from the `ul` element to `li` to the `a` (anchor) element.

The CSS is selecting the *a* element within the `ul` list:

```
<ul class="primary">
  <li><a href="#">Home</a></li>
```

And apply this CSS to the selection:

```
nav[role="navigation"] ul a {
  display: block; /* block elements
span the whole width*/
  padding: 6px 0; /*adds clickable
space above & below the text */
  font-weight: bold; /* highlight
links a bit more */
}
```

- The `display` property transforms the inline element into a `block`-level element that will span the entire width of the containing `li` element, increasing the clickable area to the right.

- The `padding` will increase the clickable space above and below the *a* element.

- Increasing the `font-weight` will help to highlight the navigation links.

The result shows increased visual and clickable space for the navigation list (**Figure 11.9**).

FIGURE 11.9
The vertical navigation list has more breathing room and clickable area.

If you hover past the right of the text, you'll see the clickable area extends beyond the text, but visually (unless you highlight the area in Photoshop) you can't really tell (**Figure 11.10**).

FIGURE 11.10
Area highlighted to show the clickable space.

STEP 11.1.4

Remember (from Chapter 5), you can help users to see this area, whether they use a mouse (using the pseudo-class `:hover`) or keyboard (using the pseudo-class `:focus`) via CSS:

```
nav[role="navigation"] ul a:focus,
nav[role="navigation"] ul a:hover {
    background: #ddd;
}
```

STEP 11.1.5

However, don't leave out the users on touch screens. While there is no :touch pseudo-class, using `:active` can help them when they press the link to see where they've pressed:

```
nav[role="navigation"] ul a:active {
    background: #ddd;
}
```

Now users get feedback when they hover or use the keyboard (**Figure 11.11**).

FIGURE 11.11
A background color now shows which link a user will select.

You've done it! Okay, while it's not taking mobile into account (yet), you've got the basics of styling a vertical navigation menu on the left side.

REMOVING UNDERLINES FROM LINKS

Back in Chapter 5, in the section about the `:hover` pseudo-class, you learned that the CSS property `text-decoration` allows you to remove underlines for links by setting the value to none. While it's not always advisable to remove the underlines from links in the body copy, removing them from navigation menus can help the links look a little cleaner and more like buttons.

If you apply the following code to the **master.css** document, all the links in the navigation examples will no longer have an underline:

```
nav[role="navigation"] a {
  text-decoration: none;
}
```

OPTIONAL: RIGHT NAVIGATION

STEP 11.1.5B

If you want to move the navigation to the right, it only requires a few simple changes and additions:

```
nav[role="navigation"] ul {
  width: 18.3333333%; /* 220px ÷ 1200px
*/
  float: right;
  list-style: none; /* removes the
bullets */
  padding: 0; /* removes the padding
that indents the li elements */
  margin-top: 0;
  margin-right: .8333333%; /* 10 ÷ 1200
*/
  margin-left: .8333333%; /* 10 ÷ 1200
*/
  border-left: 1px solid #aaa;
  text-align: right;
}
```

By changing the `float` from left to right, changing `border-right` to `border-left`, and setting the `text-align` to the `right`, you move the navigation menu to the right (**Figure 11.12**).

FIGURE 11.12
Simple changes can move the navigation menu from the left side of the layout to the right.

CURRENT PAGE

Another visual cue you can give users is to inform them of what page they're on by highlighting the navigation link that corresponds to the current page.

FIGURE 11.13
Highlighting a link can help users know what page they're on.

STEP 11.1.6

In your example, consider the page you're on to be the "Home" page. To help you set a style on the link, you'll need to add a `class` attribute with the value of `current` to your navigation list in your **01-nav-vertical.html** document.

```
<nav role="navigation">
  <ul class="primary">
    <li class="current">
      <a href="#">Home</a>
    </li>
    <li><a href="#">Electronics</a></li>
    ...
    <li><a href="#">Automotive</a></li>
  </ul>
</nav>
```

Then, returning to the **nav-vertical.css** document, add a `.current` class selector that changes the `color` and `background`:

```
.current a {
  color: #333;
  background: #ddd;
}
```

Now the "Home" link is highlighted (**Figure 11.13**).

So, if you were to create an "electronics.html" document, the navigation list on that document would have the `class="current"` attribute and value pair on the "Electronics" link.

```
<nav role="navigation">
  <ul class="primary">
    <li><a href="#">Home</a></li>
    <li class="current">
      <a href="#">Electronics</a>
    </li>
    ...
    <li><a href="#">Automotive</a></li>
  </ul>
</nav>
```

RESPONSIVE VERTICAL NAVIGATION

Now, if you narrow the browser until the border on the right of the navigation menu is touching the longest link, "Home & Garden" (**Figure 11.14**), the layout starts to break down. In this case, you might consider adding in a media query to change the layout for the navigation at this point.

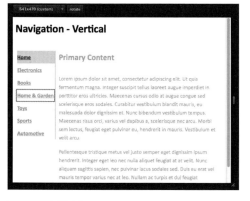

FIGURE 11.14
As the width of the navigation box decreases on mobile devices, it might be time for a media query to reposition the box.

A media query should probably be set to change the layout when the viewport width is 640 pixels or smaller.

>>> *REMEMBER, FOR LAYOUT AND FONT SCALING, IT'S BEST TO SET THE VALUE AS EM VERSUS PX: 640 PIXELS ÷ 16 PIXEL FONT = 40EM.*

The design goal is now to move the navigation menu from the left side to back above the content. To do this, remove the float from the navigation list by setting it to none. Set its width to auto (so it expands to the width of the parent container). Finally, remove its border on the right side with a value of none.

```
@media screen and (max-width: 40em) {
  nav[role="navigation"] ul {
    float: none;
    width: auto;
    border-right: none;
  }
}
```

The content below the navigation menu needs similar treatment. The following rule removes the float from the primary content box and sets its width to expand to the width of the parent container:

```
div[role="main"] .primary {
  float: none;
  width: auto;
}
```

STEP 11.1.9

This final rule adds a border on the bottom of each anchor element in the menu, to aid in visually separating the links:

```
nav[role="navigation"] ul li a {
  border-bottom: 1px solid #ccc;
}
```

When you save and then resize your browser, you'll find the navigation menu has returned to the top of the page (**Figure 11.15**).

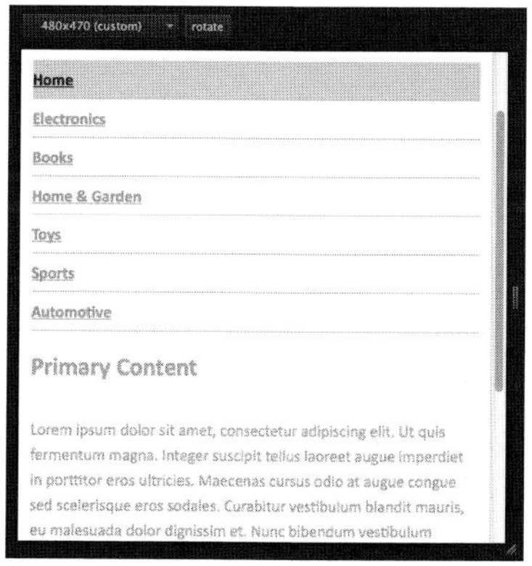

FIGURE 11.15
A basic responsive navigation solution to a narrower viewport.

>>> REMEMBER TO ALWAYS CHECK THAT YOUR DOCUMENT IS READY FOR MOBILE DEVICES WITH THE VIEWPORT META TAG:

```
<meta name="viewport"
content="width=device-width, initial-
scale=1">
```

This is a basic solution, and the navigation could be pretty long for sites with a lot of page (and sub-page) links, which would result in an unsightly whole page of links. You will, however, soon learn about how to address such issues. For now, you've laid the foundation.

On to developing a horizontal navigation bar!

HORIZONTAL NAVIGATION

While the stacked, vertical display is the default for lists, horizontal navigation bars are one of the most common patterns in navigation (**Figure 11.16**).

FIGURE 11.16
Personal websites and large corporations often utilize the horizontal navigation bar.

In your **02-nav-horizontal** document, you'll find the unordered list structuring the navigation:

```
<nav role="navigation">
  <ul class="primary navbar">
    <li class="current">
        <a href="#">Home</a>
    </li>
    <li><a href="#">About</a></li>
    <li><a href="#">Portfolio</a></li>
    <li><a href="#">Contact</a></li>
    <li><a href="#">Blog</a></li>
  </ul>
</nav>
```

When viewing the document in the browser, you'll see the stacked navigation list between the main title of the page and the content (**Figure 11.17**).

FIGURE 11.17
The default vertical navigation starting point.

STEP 11.2.1

The first step, in your **nav-horizontal.css** document, will be to style the unordered list and the list items:

```css
nav[role="navigation"] ul {
    border: 1px solid #ccc;
    border-width: 1px 0;
    list-style: none;
    margin: 0;
    padding: 0;
    text-align: center;
}
```

The first rule set above simply styles the unordered list a little by removing padding, margin, and bullets, centering the text, and adding a border on the top and bottom of the navigation bar.

FIGURE 11.18
The vertical list now becomes horizontal and centered in the design.

```css
nav[role="navigation"] li {
    display: inline;
}
```

The second rule set transforms the display of the block-level list elements. By default, they expand to the width of the containing element and create a new line, but `display: inline;` turns them into inline-level elements that sit alongside one another on the same line (**Figure 11.18**). See the sidebar about using a float in this instance.

USING FLOAT VS. INLINE

Could you have used `float: left` rather than `display: inline`? Yes, and it's also a common practice. However, floating the `li` will collapse the containing `ul` box element (**Figure 11.19**), move the all the links left (allowing for no text centering), and would require you to use the "clearfix" method or `overflow: auto` and `width: 100%`, as presented in Chapter 9.

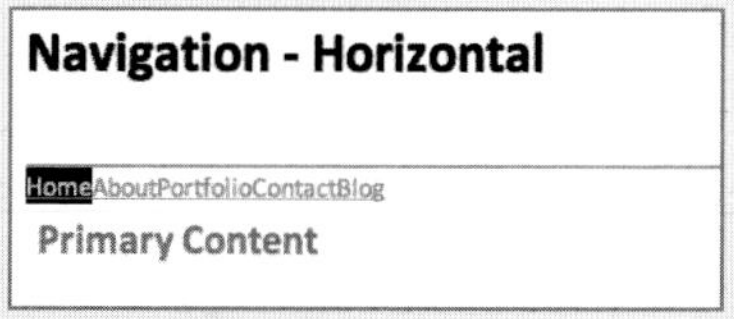

FIGURE 11.19
Using the `float` property to achieve a horizontal navigation bar.

STEP 11.2.2

The next step is to add some clickable space to the links:

```
nav[role="navigation"] a {
    display: inline-block;
    padding: 0 .625em;/* 10px ÷ 16 */
    line-height: 2.75em;
}
```

The `inline-block` value, if you remember from Chapter 9, allows you to render an element as inline, but with some block-level abilities (which is perfect for styling *a* elements). Adding the `padding` to the left and right and increasing the `line-height` centers the text nicely and provides more area to click or tap (**Figure 11.20**).

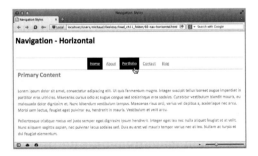

FIGURE 11.20
An inline-block element allows for space to be added on the left and right of the inline anchor element.

REMEMBER THE :ACTIVE PSEUDO-CLASS

While you don't need to worry, for this step, about the `:active` pseudo-class for the tap (**Figure 11.21**), as it's already been provided (see line 8 of nav-horizontal.css), it's something to always keep in mind!

```
a:active {
    color: #333;
    background: #F7A236;
}
```

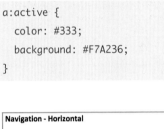

FIGURE 11.21
The `:active` area gives visual feedback when a user clicks or taps on a link.

STEP 11.2.3

If your navigation bar was small enough to fit to the right of the site name or logo, you could set the width for both the h1 and the navigation bar and float both elements:

```
h1 {
    width: 48.3333333%;
    /* 580px ÷ 1200px */
    float: left;
}
nav[role="navigation"] ul {
    width: 48.3333333%;
    /* 580px ÷ 1200px */
    float: left;
    margin-top: 10px;
    /*add space above the navigation */
}
```

This will now place the name and menu bar on the same level (**Figure 11.22**).

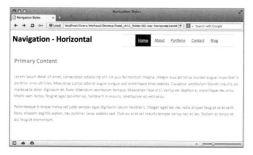

FIGURE 11.22
Short navigation bars could be on the same level as the site name and/or logo.

RESPONSIVE HORIZONTAL NAVIGATION

The final goal will be to address responsive design as the screen narrows. When the width of the design hits 693 pixels, the navigation bar moves to two lines (**Figure 11.23**). This could be a good time for a media query to adapt your layout.

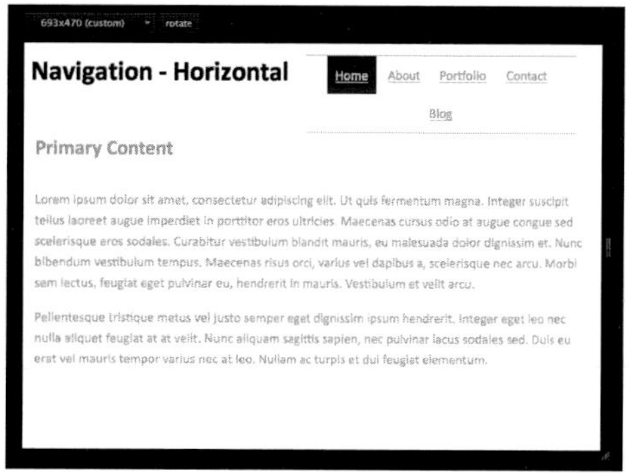

FIGURE 11.23
The navigation bar "breaks" into two lines as the viewport narrows.

>>> *REMEMBER, NAVIGATION LINKS WILL VARY IN SIZE. ALTHOUGH THE DESIGN IN THE DEMONSTRATION MAY BREAK AT 693 PIXELS, YOU'LL NEED TO TEST YOUR DESIGNS AND SEE WHERE CHANGES OCCUR ON YOUR PROJECTS.*

STEP 11.2.4

While you may not realize it, you already know the solution to this problem! Simply remove the float from the navigation bar and the h1 at a screen width of 694 pixels or less—and transform 694px into em by dividing it by 16. But you already knew that (from Chapter 10).

```
/* 694px max */
@media screen and (max-width:43.375em) {
  h1,
  nav[role="navigation"] ul {
    width: auto;
    float: none;
    margin-bottom: 5%;
    /* helps to center nav between the
    headers */
  }
}
```

The result allows the navigation bar to slip under the header (**Figure 11.24**).

FIGURE 11.24
Removing the floats allows
the navigation bar to move
under the header.

FIGURE 11.26
The navigation list is vertical
for small screens.

However, notice that the width is
becoming too narrow for the navigation
bar to retain the single line for the
horizontal layout (**Figure 11.25**).

FIGURE 11.25
The navigation bar will display on two lines
on many phones—on portrait rotation.

When viewed on a phone with a viewport
width of 320 pixels, the design is still
functional but doesn't look as appealing.

STEP 11.2.5

One solution would be to add in one
more media query that would revert your
list to a vertical display:

```
/* 360px max */
@media screen and (max-width: 22.5em) {
  nav[role="navigation"] li a {
    display: block;
    border-bottom: 1px solid #ccc;
  }
}
```

This gives you a vertical navigation bar
with some lines to help visually separate
each clickable box (**Figure 11.26**).

Can you believe what you've just
accomplished over these few pages?
You've

• Styled a vertical navigation menu.

• Styled a responsive navigation menu.

• Styled a horizontal navigation menu.

• Made the horizontal menu responsive.

• Highlighted a link to indicate what
  page the user is currently on.

• Helped those on touch devices get a
  visual response when they tap on a link.

While you can use vertical and horizontal
menus (or a combination of both) for any
website, vertical is primarily used for
long menus and horizontal for shorter
menus.

MORE RESPONSIVE NAVIGATION

This book only scratches the surface of responsive navigation. For more ideas on how to tackle responsive navigation, check out the website Adventures in Responsive Navigation, by Erick Arbe (http://responsivenavigation.net).

It is not ideal to have the navigation menu taking up the whole of the first page of a site, so for mobile apps, developers often put the menu at the bottom of the page or replace the vertical links menu with a <select> menu (or have it hidden under a single small menu button that can be clicked/tapped to reveal the whole menu).

These kinds of techniques often require a bit of JavaScript; see http://responsivenavigation.net for examples. However, you can put the menu at the bottom using the table-caption hack. See http://jsbin.com/axobun/1/edit for an example.

ADDITIONAL NAVIGATION PATTERNS

While there is more to navigation, you've developed the basic skills for creating common navigation elements. Before leaving this chapter, you'll want to know about some additional navigation patterns you may encounter in your projects.

BREADCRUMBS

Did you ever read or hear the fairytale of Hansel and Gretel? Hansel leaves a trail of breadcrumbs to follow to find their way back home as he and his sister are marched deep into the woods by their stepmother (and father, who apparently can't stand up to her). Anyway, if you haven't, read the story—you need to learn about breadcrumbs!

Breadcrumb navigation shows users where they are in the site (**Figure 11.27**).

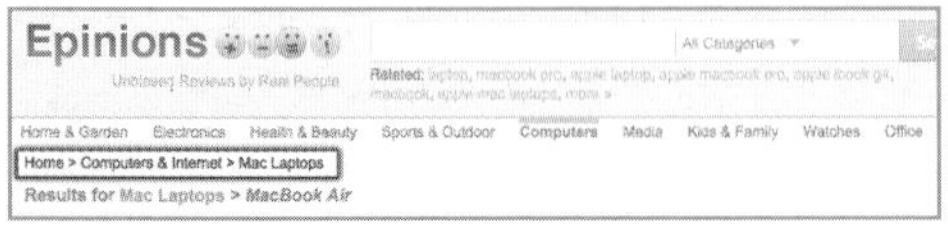

Maybe the visitor followed one link, then another, and another, and drilled down deep into a very large site. It is useful for him to know how to get back to the pages he's already visited. Of course, even for a small site, a breadcrumb can help users see the relationships between the main topic, sub-topics, and sub-sub-topics.

>>> *LEARN HOW: DOWNLOAD THE BONUS CONTENT FOR THIS CHAPTER TO LEARN HOW TO CREATE A BREADCRUMB MENU*

DROP DOWN MENUS

Drop-down menus can be "simple" or complex. The reason for quotes around "simple" is the fact that hiding and showing sub-menus is never as easy as it appears. Drop-down menus are used to show sub-topics of a parent topic, which you've probably seen before (**Figure 11.28**).

>>> *LEARN HOW: DOWNLOAD THE BONUS CONTENT FOR THIS CHAPTER TO LEARN HOW TO CREATE A DROP-DOWN MENU—THAT'S RESPONSIVE TOO!*

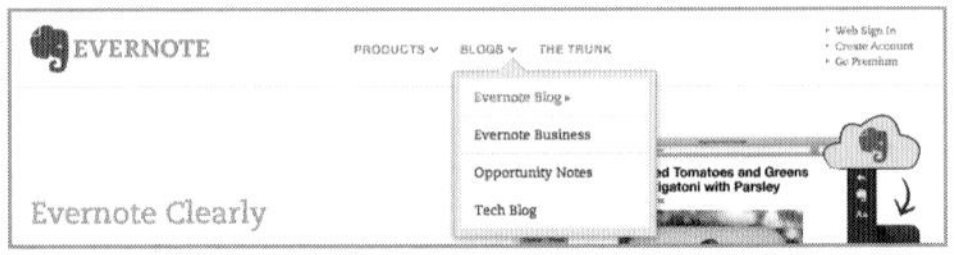

FIGURE 11.27
Simple breadcrumb navigation can help users orient themselves in a website.

FIGURE 11.28
Drop-down menus hide and reveal sub-topics as needed.

SITEMAPS

A sitemap is a list of links to pages accessible to users. It can also be useful for search engines indexing your site for search results. While you can code a sitemap by hand, for larger sites that could be very time-consuming. Some content management systems will develop a sitemap for you using server-side scripting. However, there are free online tools, like www.xml-sitemaps.com, available to create a sitemap for you that can be submitted to Google to help when their bots crawl or index your site. Although there's no guarantee as to the benefits, you certainly won't be penalized.

*>>> **LEARN HOW:** VIEW THE VIDEO TUTORIAL ON THE WEBSITE TO LEARN HOW TO CREATE A SITEMAP.*

SEARCH BOXES

Another way to find content on a site, besides using a navigation bar, is to use a search box. While you can add a search box to your website with some basic code

```
<form>
  <input name="search" type="search">
  <input type="submit" value="Find">
</form>
```

it won't do anything by itself—and how it's done is beyond the scope of this book. However, you can add a custom Google search box to your website for free at www.google.com/cse.

*>>> **LEARN HOW:** VIEW THE VIDEO TUTORIALS ON THE WEBSITE TO LEARN HOW ADD A GOOGLE SEARCH BOX TO YOUR WEBSITE.*

WRAPPING THINGS UP

Well, that's it for the foundations of developing navigation for your website. By now, you can develop a vertical or horizontal menu and add in responsive design as well. Do you think you could go back to Chapter 10 and make the navigation menu there a horizontal (and responsive) menu? A solution is provided in the Chapter 11 folder download.

Next up will be the basics on forms. While it takes more than HTML and CSS to get them to work, it's good to know some of the rudiments of creating a contact or search form.

*>>> **DOWNLOAD REMINDER:** THERE IS BONUS CONTENT TO DOWNLOAD FOR ADDITIONAL LEARNING ABOUT NAVIGATION AND AN ASSIGNMENT TO TEST YOUR SKILLS!*

FORMS

—

12

CHAPTER CODE

>>> THE CODE EXAMPLES FOR THIS CHAPTER CAN BE DOWNLOADED FROM THE WEBSITE (HTTP://FOUNDATIONSOFWEBDESIGN.COM).

Forms help visitors interact with the websites they visit. While the most common form you'll encounter is a search form (**Figure 12.1**), you've probably seen many other types:

- Account creation
- Online payment
- Newsletter subscription
- Feedback or comments

And many more.

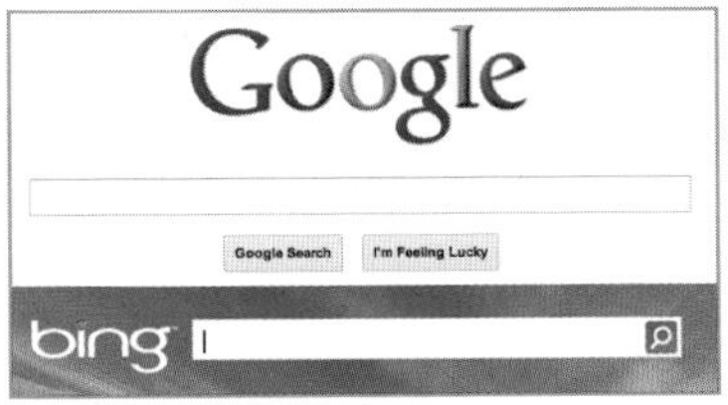

FIGURE 12.1
The search boxes on Google and Bing are good examples of a search form element in action.

HOW DO FORMS WORK?

While you've got the foundations of developing a static page, an HTML form requires a journey into developing a page that's actually interactive. Forms go beyond the basics of HTML and CSS (**Figure 12.2**). Forms are typically processed in the following steps:

- First, the visitor enters information into the required form fields

- When the "submit" button is clicked (and sometimes before) the data is checked to see if there are any errors. If there are none, the form data is submitted to the web server.

- The data is processed by a server scripting language such as PHP, ASP.NET, or Python.

- The data can then be sent to a database, file, or email (which is then sent to a company or individual).

- A response is normally sent to the visitor with a message indicating the success or failure of processing the form.

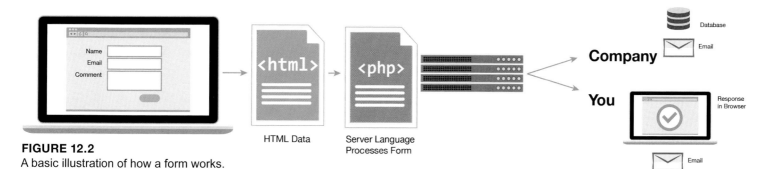

FIGURE 12.2
A basic illustration of how a form works.

SERVER SCRIPTING
LANGUAGES

Server scripting languages go beyond the scope of this book and require additional setup to run on your personal computer. Once you feel comfortable with HTML, CSS, and JavaScript, I'd suggest moving on to learning a language such as PHP.

PHP AVAILABLE

While we're not covering any PHP in this book, the website does provide a basic PHP script to help with getting your contact form to work on your web server.

FORM ELEMENTS

To begin with, you'll be introduced to many of the basic form elements—including a few from HTML5—and then you'll put them together and develop a contact form.

In your download for this chapter, open the **01-form.html** document and follow along to learn the form elements.

THE FORM ELEMENT

The `form` element establishes the form— much like the `table` element for tables:

STEP 12.1.1

```
<form>
</form>
```

By itself it displays nothing onscreen, but it does require two attributes—`action` and `method`.

THE ACTION ATTRIBUTE

The `action` attribute holds the address of where the form-processing script is on the server.

STEP 12.1.2

```
<form action="http://mywebsite.com/form-
processor.php">
</form>
```

THE METHOD ATTRIBUTE

The `method` attribute determines how the data from the form is sent to the server. This attribute accepts two values—`post` or `get`.

STEP 12.1.3

The `post` value submits the data from the form to the server, and the URL (`http://mywebsite.com/form-processor.php`) is never seen by the user. This method keeps data more secure. You should use this method for pretty much any form other than search forms.

```
<form action="http://mywebsite.com/form-
processor.php" method="post">

</form>
```

The `get` value adds values from the form into the URL address. This method is perfect for searches, as you can bookmark a URL search result (**Figure 12.3**).

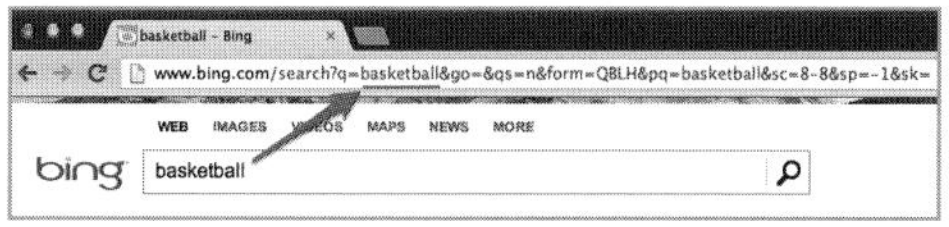

FIGURE 12.3
The `get` value adds the form values to the URL address—which can be bookmarked.

>>> **CAUTION:** *IF NO METHOD IS ATTRIBUTED TO, THE* get *METHOD IS USED BY DEFAULT.*

DATA INPUT

The self-closing `<input>` element allows visitors to enter their information in a number of ways. By assigning the `type` attribute (`<input type="value">` different values, you can set the input method to be a single line of text, a password, a radio button, a checkbox, a file upload, or a submit button.

FORM STRUCTURE MARKUP

In the initial set of demonstrations, the form will be structured using lists. While using a list (ordered or unordered) is not required, it can help denote steps in the form. Other structures may use divs, paragraphs, description lists, or only form elements.

TEXT TYPE

STEP 12.1.4

The `text` value creates a field allowing the user to enter one line of text (**Figure 12.4**).

```
<form action="http://mywebsite.com/form-
processor.php" method="post">
<ol>
    <li>Name <input type="text"
name="name"></li>
<ol>
</form>
```

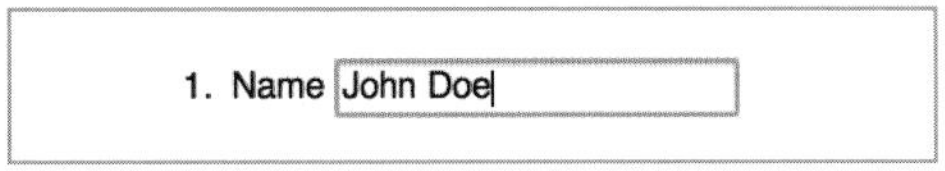

FIGURE 12.4
An input field with a `text` value for the `type` attribute.

>>> **NOTE:** *IF YOU WANT THE USER TO ENTER MULTIPLE LINES OF TEXT, USE THE* `textarea` *ELEMENT.*

The `name` attribute value aids the processing script that handles the form to identify the field.

>>> *IF THE* `input` *TYPE WAS FOR AN EMAIL ADDRESS, THE INPUT ELEMENT WOULD LOOK SOMETHING LIKE* email `<input type="text" name="email">`.

The `maxlength` attribute defines the maximum length of the field—how many characters can be entered (good for username fields that have a specific limit).

>>> **NOTE:** *WHILE SOME USE THE* `size` *ATTRIBUTE TO SET A WIDTH FOR THE INPUT FIELD, IT'S BEST TO USE CSS TO CONTROL PRESENTATIONAL SIZING.*

>>> *NARROW LOWERCASE LETTERS LIKE* f, i, j, *AND* l *ALLOW A CHARACTER OR TWO MORE TO FIT WITHIN THE VISIBLE FIELD.*

PASSWORD TYPE

If you're setting up a form that requires users to enter a password, use the `password` value. This field will not show the actual text input, to help shield the password from public view (**Figure 12.5**).

```
<ol>
  <li>Name <input type="text"
name="name"></li>
  <li>Password <input type="password"
name="password"></li>
</ol>
```

Again, you must set the `name` attribute to help the form-processing script to find the correct field. The `maxlength` and `size` attributes are optional.

>>> *CAUTION: WHILE THE TEXT FOR THE PASSWORD IS NOT SHOWN IN PLAIN TEXT, THIS DOES NOT GUARANTEE SECURITY—THAT IS A JOB FOR THE PROCESSING SCRIPT.*

RADIO TYPE

The `radio` value creates a single "button;" put multiple radio buttons together and users can select one out of a list of options. Think of them like the push buttons on an old-school radio or hi-fi, only one of which can be pushed in at a time (**Figure 12.6**).

```
<form action="http://mywebsite.com/form-
radio" method="post">
  <ul>
    <li>What size drink: <br>
      <input type="radio" name="drinksize"
value="large" checked="checked"> Large
      <input type="radio" name="drinksize"
value="medium"> Medium
      <input type="radio" name="drinksize"
value="small"> Small
    </li>
  </ul>
</form>
```

The `name` value must be the same for each separate radio button in the group.

The `value` attribute must be used and must indicate the value of the option selected.

The `checked` attribute with the value of `checked` causes the button to be preselected (no more than one radio button can have this setting per group).

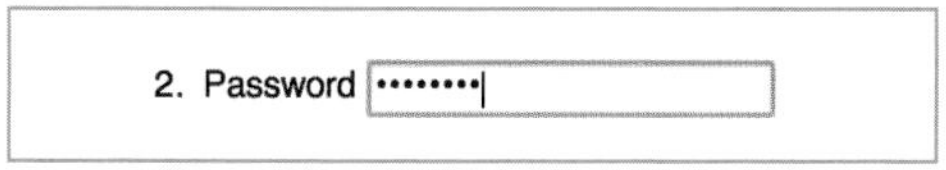

| 2. Password ••••••••| |

FIGURE 12.5
Password types hide the inputted text from view.

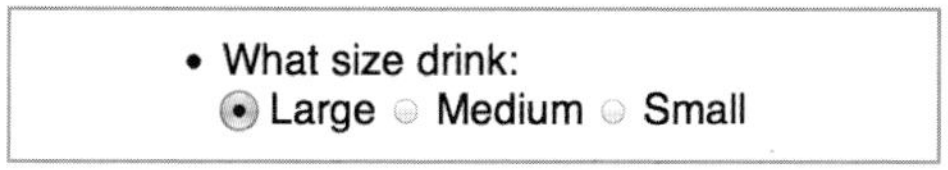

| • What size drink:
◉ Large ◯ Medium ◯ Small |

FIGURE 12.6
Buttons allow only a single choice.

CHECKBOX TYPE

STEP 12.1.7

The checkbox value creates boxes the visitor can select or deselect. Unlike radio buttons, any number of checkboxes can be selected simultaneously (**Figure 12.7**).

```
<form action="http://mywebsite.com/form-
checkbox.php" method="post">
<ul>
   <li>What fruit do you like?
   <input type="checkbox" name="fruit"
value="apple"> Apple
   <input type="checkbox" name="fruit"
value="banana"> Banana
   <input type="checkbox" name="fruit"
value="orange"> Orange
   </li>
</ul>
</form>
```

The name attribute allows the processing script to know which group the selections were from, and the value informs it of the specific choices.

As with radio buttons, you can assign the checked attribute with the value of checked to any selections you wish to preset.

- What fruit do you like? ☐ Apple ☑ Banana ☑ Orange

FIGURE 12.7
Multiple checkboxes can be selected.

If you find an element of your interface requires instructions, then you need to redesign it.

— Dan Rubin

FILE TYPE

The `file` value creates a button which, when pressed, brings up a file-select dialog box, allowing the visitor to select a file (.pdf, .doc, .mp3, image, etc.) from his computer to upload to the server (**Figure12.8A**).

```
<form action="http://mywebsite.com/form-
upload.php" method="post">
<ul>
  <li>Upload Resume
    <input type="file" name="resume"><br>
    <input type="submit" value="Upload">
  </li>
</ul>
</form>
```

After the file has been selected, the file name appears in the window (**Figure 12.8B**).

For this form to work, you must use the `post` method.

>>> SOME BROWSER FILE-UPLOAD BUTTONS WILL SAY "BROWSE" OR "CHOOSE."

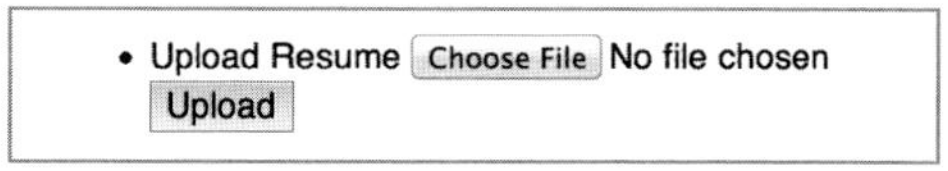

FIGURE 12.8A
The file-upload form as seen in the Google Chrome browser.

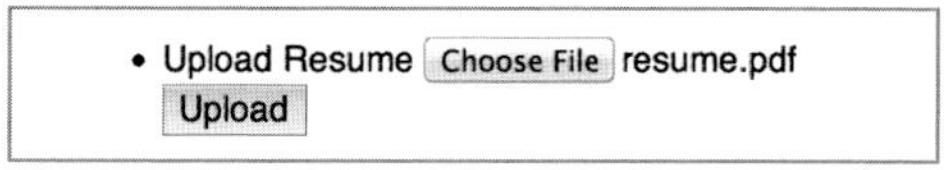

FIGURE 12.8B
A document has been selected to upload.

SUBMIT

The `submit` value creates a button allowing the visitor to submit a form for processing.

```
<form action="http://mywebsite.com/
form-submit.php" method="post">
  <input type="submit" value="Submit
My Application">
</form>
```

If the `value` attribute is not included, the default text on the button is "Submit." However, you can change the text on the button by entering in text for the value (**Figure 12.9**).

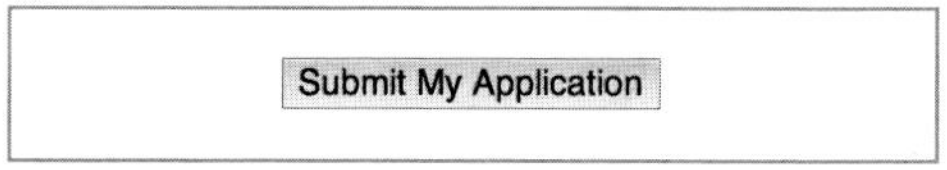

FIGURE 12.9
A submit button with a custom value.

TEXTAREA

The textarea element allows for input of multiple lines of text (e.g., comments on a blog, feedback, or requests). If more text is typed into the box than can be comfortably displayed, then a scroll bar will appear (**Figure 12.10**).

```
<form action="http://mywebsite.com/
form-comment.php" method="post">
  <ul>
    <li>Leave a Comment
    <textarea name="comment">I think...
</textarea>
    </li>
  </ul>
</form>
```

FIGURE 12.10
A text area allows input of multiple lines of text.

>>> *NOTE: THE AREA CIRCLED IN FIGURE 12.10. MOST MODERN BROWSERS ALLOW THE USER TO INCREASE (BUT NOT DECREASE) THE TEXT AREA'S SIZE AS DESIRED.*

The width and height of the textarea are controlled with the rows and cols attributes. However, as you know, it's best to control presentation with the width and height CSS properties.

If you place text between the <textarea>...</textarea> tags, and the visitor does not delete the text before submitting, it will submit with the form.

SELECT OPTION

If you wish to create a drop-down menu (e.g., to select a state or country) in a form, the `select` element defines the menu, and the `option` element populates the menu (**Figure 12.11**).

```
<form action="http://mywebsite.com/form-
menu.php" method="post">
  <li>What Month Were You Born?
  <select name="month">
   <option value="January">January
</option>
   <option value="February">February
</option>
  </select>
  </li>
</form>
```

The `name` setting, in the `select` element, helps the processing script to identify the field.

The `value` setting, in the `option` element, informs the processing script of the selection.

If you want to allow users to select multiple options, there is a way to make the drop-down menu a selection list, but checkboxes might be a better option.

>>> *NOTE: CHECK OUT THE WEBSITE FOR ADDITIONAL EXAMPLES ON HOW TO USE THE* select *ELEMENT.*

FIGURE 12.11
The `select` and `option` elements work together to develop a drop-down form menu.

LABELING FORMS

To make the form more accessible and usable, it's best to use the `label` element. It helps to connect the caption (such as "Name") with the control (such as `<input type="text" name="name">`).

- Accessibility is improved by allowing screen readers to see which `label` goes with which form element.

- Usability is improved, as the `label` makes the text associated with the form element a clickable area. This may help make radio buttons and checkboxes easier to select.

The association of the `label` element and the form control element (`input`, `textarea`, `select`, etc.) can occur in either of two ways:

- You can place the form element inside the `label` element.

```
<form method="post" action="http://
mywebsite.com/form-label.php">
  <label>Name: <input type="text"
name="name"></label>
</form>
```

>>> **NOTE:** *USING THE* for *AND* id *ATTRIBUTES CAN BE HELPFUL, AS THEY SUPPLY A VISUAL INDICATOR OF THE PURPOSE OF EACH FORM FIELD ON THE SCREEN AND GIVE THE FORM FIELDS MORE SEMANTIC MEANING. ADDITIONALLY, CSS AND JAVASCRIPT CAN USE THEM FOR STYLING AND INTERACTIVE "HOOKS."*

- You can associate the `label` element with the form element using the `for` and `id` attributes.

```
<form method="post" action="http://
mywebsite.com/form-label.php">
  <label for="form-name">Name: </
label><input type="text" name="name"
id="form-name">
</form>
```

Rendering in the browser is the same for both (**Figure 12.12**).

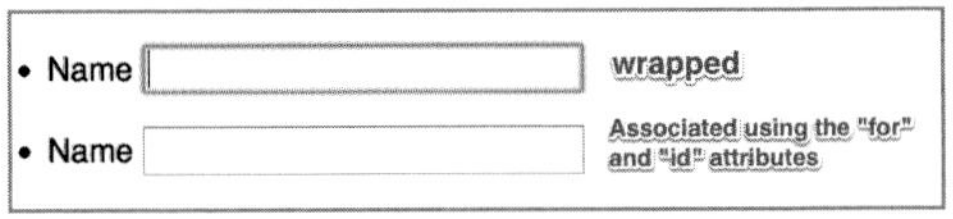

FIGURE 12.12
The `label` element does not change the appearance of the text or form controller.

RADIO AND CHECKBOX LABELS

For checkboxes and radio buttons, it's best (visually) if the `label` appears after (to the right of) the form control (radio button or checkbox). However, for accessibility, it's best if you have the `label` before the `input` element and use CSS to place it after the `input` element. Check the website for a demonstration.

FIELDSET

STEP 12.1.13

Forms can use the `fieldset` and `legend` elements to help group sections of long forms (**Figure 12.13**).

```
<form method="post" action="http://
mywebsite.com/form-fieldset.php">
<fieldset>
<legend>Address</legend>
<ul>
  <li><label>Street: <input type="text"
name="address"></label></li>
  <li><label>City: <input type="text"
name="city"></label></li>
  <li><label>Zip Code: <input
type="text" name="zip"></label></li>
</ul>
</fieldset>
</form>
```

For most browsers, the `fieldset` is displayed with a border that can be controlled with CSS.

The `legend` can help identify the grouping and appears within the `fieldset` border—it too can be individually styled with CSS.

FIGURE 12.13
Fieldsets can group sections of forms.

A CONTACT FORM

With all you've learned, it's time for you to develop a contact form.

In the download for this chapter, you're supplied with a **contact-form** folder that contains

- A **contact.html** document that contains comments to help you along

- A **contact_process.php** script that will allow the form to process

- An **autoresponse** folder with a **response.txt** document that is emailed to the person who submits a form

FORM

First, develop a basic contact form with which someone can contact you—to offer you a freelance web design gig! The form should allow the user to enter:

- His or her name (required)—already developed for you as an example

- His or her email address (required)

- A subject

- Details (within a text box) of the job offer

The submit button is already developed, as well as some other essential elements at the bottom of the form.

THANK YOU

Additionally, after the form is submitted, it will redirect the user to a "Thank You" page (thankyou.html) and send a confirmation email. Make sure you develop this page.

VIEW CHAPTER VIDEOS

To add required attributes with HTML5 elements, watch the videos online and download the "bonus" material for this chapter.

AUTOMATED RESPONSE

The **autoresponse** folder has a **response.txt** document that will be sent (by the server) as an email to the user who submits your form.

- You'll need to add your name to the document where it says "YOUR NAME HERE."

- You can modify the message.

- Don't touch {~name~}, as it uses the name the user enters in the contact form.

HELP ONLINE

If you get stuck, the video on the website can walk you through from beginning to end.

PROCESSING SCRIPT

The **contact_process.php** document has a lot going on, and most of it you don't need to worry about—and shouldn't touch. You only need to modify two lines:

Line 25: Replace your@emailaddress. here with your email address:

```
$default_destination_email = "your@
emailaddress.here";
```

Line 28: Replace Your Website's Name with your website name:

```
$site_name = "Your Website's Name";
```

I cannot stress this point enough, as many of my students forget despite numerous reminders. This form will not process until it gets uploaded to a web server or you have a local web server set up with MAMP (Mac) or XAMPP (Mac, Windows, and Linux). If you test it on your computer, you'll simply see the **contact_process.php** document code after clicking the submit button.

WRAPPING THINGS UP

By finishing this chapter, you've completed all the foundational components of HTML and CSS! Developing a form is your first transition from having a "static" website to having an interactive site. Believe me, it's a tremendous feeling when you get an email from someone who's visited your site—even when they inform you there's a problem on the site that needs fixing.

In the next chapter, you'll be introduced to the workflow of a web designer and learn the process of taking a site from idea to launch.

>>> *DOWNLOAD REMINDER: THERE IS BONUS CONTENT TO DOWNLOAD FOR ADDITIONAL LEARNING ABOUT FORMS AND AN ASSIGNMENT USING YOUR CONTACT FORM TO TEST YOUR SKILLS!*

PART

—

04

NEXT STEPS

	WORKFLOW
	LOOKING AHEAD

WORKFLOW

—

13

There is no miracle workflow.

—Trent Walton
@TrentWalton

When you work on a personal or client project, you'll find there are stages to the workflow of each. Sometimes you'll work with a team, and other times you'll work alone, but you'll find that no two projects are ever exactly alike.

One thing you'll find that's common to each project, however, is that some tasks and subtasks are always mandatory:

» Planning

» Designing

» Coding

» Launch

Quite often you'll be asked to maintain the website after launch as well.

You might think these tasks are linear (**Figure 13.1**):

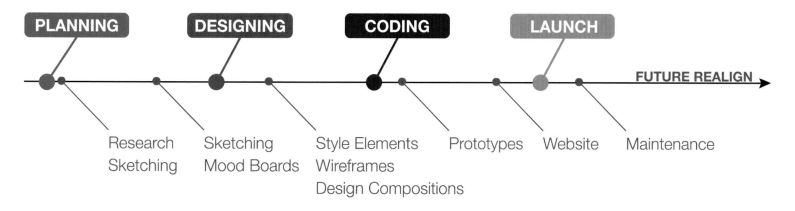

FIGURE 13.1
A traditional assembly-line approach to a project.

However, you'll come to find they will often overlap at each stage of the process (**Figure 13.2**):

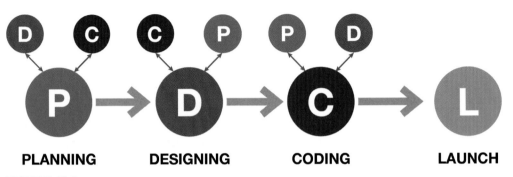

FIGURE 13.2
Each phase of a project involves various tasks of planning, designing, and coding.

During the **planning** stage, you'll find that research may include developing design elements and testing out ideas (forms, layout, menus, etc.) in code.

During the **design** stage, you'll continue to sketch out ideas, possibly research whether target users "get" the website, and code layout ideas in the browser.

During the **coding** stage, you'll research how your website works in various browsers, which will often lead to tweaking the design and content.

By the time you **launch** the website, each stage will have touched various aspects of each task. After the launch, you'll find the tasks continue with the upkeep of the website.

So, what types of tasks can you expect to face in a project? I'll introduce you to the basics of each here in the book and walk you through a small project on the website. Remember, this is not a sequential order of tasks, but it does suggest which tasks are most common to web projects.

❓ ASKING QUESTIONS

When you are developing a "plan," you're asking questions. You should always be asking questions throughout the process. You can start by using the five *W*s:

» **Who**? At the beginning of a project, you might ask: Who is the target audience? Who are the team members who are contributing to the site? Then, during the project, you may ask: Are we meeting our target audience's needs? Is the team working toward its goals?

» **What**? At the start of a project, ask: What is the site being developed for? What problems need to be solved? What content is needed? What look and feel will complement the content? Then, as you progress, ask: Are we solving the problems or are we off track?

» **Where**? When you begin the project, ask such questions as: Where will people be using the site? Where will they be coming from? During the project, see if any of these questions have been answered and whether the questions need to be asked again.

» **When**? At the beginning, you'll need to ask: When does this need to be complete? When is it good to get feedback from users? Then, during the project, continue to ask: Are we on time? Is it time to bring in people to test the website?

» **Why**? These questions ensure that you are staying on task and relate to all of the other questions.

You can see that some of these questions can't be answered all at once. Sometimes the project needs to progress before you are able to get the answers. However, start right away to ask as many questions as possible about the project (even for personal projects), and see what can be answered and what needs more time.

ORGANIZATIONAL
RESOURCES

To assist you with organizing your content, here is a list of a few applications that can help create your sitemap or mind map:

Slickplan
http://slickplan.com

draw.io
http://draw.io

MindNode
http://mindnode.com

OmniGraffle
(http://omnigroup.com/products/omnigraffle/)

Check the website for additional resources!

CONTENT

For an informational or e-commerce website, content is king. Depending upon the project, the content will be developed either by you or someone else, but that content will also need to be organized and categorized on the website.

>>> *LOW-TECH CARD SORT: SIMPLY WRITE OUT TOPIC IDEAS ON INDEX CARDS AND PLACE THEM IN A LOGICAL ORDER. GIVE THE CARDS TO OTHERS AND SEE IF THEY MATCH YOUR ORDER.*

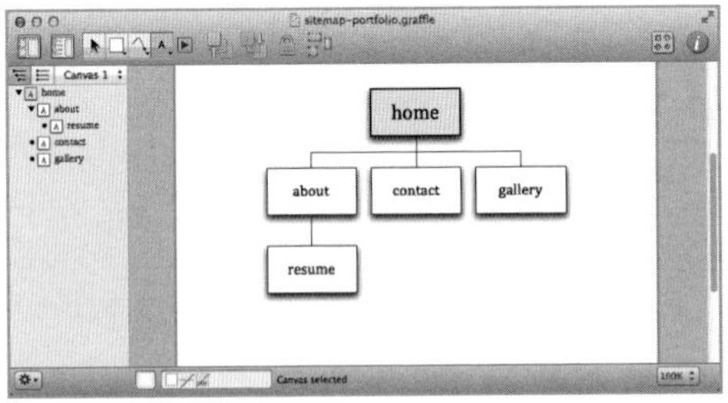

FIGURE 13.3
An example of OmniGraffle's organizational chart.

SITEMAP

A sitemap is a list of all the pages—and sub-pages—of the website. It's a way to organize the site's content without worrying about content details or design. You can write the names of the pages out on paper, use a word-processing document, or use an organizational application (**Figure 13.3**).

Sometimes, from the start, you'll know specifically what pages are required in a project; other times the sitemap will change a few times during the course of a project. If you don't know any (or all) of the pages, use a method called "mind mapping"—where you write out all possible topic names that could be pages. Later you can add, combine, or remove topics as the project gains more focus.

 **CATEGORIZE**

To plan the site content and design, you should determine what category the website falls within, such as:

» Portfolio

» Product

» Service

» News

Then, research what's already been done: what works and what doesn't work. While you don't want to rip off another website, study competing sites' content, layout, color, typography, and imagery. Then, start to ask questions: Is the content too much, too little, or just enough? Are the sites optimized for alternative devices such as smartphones, tablets, TVs? What colors are used, and why? Are there elements that would work well for your project?

TEXTUAL CONTENT

If you're developing a personal site, work on developing your content as early as possible. The text for each page doesn't have to be a final draft the first time around; the purpose is just to start writing the content for each page and refining as you progress.

If you have difficulty writing, you may need to hire someone to do it or (at the very least) have someone proofread your work—there's nothing quite like saying, "Hey, I'm a professional!" with a website full of grammatical and spelling errors!

 CONTENT AND DESIGN INSPIRATION

Design Bombs
http://designbombs.com

CSS Drive
http://cssdrive.com

CSSelite
http://csselite.com

Dribbble
http://dribbble.com

Visit the website for additional inspiration resources.

VISUAL LANGUAGE

If you're trying to figure out what type of mood and feel the design should have, a mood board is a great tool for inspiration. A mood board is a collection of colors, textures, patterns, images, and type related to the theme you're developing. While you could rip out pages from magazines and books (that you own), you could also take screenshots (see application list in the sidebar) of images and websites on your computer. You can compile the images in one large layout in an image editor or print them out (**Figure 13.4**).

FIGURE 13.4
An example of mood boards.

To take snapshots of websites, you can use the built-in screenshot feature on your computer.

OS SCREENSHOT

It can be very helpful to grab images from the screen when working on design ideas. Luckily there is built-in software to accomplish this.

MAC

» **Full Screen:** Command+Shift+3 allows you to take a screenshot of your entire monitor.

» **Single Window:** Command+Shift+4+Spacebar gives you a little camera icon that you can use to click on a window to get a window screenshot with a drop shadow.

WINDOWS

You can find a few different methods for Windows users at www.wikihow. com/Take-a-Screenshot-in-Microsoft-Windows.

» **Full Screen:** The Print Screen key may be labeled "Prt Sc," "Prnt Scrn," "Print Scrn," or similar. On most keyboards, the button is usually found next to the F12 and Scroll Lock keys. On laptop keyboards, you may have to press the Fn or Function key to access "Print Screen."

» **Single Window:** If you want to take a screenshot of just one window, make sure that the window is the "active" window on your screen. This means that it should be in front of all your other windows. Then, hold down the Alt key and press Print Screen.

You can also use an application (see sidebar).

SCREENSHOT TOOLS

PicPick (PC)
http://picpick.org/en/)

Skitch (PC/Mac)
http://evernote.com/skitch/

Awesome Screenshot (browser extension for Chrome and Firefox)
http://awesomescreenshot.com

Voila ($ Mac)
 http://globaldelight.com/voila/

Ember ($ Mac)
http://realmacsoftware.com/ember/

Snagit ($ PC/Mac)
http://techsmith.com/snagit.html

See the website for more mood board resources and demonstrations.

To organize a mood board a bit further, you could consider using a "Style Tile" (see sidebar resources), developed by Samantha Warren, that can help you define your visual language (**Figure 13.5**)—much like an interior decorator uses swatches of cloth, paint chips, and illustrations to describe his or her vision of a room to a client. While many templates are for Photoshop, you could use applications such as PowerPoint or Apple's Keynote, or any application you can add images to.

FIGURE 13.5
An example of a style tile to help convey the visual language of a project.

STYLE TILES AND ELEMENT COLLAGES

Visual language elements can be developed online or with a desktop application.

ONLINE

The Matboard
http://thematboard.com

Pinterest
https://pinterest.com

APPLICATIONS

Evernote
http://evernote.com

PHOTOSHOP TEMPLATES

Style Tiles
http://styletil.es/

404 Creative
http://bit.ly/16ioox

Check out the website for more style tile resources and demonstrations.

SKETCHING

Sketching is useful in all three areas (planning, designing, and coding)—you'll find yourself sketching out ideas (in part and in whole) throughout the project. Sketching allows you to draw out lots of ideas quickly, without having to worry about the content, before opening an image editor or text editor (**Figure 13.6**).

Let me stress this point: you don't need to be an artist to sketch out ideas—simple shapes (boxes, circles, lines, etc.) are very helpful for capturing ideas. However, you'll find the more you sketch, the easier it becomes.

Here are a few of the basic tools:

» Pencil: A nonintimidating tool that allows you erase errant marks—but try not to erase ideas (a previous idea may work out best).

» Pen: Helps to highlight areas and is easier to see if you need to scan an illustration.

» Paper: A sketchbook, plain paper, and grid paper are all useful to have.

» Ruler: Helpful when you don't have grid paper—even I can't draw a straight line.

WEBSITE SKETCH PAPER

Sneakpeekit
http://sneakpeekit.com

Zurb (responsive-sketchsheets)
http://zurb.com/playground/

See the website for more sketching resources and demonstrations.

>>> *TABLES: IF YOU'RE A REALLY TECH SAVVY SKETCHER, A TABLET AND STYLUS ARE GREAT DRAWING TOOLS. CHECK THE WEBSITE FOR APPLICATIONS AND STYLUS RECOMMENDATIONS.*

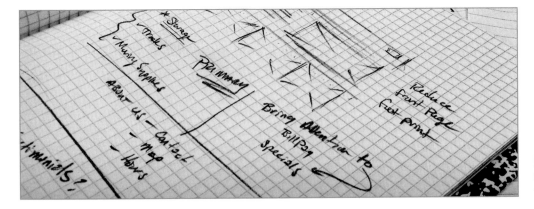

FIGURE 13.6
Sketches help you work through your ideas.

 **WIREFRAME**

A wireframe is a static mockup of the website—much like a blueprint for a house. It can help you create a more consistent layout from page to page and help you arrange elements within the layout (**Figure 13.7**).

The difficulty with wireframes is they are normally static and don't indicate how the design will respond to different viewport sizes. However, there are some great applications being developed that can help you construct basic to complex responsive wireframes! As with mood boards, you don't need to use an expensive application to develop a wireframe. Any application (online or on the desktop) that can draw boxes can help you make a basic wireframe.

The front page layout grid allows for easy eye scan down the page promoting the design widget and categories of creations. The user call to action is to register and start creating.

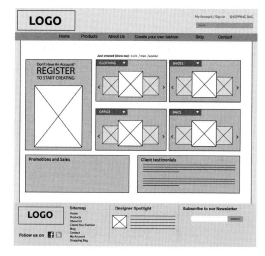

Unique design for the widget—reflection commonly used image applications. Breadcrumb allows for quick navigatdion within the widget.

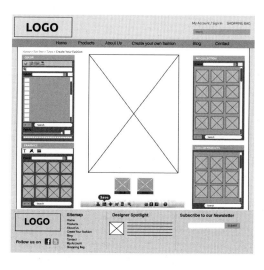

FIGURE 13.7
A sample wireframe.

 ONLINE APPLICATIONS

RWD Wireframes
http://lifeishao.com/rwdwire

Wireframe.cc
https://wireframe.cc/
minimal wireframing application

Visit the website for more wireframe resources and demonstrations.

CODING

In the end, you're striving to bring your project on to the web through the browser, and this of course requires you to write some code to do the job. To make sure the content and presentation work well across different browsers and viewport sizes, you'll need to test, test, and test some more within the browser.

PROTOTYPES

A prototype is a simply a preliminary model for something that could be a final feature of the website. You could code a prototype of a portion of the site, a whole page, or multiple pages. Early on in the project, you might want to test how your two-column layout, gallery of images for a portfolio, or contact form is going to perform (**Figure 13.8**).

TESTING

The difficulty here lies in how to test your prototypes in different devices, browsers, and operating systems. There is a lot to consider with testing, and sometimes (in the beginning) the only option is to test in a couple of browsers you have installed on your computer. As you progress and work on client projects, you may want to consider using a third-party service that will show you how your website looks on more devices than you could test on your own (**Figure 13.9**).

There are a number of online resources you can try out for free—some providing only screenshots and others providing live (interactive) results!

BROWSER TESTING TOOLS

Browsershots
http://browsershots.org/

Browserling
https://browserling.com/

Check out the website for more browser testing resources and demonstrations.

FIGURE 13.8
Prototypes allow you to test ideas early and often within the browser and on different devices.

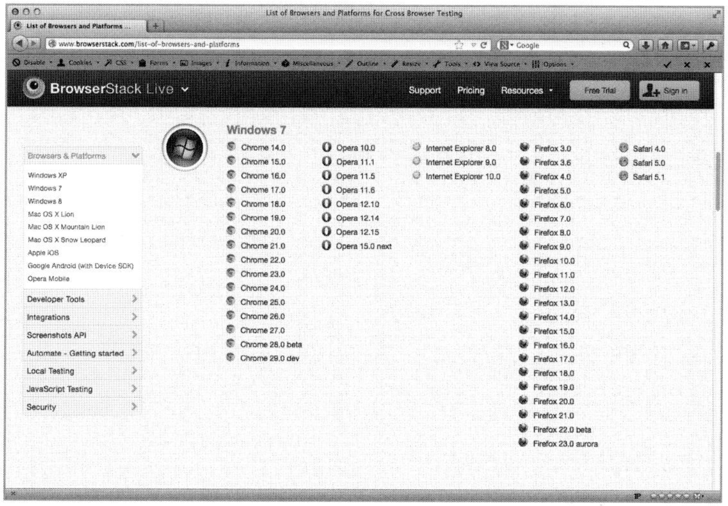

FIGURE 13.9
Online services offer testing in multiple browsers and operating systems.

WRAPPING THINGS UP

The workflow of a web designer can change from project to project, but you'll come across common tasks—and find that those tasks overlap among phases of a project's timeline. To start, keep the tasks (planning, designing, coding) and their subtasks (questions, sitemaps, sketches, mood boards, wireframes, prototypes, etc.) simple; over time you'll progress into more advanced techniques.

In the last chapter, I want to give you a taste of what else a front-end developer/designer should consider.

LOOKING AHEAD

—

14

ONLINE JOB BOARDS

To get an idea of what employers are looking for in the field of web design, view the following online job boards:

Authentic Jobs: http://authenticjobs.com

Krop: http://krop.com

Smashing Magazine: http://jobs.smashingmagazine.com

Look for job titles such as

• Front-End Developer
• Web Designer
• Front-End Designer
• UI/UX Designer
• UI Developer

and anything else pertaining to "Front End" or Designer.

You've come a long way in learning the foundations of HTML and CSS. However, there is more a web designer needs to add to his or her toolkit. If you wish to work as a web designer, web developer, front-end designer, UI/UX designer, etc., you'll need to continue your education beyond the basics. You will always be learning, as the landscape is always changing. Two of the important skills you'll need are the abilities to work with moving targets and to digest new information quickly. If you look at online job boards (**Figure 14.1**), you'll see some of the following requirements:

» Ability to hand-code standards-compliant HTML/CSS

» Possess an exceptional knowledge of current web development languages including, but not limited to HTML/CSS3, JavaScript, and jQuery

» Develop HTML, JavaScript, and CSS solutions that make the magic happen

» A black belt in HTML, JavaScript, CSS, Adobe Photoshop, and Illustrator

» Mastery of CSS3, HTML5, and JavaScript; able to produce clean, standards-compliant markup

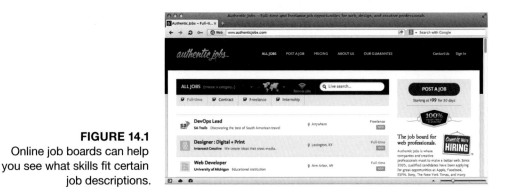

FIGURE 14.1
Online job boards can help you see what skills fit certain job descriptions.

Do you see any common themes in job description requirements? HTML, HTML5, CSS, CSS3, web standards, JavaScript, and jQuery. You're already getting a strong grip on HTML and CSS; now you need to move on to the latest trends with HTML5 and CSS3—some of which you have been introduced to in this book and in online videos. However, there's more to take in.

Additionally, JavaScript (not to be confused with—although it always is—the Java programming language) is a wonderful complementary, and necessary, programming language specifically developed for the Web. It's been around pretty much as long as the Internet, and it helps to add a layer of interactivity that "really makes the magic happen," as one job description above noted.

 ## WHAT ARE UX AND UI DESIGN JOBS?

UX stands for User Experience. UX designers work behind the scenes figuring out the best possible solutions for the tasks users will be performing on the website, to ensure the best possible (most pleasurable) experience. They are also responsible for how the design of a website fits in with the overall branding and experience of a company.

UI stands for User Interface. UI designers focus on the user's experience and interaction with a website. The goal is to make a user's interaction with the website as simple and efficient as possible—to avoid making people struggle with (or even think about) what they're wanting to do or trying to find.

 ## DEVELOPER VS. DESIGNER

Front-end developers and designers can have many overlapping roles in the creation of a website. Developers might do more coding of HTML and JavaScript for optimal and accessible interactive content delivery, but a good knowledge of CSS is still important for the overall experience. Designers may focus more on the use of Photoshop and CSS to create effective visual elements, but familiarity with properly structured HTML is still vital for creating the right visuals to fit in with the structure. However, there are job descriptions where you'll find a developer needing the skills of a designer and a designer needing the skills of a developer.

HTML5

HTML5 introduces many cutting-edge features that enable developers to create apps and websites with the functionality, speed, performance, and experience of desktop applications. But unlike desktop applications, apps built on the web platform can reach a much broader audience using a wider array of devices. HTML5 accelerates the pace of your innovation and enables you to seamlessly roll out your latest work to all your users simultaneously.

—HTML5 Rocks
www.html5rocks.com/en/why

While the book and online resources have skimmed the surface of HTML5 tags and attributes, it's another area in which you'll need to develop more knowledge to be competitive in the marketplace. There are a number of new HTML structural elements—header, footer, hgroup, article, section, etc.—that you'll need to familiarize yourself with. If you wish to be a front-end designer or developer, the structural elements will be useful to know as you develop layouts and mobile applications.

Additionally, there are multimedia elements, audio and video, that treat media more as a native object than an embedded object (from YouTube or Vimeo). You can also use CSS and JavaScript along with HTML5 to create custom audio and video players (**Figure 14.2**)!

RESOURCES: BOOKS

HTML5 for Web Designers, by Jeremy Keith

Introducing HTML5, by Bruce Lawson and Remy Sharp

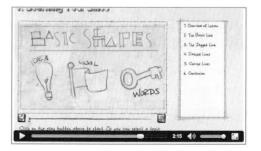

HTML5 Multimedia: Develop and Design, by Ian Devlin

RESOURCES: ONLINE

» HTML5 Rocks: http://html5rocks.com

» Dev.Opera: http://dev.opera.com/articles/tags/html5

» An Advanced Guide to HTML & CSS: http://learn.shayhowe.com/advanced-html-css/

» Mozilla Developers Network: https://developer.mozilla.org/en-US/docs/Web/Guide/HTML/HTML5

>>> *REMEMBER: CHECK OUT THE WEBSITE FOR ADDITIONAL RESOURCES FOR LEARNING HTML5.*

FIGURE 14.2
HTML5 video players can be styled using CSS and JavaScript.

CSS3

Most of what you've learned about CSS in this book is considered CSS1 and CSS2—both of which have been around for a very long time. While CSS3 has been around longer that you might imagine, this book purposely contains limited coverage of CSS3 to keep things straightforward. However, you'll want to start employing CSS3 features in your work as soon as possible, as they will build on top of what you already know to provide more power, flexibility, accessibility, and ease of implementation.

CSS3 mostly provides simpler and more flexible solutions to problems designers and developers have been solving on the Web for a long time, but often in complicated ways involving hacks and inefficient code; for example:

» Using custom fonts on a web page previously involved using images of text to provide heading visuals, with the real text placed offscreen for semantics/accessibility. Now you can use CSS3 web fonts to simply provide the required font along with the website download.

» Using graphical features like rounded corners, drop shadows, and gradients on a web page used to involve lots of image files and extra nested divs to include those images on the page as CSS background images. Now you can create such features programmatically (**Figure 14.3**).

» Creating complex layouts has traditionally been really difficult in CSS, but CSS3 is starting to provide much simpler, more logical layout properties.

CSS3 also provides some new features that you'll enjoy getting to grips with, such as:

» Animations for more interactivity and smooth transitions between states

» Media queries to apply different rules to your markup conditionally, depending on device features such as browser viewport width and resolution

There are a lot of new things to learn in CSS3, so start digging into the resources I've listed below and have fun.

FIGURE 14.3
A simple example of CSS3 styling features for text and boxes that would have required several images just a few years ago.

RESOURCES: BOOKS

CSS3 For Web Designers, by Dan Cederholm

CSS3: Visual QuickStart Guide (6th Edition), by Jason Cranford Teague

Practical CSS3: Develop and Design, by Chris Mills

Stunning CSS3: A project-based guide to the latest in CSS, by Zoe Mickley Gillenwater

RESOURCES: ONLINE

The following sites are good starting points and lead to additional blog posts specific to CSS3:

» CSS3.info: www.css3.info

» Learning CSS3: A Reference Guide: www.smashingmagazine.com/learning-css3-useful-reference-guide/

The following three sites will help you play around with—and generate—CSS3 rules:

» CSS3 Generator: http://css3generator.com

» CSS3.me: http://css3.me

» CSS 3.0 Maker: http://css3maker.com

>>> *REMEMBER: VISIT THE WEBSITE FOR ADDITIONAL RESOURCES ABOUT CSS3.*

JAVASCRIPT

JavaScript is utilized by all standards-compliant browsers and allows you to add interactivity to your document—much like CSS adds styling to your document. While you may feel a little intimidated or overwhelmed to consider learning another language, it's an essential tool for web designers and developers. This section is not going to go into the history or structure of JavaScript, but it will give you some resources and show you some simple possibilities to help whet your appetite.

TABBED BOXES

Tabbed boxes allow you to show and hide content according to the user's needs—much like tabbed folders in a file cabinet (**Figure 14.4**). Tabs can be useful if the site has large amounts of content on a single page.

They can also show the content if the user disables JavaScript (**Figure 14.5**).

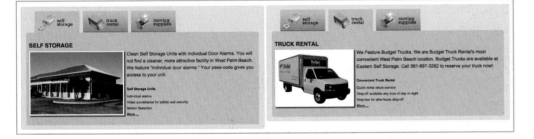

FIGURE 14.4
Tabbed content can be hidden when other content is visible.

FIGURE 14.5
All tabbed content will be shown if JavaScript is disabled.

LIGHTBOX GALLERY

Lightboxes are ways to display a single piece of content on top of other content in what are called "modal windows," where a child element displays on top of a parent element (**Figure 14.6**). You may know modal windows from seeing an error or alert message in an application or operating system (**Figure 14.7**).

While tabs and lightboxes are common interactive elements you can create with JavaScript, there are other possibilities to explore:

» Drag and drop

» Custom control buttons

» Animation

» Dynamic data update

FIGURE 14.6
A lightbox modal window showcasing an image while the content behind is slightly hidden.

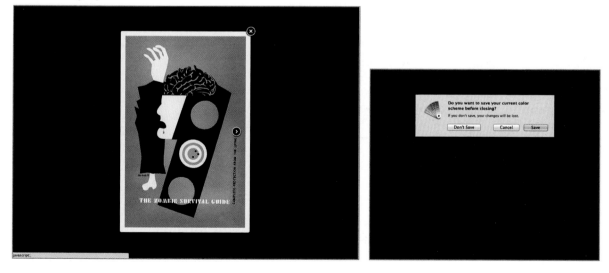

FIGURE 14.7
A modal dialogue in an application asking if you wish to save the document before closing to avoid losing your information.

CSS3 AND JAVASCRIPT

Interestingly, some of the interactive design features that used to belong within the domain of JavaScript are now available with CSS3!

JAVASCRIPT LIBRARIES

While you should first learn the basics of programming with JavaScript, there are libraries—prewritten JavaScript—that enable easier application development. There are many different types of libraries you can choose from; some of the more popular are jQuery, Dojo Toolkit, MooTools, and Angular.

JQUERY

For front-end designers and developers, jQuery (http://jquery.com/) is one of the more popular libraries because of its large community, its use in a number of small and large business websites, and its learning curve, which is a little less daunting than pure JavaScript. The documentation is pretty extensive, and there are a number of great learning resources for beginners to advanced users.

RESOURCES: BOOKS

Modern Javascript: Develop and Design, by Larry Ullman

JavaScript: Visual QuickStart Guide (8th Edition), by Tom Negrino and Dori Smith

Applied jQuery: Develop and Design, by Jay Blanchard

>>> *NOTE: THE WEBSITE HAS BASIC VIDEO TUTORIALS ON HOW YOU CAN INTEGRATE TABBED BOXES, LIGHTBOX GALLERIES, AND SLIDESHOWS INTO YOUR PROJECTS.*

RESOURCES: ONLINE

There are many resources online and in print to help you learn the basics of JavaScript. If you want to jump right in, and you like to learn online, you can check out

» Codecademy
  http://codecademy.com/tracks/javascript

» appendTo:
  http://learn.appendto.com/lessons

» Try jQuery:
  http://try.jquery.com/

REMEMBER: VISIT THE WEBSITE FOR ADDITIONAL RESOURCES FOR LEARNING JAVASCRIPT.

WRAPPING THINGS UP

This is simply an overview of the next steps in your journey into becoming a front-end designer or developer. CSS3, HTML5, and JavaScript all are necessary tools in web designers' kits, and there are a lot of great print and online resources for learning them. With JavaScript, you'll also want to look into the options of prewritten libraries and APIs to help simplify some website and application development, as they too are a part of the requirements you'll find on online job boards.

Good luck with your continued learning, and I hope you share your midterm and final project creations with me on the website!

INDEX

WATCH
READ
CREATE

Unlimited online access to all Peachpit, Adobe Press, Apple Training and New Riders videos and books, as well as conten[t] from other leading publishers including: O'Reilly Media, Foc[al] Press, Sams, Que, Total Training, John Wiley & Sons, Course[ ]Technology PTR, Class on Demand, VTC and more.

No time commitment or contract required!
Sign up for one month or a year. All for $19.99 a mont[h]

creative
edge

SIGN UP TODAY
peachpit.com/creativeedge